A TOUCH OF
MISTLETOE

Also by Barbara Comyns

Sisters by a River
Our Spoons Came from Woolworths
Who Was Changed and Who Was Dead
The Vet's Daughter
Out of the Red, Into the Blue (A Memoir)
The Skin Chairs
Birds in Tiny Cages
The Juniper Tree
Mr Fox
The House of Dolls

A TOUCH OF MISTLETOE

BARBARA COMYNS

With an introduction by Megan Nolan

DAUNT BOOKS

First published in the United Kingdom in 2021 by
Daunt Books
83 Marylebone High Street
London W1U 4QW

1

Copyright © Barbara Comyns, 1967, 2021
Introduction copyright © Megan Nolan 2021

First published in 1967 by Heinemann, London

A CIP catalogue record for this title is
available from the British Library.

ISBN 978-1-911547-86-0

Typeset by Marsha Swan

Printed and bound by TJ Books Ltd,
Padstow, Cornwall

www.dauntbookspublishing.co.uk

INTRODUCTION

I discovered Barbara Comyns a few years back, the result of a chance encounter with an old English teacher of mine. It was Comyns's 1947 debut *Sisters by a River* I landed on first and I was drawn in by its sheer oddness. Where I had expected pastoral frolics of limited consequence, I found the shapes of such familiar scenes burdened unexpectedly by menace and decay. While I was beguiled, and found much to admire, I was also jarred by its misspellings and grammatical errors. They were included, I assumed, as a stylistic flourish by Comyns to capture a child's eye view. 'Mary was the eldist of the family, Mammy was only eighteen when she had her, and was awful frit of her,' goes an introduction to one of the book's five sisters. Such a gimmick seemed to me at odds with the originality and intelligence of the writing as a whole.

I was interested, then, to learn that some of these mistakes were originally genuine errors, omissions of knowledge which resulted from sporadic education in Comyns's formative life. The mistakes were not only allowed to remain by the book's publisher but heightened and multiplied, the better to create a sense of unvarnished ingenuity. *Sisters by a River* was also serialised in *Lilliput* magazine before its eventual publication, under the title *The Novel Nobody Will Publish*. The combination of these two facts came together to impress something on me about the manner in which Comyns's work had been received. There was appreciation, certainly, for what was undeniably compelling and singular fiction, but there existed an inclination to appreciate it through the prism of an assumed innocence, or even ignorance, on Comyns's part. Even the most unimpeachably literary praise she has won – Graham Greene was a fan and supporter, and Alan Hollinghurst blurbs a 1985 reprint of *The Vet's Daughter* – concentrates on her innocence and childlike naivety.

This book, *A Touch of Mistletoe*, is for me the great rejoinder to any idea that the freshness and simplicity of style which characterises Comyns's work can be attributed to a mere unknowing ingénue. In fact, here is something sophisticated and rare – the ability to contain many moods in a single, matter-of-fact tone. This tone is not glib, nor purely comic and wry in a way which flattens emotion (though there are many very funny moments). It is instead simply accepting of the vagaries of fortune, as our narrator Victoria Green is also.

A *Touch of Mistletoe* follows Victoria from the age of almost-eighteen (an important distinction from seventeen) in the 1930s through to the 1960s, taking in a life made up of marriages, poverty, addiction, mental illness, a love of art, children, and war. We meet her sitting with sister Blanche on a June evening after the funeral of their grandfather. The two have been living a strange sort of half-life in his estate, alongside their brother and a mother who is constantly busied with either drinking or feverish domesticity. The lack of social mixing and norms in their youths have made the sisters seem and feel younger than they really are. They are unseasoned and unprepared for what comes next, but no less eager to jump into it for that. Victoria is antsy in her undefined role in the home, wafting about, cleaning up a bit here and there, waiting for something to happen or for a proper and right course of action to be forced upon her. She jealously regards those with more permission than herself to make good and pleasurable use of the world: 'I tilted my chair back and, frowning, watched a cart pass the window. It rumbled past the house, the young driver standing up in the cart, his cap on the back of his head, laughing to himself. I felt how brave and free he was, while I sat in a room with stuffy red wallpaper eating chocolate cake and being scolded by my mother.'

She has a great yearning for the unknown *something* she understands to lie beyond daughterhood. While men may prescribe their own course toward this something, she is lectured by her mother, her brother and the family lawyer about the necessity of choosing a sensible path. Instead, she takes the two hundred pounds her grandfather has left her in his will and uses it to embark on a trip to Holland to work as a family-help. She begins her first foreign voyage with satisfaction and exhilaration but it quickly sours into a comically abject failure. Hungry and forlorn, she lies down in a frozen field with a bag of monkey nuts and 'slowly munched them as tears of misery and cold ran down my cheeks.' A bite on her finger from one of the Dutch family's wretched dogs becomes livid with infection as she traipses the streets, calculating a return to Britain.

This first, failed attempt at romance and adventure is a key example of what endears me to *A Touch of Mistletoe*. In the kind of conventional coming-of-age novel one might mistake this for, Victoria would be a pluckier sort of heroine. Her desires would be clearly defined, the path toward them perhaps rough, but reachable with determination and grit. Instead Victoria has a far more touching, true kind of appetite, which is to say the general and clueless and searching kind. She hasn't any conclusive ambition to find a man, to be a film star, a society girl, a genius, or rich. She doesn't have a burning wish that fuels her life's course. She wants everything or at least *a* thing to happen, she wants action, she hungers in the sincere but aimless way that most of us do in youth.

The failed European trip accomplishes one thing at least, making her hardy enough that even seedy old London seems comparatively soft. 'I had now lost my fear of public transport,' she says, and moves with Blanche to a hostel for young ladies. On Saturday afternoons in Camden Town they buy 'grim little oranges for two a penny' and bags of broken biscuits, and after one ill-advised attempt at securing some nutrition, a cabbage which languishes stinking in their cupboard. Their hardship is not drawn as comedy or tragedy but as an ordinary fact of life. Where they can take some small pleasures they do so, and when they cannot they hold towels against their faces to cry into. They do, though, live in a state of perpetual struggle and hunger and their shared experience of poverty will shape them both in very different ways. Blanche lacks the curious hope for adventure that Victoria harbours. She is focused on accruing manners and beautiful clothes and, through those things, a husband who can keep her well. She is burned, traumatised really, by the feeling of always scraping by, the mystery of where next month's rent will arrive from.

Victoria has a different relationship to poverty. Rather than being haunted by the feeling of wondering where things come from, she finds at least a little reviving wonder in the fact that they do always seem to come, in the end, in some way. One afternoon, walking around Hyde Park in the throes of hunger: 'We were nearly crying and I was saying "Fortitude" over and over again. Blanche stopped me with "Damn fortitude! The only thing I want is roast beef with roast potatoes and Yorkshire pudding."' Several minutes later, a car pulls up full of inconsequential boys who fancy them and want to take them for lunch. They eat their magical roast beef and never see the boys again, satisfied by the unlikely sleight of hand luck has turned for them.

I have a distrust of fetishising make-do attitudes when it comes to poverty, and as the novel circles World War Two the potential for this to be romanticised is even greater. But the sanguinity of Victoria's making do is never laden with forced cheer. Poverty is not ennobling but nor does it rob her of her sense of self or her will to enjoy life. Money behaves as misfortune does in the book, always coming and going, as inevitably variable as the weather, nothing there is any point in despairing over.

The clear-eyed approach to the world spills over into her artistic ambitions. She sincerely loves art, well enough to recognise that her own talents are too modest to compete with the greats: 'From studying paintings in galleries I knew I would never be a serious painter myself, though I had a chance as a commercial artist.' This fact does not cause her any long nights of the soul. She moves along swiftly as ever and finds work in studios and animation. Her frequenting of museums leads her to the great love of her life, her first husband Gene. He is a half-French and entirely passionate young art student who follows Victoria around the Tate one afternoon before taking her for a coffee and beginning a dreamy romance. His profession and lack of solid prospects cause Blanche worry before she meets him, whereby she too is taken by his earnest eccentricity ('Perhaps he's a genius or something,' she wonders).

Gene is the source of many of the novel's most memorable comic and tragic moments. He proposes by ranting around their bedroom for half an hour about the petit-bourgeois trappings of marriage, a thing he could never countenance, before collapsing, spent, down on the bed beside his love and saying, 'All the same I think we had better get married, don't you?'

His hatred of what he sees as aesthetic excess – anything with bows or frills or prettiness – sends him into spirals of fury: 'Once a friend took us for a drive in his father's car and Gene got so worked up about the houses on the Hendon By-pass that we had to return another way at dusk.'

The generalised desire of Victoria's earlier youth develops into a realisation of the happiness of homemaking. I mean this in the literal sense – I do not mean that she enjoys practising servitude, but that she comes to value the pleasure of making one's surroundings comfortable and filled with love. Her illustrations give her pleasure too, but work is not the provider of meaning and substance in her life.

Nor, really, is Gene specifically, nor even their child Paul when he arrives. They are all crucial parts of a wider picture, that simplest and most difficult of goals; a life lived as well as one's means and circumstances allow. Perhaps this foundational aspiration is what stops her sinking beneath the misfortunes which would engulf a less industrious, sturdy person. Chief amongst these is the loss of her beloved Gene, with whom she knows her happiest days have now been spent and are gone forever. But she does not go under, does not even falter for very long – she perseveres not through any overtly inspirational triumph of spirit, but with her same old sense that things will continue happening and some will come good and some won't and one must keep going with a slightly detached curiosity about which one it will be this time. It's an attitude that can be applied to everything from a disappointingly mediocre lunch to a world war, from the first laugh of your only child to a satisfying amble in an art gallery.

This equanimity about life's pleasure and its suffering is the most humbling achievement of A *Touch of Mistletoe*. Like Comyns herself, Victoria experiences an early life which prepares her for fluctuating fortunes and the bottom dropping out of things, for the optics of success coinciding with the reality of collapse. Blanche, beautiful and beloved and darling as she is, seeks to hammer possibility flat and chase the safest bet. Victoria has chosen to accept the manner of things, and lives accordingly. Neither path is drawn as the objectively more attractive one. At the book's close, both women see in each other those parts of life they could not have had themselves, the ghost imprints of abandoned options. Two women who could not have it all, looking at each other at times with envy or distrust, but finally with frank curiosity and love. It is one startlingly modern and moving moment of many in this fierce and compelling book, which I hope will have a well-deserved brand-new life of its own now.

Megan Nolan, 2021

PUBLISHERS' NOTE

This book was originally published in 1967. It is a historical text and for this reason we have not made any changes to its use of language.

ONE

WE SAT IN THE June dusk discussing our brother Edward, and Blanche, my younger sister, took the plait of hair she was chewing from her mouth to say: 'Did you notice he broke the glasses the undertakers had drunk from – sherry glasses?'

I moved uneasily on the stone step I was sitting on; it was growing chilly and Marcella said cold stones gave you piles. 'No, but it's the kind of thing he does,' I said gloomily. 'Do you realise he always puts his feet on the opposite seat when he travels in a train? In case there's an accident, you know. He worries about his legs getting chopped off. But why break the undertakers' glasses?'

Blanche stood up and stared across the darkening garden. 'Oh, I don't know,' she said. 'Perhaps he thinks death is catching, that undertakers sort of spread it about to get customers. He says he's the head of the house now Grandfather's dead and he wants to order us about, although he's really terrified of everything. Let's go in; it's cold and bats are flapping their wings in my face.' She held out a long hand and tugged me to my feet. We stood for a moment watching the moon rising above the pine trees that grew close to the river, then we crossed the verandah and entered the house through the French windows. We could hear a distant cat-like voice wailing our names: 'Vicky, Blanche, I want you both.' It was our mother's voice and reluctantly we walked towards it.

Old Mr Green, our grandfather, had been buried that day among the yew trees in the village churchyard, our great-grandparents on one side and the terrible Mrs Willoweed in front of him. If they had had eyes to see with they would have had a clear view of the river and the water meadows where the kingcups grew and just a glimpse of the fine Norman bridge and the Broadway hills in the distance; but they lay and noticed nothing. Grandfather had been a Civil Servant in India and had returned to his family house when he retired on a comfortable pension, and he must have been very contented there surrounded by the things he knew and loved. His wife had been mislaid years earlier. I think she had run away with a young officer and was never mentioned. For years we thought her dead. But Grandfather had his son and when the son became an architect with an office in Cheltenham, he frequently visited his home and after he had married and had us children, we all used to come along too. Then our father was killed during the second year of the 1914–18 war and Mother brought us all to stay with Grandfather. At first this was a temporary arrangement while she looked round, but, as she only had an army pension to look round on, we stayed on and on until Grandfather's house became our permanent home.

The house was large and he seemed quite pleased to have us. It was Mother who hated living there. At first she eased her boredom by organising a committee to deal with Belgian refugees, and for several years there were fêtes in the garden in aid of some good cause and a great white bundle called the Maternity Bag which provided linen for the village women's lying-in. But gradually she became thirsty and almost retired from village life. Grandfather's dreamy pink face began to wear a bewildered look and he shut himself up in the billiard room as much as possible. 'I'm afraid my daughter-in-law is poorly' or 'Your mother isn't quite herself today, poorly, you know' were words that frequently crossed his lips, and when we children heard the word 'poorly' applied to anyone who was ill, perhaps an innocent child suffering with measles, we took it for granted that they had been drinking bottles of port or sherry. Our mother rather lost interest in us after the thirst got hold of her and, although our grandfather was vaguely fond of us, he certainly wasn't interested. Edward was sent to a second- or perhaps third-rate school recommended by the vicar and Blanche and I had to make do with ever-changing governesses who seemed to know they were doomed as soon as they arrived and hardly bothered to unpack their boxes. The last one was a Miss Baggot, who was old and finding it difficult to get work; although she was frequently in tears, she stayed for nearly a year. Mother finally hit her with a parasol and she left after that. The day she departed we explored her room in the hope of finding discarded treasures. We had once found a bundle of love letters. There was not much love in them, mostly regard, but we read them out loud to each other for weeks. This time we discovered a number of cheap novels behind the wardrobe, most likely hidden from servants' eyes and forgotten in her hurried packing: Ethel M. Dell, Elinor Glyn, the less interesting Ruby M. Ayres and Bertha Ruck. We sat up in trees devouring these books and they kept us so quiet our ageing Grandfather and poorly mother almost forgot we existed and nothing was done about engaging another governess. I was nearly sixteen at the time and Blanche fourteen.

Although I had been taught to draw single flowers in fish-paste jars, I drew and painted, when I had any paints, everything I saw, even copying the designs on china; the more complicated the design, the better I liked it. On fine days I would take a sketch book into the fields and draw animals as they grazed or make detailed studies of wild flowers. It was my ambition to become an artist, perhaps an illustrator. Blanche could not draw, but she had the very special gift of romantic beauty. She was extremely tall and willowy, with a flowing mass of almost black hair, classical features and a pale moon face, her skin as fine as the skin inside egg shells. Although I was proud of her beauty, I could not help a feeling of jealousy coming to the surface from time to time. I was pretty enough, with firm, red-brown cheeks and bushy black hair that only grew as far as my shoulders. People always said my eyes were my best feature and I felt that there was something slightly damning about the remark. I put castor oil on my eyelashes most nights to make them grow even longer than they were, but found the smell depressing in bed.

When Grandfather died I was nearly eighteen and Blanche sixteen, but we had mixed so little with other people we appeared to be much younger. Edward was nineteen, good-looking with the same classical features as Blanche. He was vain of his appearance and often spent a quarter of an hour gazing at his reflection, particularly when he had a pipe in his mouth or his overcoat collar turned up. In spite of his good looks he was extraordinarily timid, and terrified of losing people's regard or appearing unconventional. He must have suffered agonies over the way Mother behaved when she was poorly. He never mentioned that she drank. It was always 'Pity about Mater's health' or 'The Mater's not quite the thing' and there she'd be, glassy-eyed and swaying and saying terrible things. He had left school when he was seventeen and as he had no ideas about a career and no one else had either, he spent a year mooning about at home; and, when the few visitors who came to the house enquired what he intended to do for a living, he would flush and look away as he mumbled 'It's not quite settled yet.' Eventually Grandfather arranged that he was to become a clerk in a Birmingham estate agent's office. I think Grandfather had to pay a premium which was returned as a very small salary which just covered Edward's season ticket and lunch. Every day he ate the same lunch in the same restaurant he had been taken to on his first day in the city – sausages and mashed potatoes followed by trifle. One day he heard the waitress say 'Here comes Sausage and Mashed,' and, feeling hurt, he daringly ordered mutton chops and as time went on bravely travelled through the menu. Although we did not get on very well with our brother, we loved him and wanted him to love us. Perhaps he did in a way, although he regarded us as potential embarrassments.

Since Grandfather had been found dead in the billiard room, just sitting at his desk with his pen clutched in his hand, Mother's thirst had left her as it sometimes did; but this time there was a new purpose in her oyster-like eyes and, instead of wandering unsteadily round the house and garden in her usual listless way, she walked about the house opening and shutting cupboard doors or sat at her writing table answering letters of condolence and making lists. Grandfather had bequeathed her the house and its contents, but his pension had died with him. To each of us children he had left two hundred pounds to be paid on our eighteenth birthdays, which meant that Edward would have his money immediately and that I would only have to wait a few weeks for mine; so, when Hobbs the lawyer's black back disappeared behind the front door, we immediately started discussing our legacies. Two hundred pounds seemed a very large sum to us and I said I'd spend mine on painting materials and travel. Edward thought it would be nice to open a bank account and take out a pound a week for four years and said rather wistfully, 'I've always wanted to write cheques, but I'm sure Hobbs won't hand over the money; he'll say it's for the Mater; as I'm the head of the house now, I'll have to look after her.' I protested that Mother would be a rich woman as she owned a whole house and its contents, but it seemed there was something called a mortgage that would have to be paid off. Edward said, 'Of course I know all about mortgages, we deal with them every day in the office, but I'm surprised that Grandfather had one. He always seemed so rich.' I considered this for a moment, then said, 'Perhaps he was before we all came to live with him.' Edward polished his pipe against his cheek, smiling vaguely, 'I wouldn't say that. Mother has her pension so we didn't entirely depend on him. Anyway, the old man must have loved having us here brightening his last days.' Then, nervously, 'You didn't mean that about going abroad. People would think it queer when you're so young. If you do get the money you had better spend it on learning something useful, something a lady could do – office work for one of Grandfather's friends, for instance. Miss Leake in our office earns two pounds a week and that's a lot for a woman, but of course she's been there for years, about twenty, I think.' He was warming to his subject, but I stopped him impatiently with, 'How can you suggest such a horrible thing. You do have the most dreary ideas. I'd rather be dead than spend twenty years in an office with a lot of old bores. If I can't travel, I'll go to London and study art and I'll take Blanche with me.' Edward spluttered, 'You wouldn't be allowed to. You don't know what you are talking about, you silly little fool.' I laughed, the first time I'd dared to since Grandfather died. The prospect of money and freedom gave me a wonderful feeling of exhilaration and I ran from the house into the dusky garden making swimming movements with my arms. I could smell the tobacco plants that grew in a round bed in the centre of a round lawn and the swallows were swooping above me searching for a last meal of the gnats that danced about in small grey groups. I could see Blanche sitting disconsolately on the verandah steps and guessed that she was disappointed about having to wait two more years before she had her money. I joined her on the steps, one of our favourite talking places, and told her about Edward's appalling suggestion for me to spend my money and waste my life in some old man's office. It was while we were sitting there that we heard Mother's voice wailing and calling.

We followed this voice to the kitchen where she was pawing over the silver with one of the servants – Marcella Murphy. Marcella stood by the table, her large empty hands hanging down by her side; but her lopsided face wore a smug expression because she was the only servant who had not been dismissed by Mr Hobbs. She worked for very small wages because she had the misfortune of having only one nostril to her nose and found it difficult to obtain work. Mother had been poorly when she engaged her and had not noticed anything particularly odd about her appearance. The table was littered with green baize bags with teapots and jugs protruding from them. Tarnished silver cups stood on black stands, cups that had been won by Grandfather in his youth for jumping and sprinting faster than other young men, and Sheffield plate candlesticks with the copper gleaming through the silver, and an extraordinary contraption for boiling eggs at the breakfast table.

Mother had called us in to help Marcella polish the silver which was to be sold. 'I can't imagine anyone wanting these cups,' she said as she absent-mindedly tapped one with a fingernail. 'But Hobbs says I'm to sell everything we don't use – everything in the billiard room for instance and the spare-room furniture. That great ugly brass bed with the curtains, I shall be glad to see the last of it. The rooms that are emptied are to be locked up and we must try and forget they exist. It's either that or moving into some frightful little villa he has his eyes on.' Suddenly her briskness left her and she cried in her floating voice, 'If only we could have gone to Cheltenham. I hate this wretched village and it's no place for you girls, who'll marry you here? Mark my words, you'll both end up as old maids.' She glared at us reproachfully as if it was our fault we were going to be old maids. 'He says there isn't the money and they know me here. What does he mean by that? They knew me in Cheltenham, many people must remember pretty Ann Fenwick when I was the leader of all the young girls; they copied me, my clothes and so on, and I was the first to marry. Oh, it's so lonely here and there'll be all those empty rooms.' She turned away from us and trailed from the kitchen and Marcella Murphy said, 'Now, dears, I'll put on the Goddards and you can do the polishing,' and she poured methylated spirits into a saucer of pink powder.

It took us about a month to clear the house of the things that were not needed. Mother stood out about the contents of the cellar being sold. We kept finding more and more things that we didn't need, like the carriage and pony trap in the coach house and an old bath chair, Grandfather's guns and fishing rods. His bedroom, where photographs of school groups used to hang, was completely empty, with just marks on the walls where things used to be, and the billiard room was empty too except for a few stuffed fish in glass cases and some animal horns. Mr Hobbs had plans for hiring it out as an assembly room. The thing that saddened us most was the boats going to the Pleasure Boat Inn and they had new names painted on them. There was the summer river flowing past and we couldn't use it. We had no gardener any more and the lawns were growing long and threatening and you could tell they were planning to take over the entire garden. As the autumn came Blanche and I tried picking the apples from the trees; but it was harder work than we had imagined and impatiently we bashed the fruit with poles and it fell bruised and battered among the twigs and leaves.

When the surplus servants and furniture left the house Mother developed a terrible passion for cleaning. In spite of the rooms that were locked away there was an enormous amount of space that needed cleaning, two flights of stairs, a great hall, several landings, and long dark passages with stone floors and rows of bells hanging from the walls. Then there were china pantries and butler's pantries and two kitchens and a scullery, where the water was pumped up from a well under the floor; but worst of all were the carpets from India and Kidderminster – stair carpets, bedroom carpets with roses, dining-room and sitting-room carpets and they all needed sweeping. These carpets were turned over to Blanche and me and we had to sweep them with a long broom with yellow bristles or crawl about on our hands and knees with a dustpan and brush. Either way horrible fluff flew into our faces and down our throats and we felt we were choking with the stuff and begged to be given some other work;

but Mother was unrelenting: 'How would you like to wash the floors?' she gasped. She had taken to speaking in gasps. 'Look at my hands, would you like to have hands like these?' She was grovelling about on the hall floor with her stockings all twisted round her thin legs in front of a bucket of dark water. She held up her sodden hands for our inspection. The nails had become short, the cuticles long, so we agreed we did not want hands like that and returned to our sweeping. Although Marcella was slaving away all day, Mother got up earlier and earlier to attack the housework and expected us to do the same. She wore her hair hanging down in a sad-looking pigtail which hung over her shoulder as she worked and instead of an overall she wore a dreadful brown knitted dress that hugged her figure in an embarrassing way. Wondering where it came from, we hated it, looking on it as a symbol of poverty. Eventually Blanche crept behind her with a pair of scissors in her hand and snipped it in several places so that it slowly unravelled to Mother's surprise. 'How strange!' she said, 'it must have been eaten by moths.' Even as she spoke it continued to unravel and she seemed to be wearing a kind of hula skirt.

On autumn afternoons the old and not so old ladies of the village called and sometimes stayed to tea, munching buttered scones with their large false teeth which had their own pink gums. Their clothes were grey, black or brown and perhaps an occasional purple, and from the back one could see a distinct line where their corsets began and ended. If Mother was expecting them the house was polished and scoured even more ferociously than usual, even the places they would never enter, like the maid's lavatory and larder. We dreaded these visitors and almost wished the old poorly days would return. Sometimes in the evening Mother's words would become slurred and she would cry or fall asleep in her chair, but the following morning the frenzy of cleaning would start at the same ghastly hour. The milkman told us our mother was a marvel, working her hands to the bone and the more spiteful village women would ask, 'How's your mother, girls, I hear she is in better health, and does not have those giddy turns she used to suffer from. I wonder what caused them?'

Edward, as the only breadwinner of the family, lay in bed in the mornings oblivious to the sound of buckets and brooms. He arrived downstairs to eat a hurried breakfast, then rode a bicycle to the station, often with a piece of toast in one hand. The firm he worked for had increased his salary by a pound a week, which he gave to Mother and thereby felt he was keeping the whole family from starvation. When he returned home he was given a meal of luncheon leftovers heated up between two plates which he ate without complaint, telling us about his day between mouthfuls. The very fact that he travelled on a train every day seemed wonderful to us.

The coach house and loft above it were sold to an ironmonger who turned it into a shop by the simple operation of making an opening on the side that backed on to the village street. The sale enabled Mr Hobbs to pay off the mortgage, but poor Edward turned his eyes away every time he passed the shop with its display of buckets, hip baths, coal scuttles and rat traps. He felt it was a terrible disgrace. Worse was to come. The billiard room was hired out to Buffaloes and corsets, Buffaloes at night and Slimu corsets in the afternoon. A woman called Miss Noakes was an agent for these corsets and the billiard room made a good fitting room. Twice a week women walked or rode on bicycles from miles away, all heading for our billiard room. They left their prams and bicycles by the back gates and walked through the yard and up a narrow garden path, discreetly looking away if they saw any of the family. We didn't really mind them coming but hated the little notice painted on one of our gateposts. It just said, 'Slimu'. The Ancient Order of Buffaloes usually met on Saturday evening. It was funny to think of them sitting there among the corsets and stuffed pikes and once Blanche and I listened at the door and thought we heard someone say, 'Pass the weed,

Brother,' but it may have been 'mead'. Our ex-gardener was one of these Buffaloes and when he walked up the garden path and saw what was happening to his lawn, he said it brought tears to his eyes. It is extraordinary watching a garden do what it wants to do, and the more overgrown it becomes the smaller it looks.

When all these changes had taken place Mr Hobbs was pleased with what he had done, but no one thanked him. He visited the house quite often and went to considerable trouble to sort out our affairs and make us reasonably comfortable. He called Mother 'dear lady' although he did not like her. Perhaps he didn't care for any of us, but he had been Grandfather's friend and felt responsible. It was not long before he was worrying about Blanche and me. 'What do you intend to do with these girls, dear lady?' he asked. 'They don't appear to have had much education and it's imperative that they should earn their livings. They must be trained to do something useful, teaching or secretarial work, perhaps.' Mother said she would think about it and, when he had gone, became quite enthusiastic about our careers. I said I'd like to study art, but that was brushed aside with, 'What about dancing? You could both learn to dance and make your fortunes on the stage, dancing sisters you know, like the Dolly Sisters.' No one could have looked less like the Dolly Sisters than Blanche and I and we burst out laughing. Slightly hurt, Mother said it was only a suggestion and much better than being a grubby art student. For several days she combed through the personal column in our daily newspaper and eventually came on an advertisement inserted by a 'Lady of title, who offered to train the daughters of gentlemen as mannequins, fifty pounds for a six-week course and work guaranteed'. Mother knew that mannequins had to be tall and beautiful, so what could be more suitable as a career for Blanche who was five feet ten inches tall and a budding beauty. She looked up from her newspaper to give Blanche a critical glance and had to admit that she needed 'grooming'. Her long black plaits were bound with elastic bands and her hands were none too clean; her lisle thread stockings twisted round her thin legs and one cheek bulged with a pear drop. She was resentfully laying the table for luncheon and the damask cloth, far too large for the table, hung down to the carpet on one side and the silver looked as if someone had been playing skittles with it. Mother remarked thoughtfully, 'You don't appear to be the domestic type, child, but I do wish you would take more care with your appearance. With a little attention I'm sure you would make a most successful mannequin. It would be just the thing for you and it's quite likely you would end up by marrying a lord; they always marry well, I believe.'

Blanche swallowed her pear drop at Mother's suggestion with enthusiasm, declaring a mannequin was what she had always wanted to be. Although the idea had never entered her head before, she was convinced it had always been there. Mr Hobbs was a little dubious about the suggestion although 'Lady of title' and 'gentleman's daughter' appealed to him; it was the thought of London that he found disturbing. The remark he had often heard about girls ending up on the streets of London kept coming to his mind and where was the fifty pounds to come from? Nevertheless, the lady of title was written to and a pretty brochure accompanied by a charming letter came by return of post. It was slightly disappointing that the title turned out to be only an Honourable, but she said that many débutantes attended her Mayfair establishment. 'Think of the friends the child will make,' Mother pleaded with the lawyer. 'It is dreadful to think of her buried here, indeed it is dreadful for us all. It would have been different if we'd moved to Cheltenham, but you wouldn't allow us to do that,' she reproached him. 'My dear lady,' he replied sharply, 'it wasn't I that wouldn't allow you to have your own way about Cheltenham, but lack of funds. Anyway, where's the fifty pounds to come from, tell me that?' Eventually he was won over and the money for the fees was advanced from my two hundred pounds which had not been handed over to me, although I had asked for it the first time Mr Hobbs had called after my birthday. Instead of producing two hundred-pound notes, as I had expected, he exclaimed irritably, 'Surely you don't think I would give you a sum like that to fritter away on hair ribbons. When you have made up your mind what you want to do, then will be the time to talk about your money.' Disappointedly I cried, 'But I have. I want to study art and travel.' Then, glancing at his disapproving face, I said more calmly, 'Anyway, I'd like to go to an art school.' Mr Hobbs looked down at me, jingling the money in his pockets, and said with forced patience, 'My dear child, art students are notorious for the way they live and you would never make a living from selling paintings, no one does.' I suggested commercial art, posters and advertisements and working in a studio where they would pay me a salary, but all the satisfaction I got was a promise to look into it some time. 'Mannequins and artists! What would your Grandfather have said about all this nonsense. Edward is the only member of the family with a grain of sense.' And he left the house coughing bronchially into the afternoon rain, wishing, no doubt, that his old friend had asked someone else to look after his son's family.

A few days later Blanche and I were sitting huddled up over one of the first fires of autumn. It was not cold but rain was running down the windows and we could hear a dismal dripping. Blanche was trying to save the life of a woodlouse that was rushing about on a burning log and I was absent-mindedly reading a column of advertisements for household servants. Suddenly the word 'Holland' caught my eye among the wanted cook-housekeepers, cook-generals, parlour-maids and butlers. 'Young Lady,' I read, 'required to help in house and kennel. Live as family,' and there followed an address in Amsterdam. I showed the advertisement to Blanche, who had returned to the fire after putting the rescued woodlouse out of the window and was muttering something about it going through an ordeal of fire and water. She read the advertisement and said, 'You wouldn't like it there. All those fat boys with patches on their trousers and they are supposed to be a dreadfully clean nation. We've had enough of cleaning lately.' 'Mmm,' I agreed dreamily, 'but it would be abroad and I'd be seeing something of the world. Windmills creaking in the wind, canals, foreign food and the chance to learn another language. I think I'll try it, anyway I'll write.'

With the aid of a dictionary we composed a letter by the fire, in fact several letters and the one we considered best was put in an envelope and posted that evening. Even the stamp costing more was exciting. I did not mention what I had done to Mother because it was not one of her good days and she was singing shaky songs to herself in her bedroom.

The letter to Holland was posted a few days before Blanche was due to leave for London. It had been arranged that she was to stay in the Bayswater house of one of Mr Hobbs's cousins – 'a most trustworthy and respectable woman; it is some years since I have seen her, but we have continued to correspond. She is not very well off, poor dear, so she sometimes takes gentlefolk into her house as paying guests. She's very careful of course, and only has those with first-class references.' He made her sound like stale, damp bread and Blanche began to dread living in such an atmosphere. 'If it wasn't for the chance of escaping to London, I couldn't face it. My clothes are worrying me too. That tweed coat hanging on the door has a hump on the back from the way it's been hanging and it's miles too short and my skirts are all bunchy. I know the débutantes will think me a freak.' I consoled her with the thought that the clothes only had to last a few weeks, then the money would pour in and she'd be able to buy all the clothes she wanted. 'Yes,' she agreed blissfully, 'a coat with a huge fur collar, high-heeled shoes, a really low-necked evening gown, and perhaps a gold evening bag. A muff would be nice but people don't use them now. Do you remember when we were little, we used to borrow Mother's on cold days and take turns to use it. I felt so grand walking through the village with my hands in that huge muff. It had a sort of bitter smell, like chrysanthemums.'

It was Blanche's last night at home and we sat humped up in our beds in the candlelight. An open trunk stood between our two beds. It was new and made of brown canvas, cardboard and wood. I had painted a large B.G. on the lid and added three four-leafed clovers for luck. 'How I envy you,' I sighed. 'Think of me left here with no one to talk to, just Edward and Mother and that awful cleaning. Neither of them know a thing about life, the sort of life we want to live. I suppose we don't know much except from the books we have read, but at least we want to live.'

We talked through the night, sometimes dozing, but then waking up again and chirping like sparrows. Edward knocked on our wall several times in the hope of silencing us, but we shouted, 'You are waking us up with your hammering, leave us alone.' When we were least expecting it, the morning came and the last things were thrown into the new trunk and a clean towel was carefully arranged on top. Breakfast was hurriedly eaten and Edward pedalled away after saying goodbye to Blanche and warning her against strangers and Mormons. We stood in the hall, with Marcella crying in the background, waiting for the hired Ford that was to take us to a station some miles away where an occasional London train stopped. When we reached the station we had to wait for nearly half an hour and spent it alternately in the waiting room, where there was a delightful picture of a Highlander leaping through a window with a bottle of whisky in his hand, and pacing up and down the narrow platform, where we had a good view of Blanche's trunk on the opposite platform, just her trunk and a little white calf attached to a rope. Blanche and I were silent as we walked up and down; but Mother spoke of London: 'I haven't been there since your father's last leave in 1916, but I don't expect it will have changed. Of course, London will be empty just now but the little season starts soon and in the spring there will be the boat race to look forward to and I expect you'll be asked to Aintree for the Grand National. They say the summer season really starts with the private view of the Academy – Burlington House, you know. You mustn't miss that. I went one year with some cousins – the Scobys – I'll always remember the women's dresses and their hats, really lovely. We went to Ascot the same year, but I thought the clothes rather exaggerated. My dear child, you have so much to look forward to.' Mother spoke so eagerly that I could see how she used to look before she became poorly. I'd forgotten how pretty she had been, and now her poor face had become blurred and her eyes jellied, although sometimes, when she smiled, her real face showed and she still had white, even teeth and a pretty mouth.

At last Blanche boarded her train and we returned to the back seats of the hired Ford, Mother still talking about the delights of London. She chattered happily as we bumped over the country roads, but as soon as we entered the house, her cleaning mania overcame her. She looked in horror at the dining-room table where the breakfast things still stood on the table, pieces of toast with bites taken from them, teeth marks clear in the butter, and autumn flies buzzing round the uncovered marmalade. 'What can Marcella be doing? Hurry Vicky and clear the table; I think there'll be time to give the room a thorough turnout this morning. I'll run upstairs and change; then we'll start.' As she went upstairs, I heard her muttering, 'Just salad and cold meat for luncheon, or we'll never get through the work – well, perhaps some bubble and squeak.'

A letter from Holland arrived by the second post. I retired to the downstairs lavatory to read it and, sitting on the mahogany seat, I read the stilted English over and over again. Am I hygienic in my habits? No, filthy, I read letters in the lav. References. Who would give me a reference? A salary that equalled fifteen shillings a week in guilders. Guilders! How foreign and romantic that sounded. When will I be free? 'Please, God,' I prayed, 'let me be free to travel, don't let them stop me!'

I handed the letter to Mother as we sat over the tea table, crumbling a piece of chocolate cake on my plate as I watched her expression, first puzzled, then slightly irritated. Sighing, she laid the letter on the table and said, 'You can't possibly go to Holland, who would help me clean the house and "Hounds of Pleasure" sounds so peculiar. I must say, it was most deceitful of you to write without telling me.'

I tilted my chair back and, frowning, watched a cart pass the window. It rumbled past the house, the young driver standing up in the cart, his cap on the back of his head, laughing to himself. I felt how brave and free he was, while I sat in a room with stuffy red wallpaper eating chocolate cake and being scolded by my mother. I left the table and stood looking down at her with what I hoped was a determined expression on my face. 'All the same, I think I'll go,' I said firmly. 'They have offered to pay my fare and if I'm unhappy there, I can always return. Holland isn't very far away and think how clean the house will keep with only you and Edward living in it.'

Mother shrugged. 'Oh well, perhaps there is something in what you say, but I don't wish to discuss it now; I'm feeling done up. Ask Mr Hobbs about it when he comes tomorrow.' She got up to leave the room and said over her shoulder, 'I'm going up to my room to lie down a little; it's been a tiring day.' She left the door open behind her and I heard the click of her wedding ring as it came in contact with the banisters, then the opening and shutting of her bedroom door, the screech of the wardrobe being opened, then the unmistakable sound of a cork being drawn from a bottle.

TWO

WHEN I WAS PASSING through London a few weeks later I heard from Blanche about her meeting with Minnie Dawes. She told me that as soon as she put her foot on Paddington Station a little figure in royal blue hurled herself at her, kissing and patting, smiling and chattering. 'I knew you by your height and pigtails, I knew you at once.' Excited exclamations poured through the rouged lips, and the huge blue hat, pinned back in front with an artificial rose, bobbed up and down. Surely this flamboyant woman was not Miss Minnie Dawes, the cousin of Mr Hobbs. Far more likely to be one of the strange women who haunted stations in search of young girls. The strangers that Edward had hinted about that morning.

'You must take care, Blanche,' he had said in a low warning voice over the breakfast table. 'I hardly like to mention it, but there are wicked women in London, the pavements are thick with them at night, but it's the ones on stations that are worst. They are searching for girls to ship off to South America and stick at nothing, drugs and hypodermic needles are just in the day's work. There are Mormons too, searching for extra wives. Well, just beware, don't speak to anyone. Oh, and cars, don't accept lifts. I shouldn't go out at all except with Miss Dawes.' Blanche had exchanged amused glances with me at Edward's concern, but here she was being accosted by a white slaver as soon as she left the train.

Blanche leapt away when this queer little woman went to take her arm and cried out, 'I don't know you, I'm waiting for someone.' She was told in a soothing voice, 'Of course you are, dear. You are waiting for me.' Her arm was firmly taken again. 'My cousin told me what a tall girl you are, so I picked you out at once. I expect you are surprised to see someone as young as me, imagined I was an old fossil, no doubt; but we'll be like sisters, you'll see.' She steered Blanche towards some waiting cabs, a porter following with the luggage on a trolley. 'Come along now, dear, you must be tired after your journey.' Blanche reluctantly followed her new sister into the taxi, feeling uneasy until she heard the correct Bayswater address given to the driver; then she settled back in her seat and frankly stared at her companion. Not only her lips were painted, but her cheeks and her nose and chin were startling white and chalky as if sprinkled with Eno's fruit salts. Brilliant blue eyes, with the whites showing above the irises, twinkled through a little veil and there was one gold tooth that dominated the white ones like a king among his subjects. I only met Miss Dawes once and, although I knew what to expect, her appearance was still a shock.

Blanche was favourably impressed when the taxi drew up outside a tall Victorian house with cream pillars either side of the black front door. There was a small argument between the driver and Minnie Dawes before they entered the long narrow hall which ended in a gilt mirror. A battered maid appeared and helped the taxi driver take the luggage upstairs and Blanche was taken into a small back drawing room by Minnie Dawes. The walls were covered with photographs of past and perhaps present lodgers. Several haughty army officers stared sternly at girls wearing short skirts and white high boots or girls with chiffon round their bare shoulders, and there were portraits of exaggeratedly Scots Scotsmen and stout men in top hats. Except for the officers, no one resembled anyone Blanche had seen before and she asked if they were wearing fancy dress. 'Oh no, dear, not exactly fancy dress; they are in the profession, the stage, you know. I haven't any professionals now, just Mr Mason, and he's given up the stage for fortune telling – he calls it spiritualism. He does not practise here, of course; I wouldn't have anything like that in the house.' Miss Dawes took off her blue hat and, looking at it lovingly, carefully adjusted the pins as she said shyly, 'As we are going to be sisters to each other, I hope you'll call me Minnie.' Blanche said her hair was exactly like tobacco, but, when I saw it, it was covered by the big blue hat. She took her eyes away from the hair and assured her hostess she would call her Minnie; but she never managed to bring herself to do it.

Miss Dawes said, 'I'll take you up to your room now, dear. I'm afraid it's at the top of the house, but your legs are young and you won't notice the stairs.' They climbed and climbed and eventually came to a small landing with a dirty skylight in the ceiling. Miss Dawes opened a brown painted door and they entered an attic room with a dormer window built so high it was difficult to see the view of chimney pots against the evening sky. To Blanche the room had a certain charm although it was small and meanly furnished. She liked the rose-patterned wallpaper and the white iron bed decorated with brass knobs. It meant nothing to her that her clothes would hang behind a curtain, or that there was no fireplace and that the looking- glass would only reflect her head and shoulders. It was very much a servant's room.

Miss Dawes stood by with a worried expression on her rubbery face until Blanche turned to her, smiling for the first time since her arrival, to say that she was pleased with the room. The landlady beamed. 'That's right, dear, I knew you would be. You can use the back sitting room for your meals and to sit in, we'll eat together, just the two of us. My gentlemen all eat out except for their breakfasts which they have in their rooms. Well, I'll leave you to unpack and to make yourself at home. Supper at seven.' She tripped away leaving Blanche in possession of her first London room. She immediately stood on a chair and, opening the window, sniffed the London air. Sooty, but nice, she thought. She could see the gaunt backs of houses decorated with tortured plumbing. Lights were appearing in windows and curtains were being drawn. She could see two children playing with balloons in a bedroom, climbing onto their beds and tossing the balloons to the ceiling, and there was a maid frying on a stove in an upstairs kitchen converted from a conservatory. She turned from her window to give her room an almost tender glance because it was her first London home and her real life was about to begin. She hung her humpbacked coat behind the curtain and unpacked her school-girlish clothes, carefully putting the four pairs of real silk stockings that she had been hoarding since Christmas, in the top drawer of the varnished chest of drawers. She wound up the green travelling clock that her grandfather had given her on her sixteenth birthday and placed it on the dressing table next to the sixpenny pot of cold cream and the hairbrush with bristles set in rubber. She tried twisting her plaits into a bun at the back of her head, but was not pleased with the result; bounced on the bed to try out the springs; looked under it in case there was something dreadful lurking there and found a button; then decided it was time she went downstairs to face her supper with Miss Dawes. She walked down the stairs, the top flight covered in linoleum, the next in grey underfelt and the last two flights in florid Turkey carpet and the further she went down the more lonely and homesick she felt.

In the morning Minnie Dawes took her to the Honourable Mrs Mostin's Mannequin Academy. They walked down a wide street that appeared to have a little girl with a bucket kneeling on every step, their matchstick legs in holey stockings sticking out towards the street. They passed a convent with a grille in the iron-studded door and came to a street teeming with traffic and double-decker omnibuses, the first Blanche had seen. Then they were actually riding in one, but not upstairs because Miss Dawes said it was better to sit on the seats near the entrance, which gave one ample time to board and leave the bus, so they sat on the side seats under an advertisement saying 'Cats White, Homes Bright', Miss Dawes's feet only just touching the floor. They passed Hyde Park – Blanche thought it was the open country and wondered at the absence of cattle – and alighted opposite a black and disappointing Ritz. 'More like a cellar than a hotel, but perhaps it's good for the wine,' Blanche thought as she tried to peer through the heavily curtained windows.

Mrs Mostin's Academy was on the second floor above a tailor's in Sackville Street. It consisted of one large room, an office and cloakroom. There was no lift, so Miss Dawes left Blanche at the bottom of the staircase because she had enough of stairs at home. 'Second floor, dear,' she called brightly and turned away into the autumn sunshine. Blanche stood with one foot on the first step feeling hollow with nerves. She studied the names painted on the doors of the first landing, but saw no sign of a Mannequin Academy; so she climbed the next flight and there it was on a shining new door. 'Third floors must be called second floors in London,' she thought as she nervously rang the bell. A heavily made-up girl wearing glasses opened the door and, when Blanche told her she was a new pupil, the girl muttered something which could have been 'another sucker' and showed them into Mrs

Mostin's office. There was the lady of title sitting with her back to a muslin-curtained window. She was as brittle as glass, with pointed features and frozen eyes, half hidden by heavy lids. She seldom smiled because the gums showed above her teeth and her blue eyes never changed, just stayed dead like glass eyes. After questioning Blanche for a few minutes in her drawling voice, she told her that she had the perfect figure for a mannequin and took her to the room which was the 'Academy'. There were several girls lolling against walls and they vaguely nodded to Blanche when she was introduced to them and went on discussing something unintelligible in bored voices. Some of them had their arms loosely folded and others swung large leather handbags as they talked. They all wore well-cut straight skirts and silk blouses or cashmere pullovers and their hair was cut in more or less the same style, parted on one side, leaving a flop of shining, soft hair falling over one eye. A few more girls arrived and the lessons started. They consisted of walking round the room with trays balanced on the girls' heads, a few exercises, instructions on how to put a coat on and take it off, how to open a coat to display the lining, how to open and close a parasol or umbrella, how to walk into a room gracefully, pose, then walk so many steps, pose again and so on. When the lessons ended Mrs Mostin drew Blanche aside and said, 'Please wear court shoes tomorrow, Miss Green, and your coat, you really can't . . .' She faintly shrugged her shoulders and turned to another girl who was standing impatiently by. 'Oh, Mrs Mostin,' she heard, 'have you anything suitable for me yet? It's over a week . . .' Mrs Mostin patted her arm almost affectionately. 'Yes, Beryl, I have. Come early tomorrow, about nine o'clock, and I'll give you the address; these things take a little time, you know.'

Miss Dawes's servant was waiting in the entrance to take Blanche back to Bayswater. 'You'll have to manage by yourself another day, Miss. I've got more than enough work to do as it is,' she said crossly as she hustled Blanche towards Piccadilly. Even in the fresh air her mackintosh smelt of fried fish, which was not surprising as her parents kept a fried-fish shop; she became quite friendly as she told Blanche about it. 'It's real lovely the frying and sizzling and the smell's as good as a meal, passers-by say. As soon as we expand I'll leave off being a skivvy and help in the shop, and no more breakfasts to lug up them stairs.'

Blanche went to Mrs Mostin's every morning, sometimes learning to curtsey gracefully or to manage a stole or shawl. She had by now learned how to sit and discovered there was an art in getting in and out of a chair. 'Head up, Miss Green,' or 'Don't stoop, Miss Green. No, relax child, you're as stiff as a birch.' At the end of the six weeks Blanche's head had lost its drooping snowdrop look and her walk had become consciously graceful, so her fifty pounds was not entirely wasted. She found the afternoons hard to get through. Sometimes, feeling rather daring, she walked in Hyde Park practising her new walk; but men she had never met kept asking her the way or remarking on the weather, even Indians in turbans. She supposed they wanted to be friendly, but wished they would leave her alone. Occasionally they followed her to Miss Dawes's house and paced up and down the street as they gazed up at the windows. When she mentioned these men to Miss Dawes she told her they were dangerous men who wanted to 'pick her up' and she must ignore them or call the police. On Thursday evenings Miss Dawes would take her to the cinema. They both enjoyed sentimental films and usually came out red-eyed. On Saturday mornings the maid went shopping in the market at Shepherd's Bush, because everything was cheaper at the Bush, and sometimes Blanche went with her although she was ashamed of carrying the untidy baskets. You could buy anything there, including live goslings and clothes. She said she preferred these shopping expeditions to her Sunday morning walk in Hyde Park, with Miss Dawes dressed in her brilliant best attached to a puffing Pekinese wearing a large bow on its knitted harness. She called this outing 'church parade'.

When it became October a small fire was lit in the back drawing room and Blanche would sit there looking out of the window at the well-like garden where ivy climbed over clinkers and a few trails of periwinkle grew. A wall topped with trellis divided it from the next-door garden where the paths were ornamentally tiled. An old man with his hands clasped behind his back sometimes wandered there, occasionally barking like a dog. When real dogs barked he unclasped his hands and shook his fists. As the evenings drew in, the children from the poor end of the street rumbled about on roller skates and Blanche would have liked to have joined them.

She made no friends among the girls at the Academy. They seemed so much older than she was and talked about things she did not understand. They talked glibly of famous actors and said they were creaking at the knees; they spoke of dances, parties and theatres they had been to and made allusive jokes. Once she thought she had caught the meaning of a humorous remark and after a few moments had passed started to laugh and say how funny she thought it; but someone snubbed her with 'Joke over'.

She knew that she was missing the real London. It was like a fascinating book printed in a language she could not understand, and names like Temple, Monument, Park Lane, World's End flashed past on buses she dared not board. After the first week she did explore Piccadilly and Regent Street although she kept retracing her steps because she was afraid of losing her way. Losing her way became an obsession with her. Her only pleasure of those first days was gazing hungrily at clothes displayed in shop windows and comparing them with the kind of clothes that had come her way before. The old ladies of the village had dressed as crows and the middle-aged in their greys and mauves, their corsets creaking and with stiff felt hats on their heads, and the young women – there were very few of them – had worn cardboard tweeds or limp summer dresses with Peter Pan collars. Our mother's clothes had once been elegant but had become sad-looking like the things one sees hanging up in second-hand clothes shops. Blanche soon realised that, dressed as she was, she was unlikely to find work as a mannequin even if she did possess the perfect figure. She saw her reflection superimposed on the plate-glass windows so that she almost became part of the window display. There was the humped-backed coat and the heavy brown leather gloves that smelt of Bovril. In despair she wrote to Mr Hobbs demanding five guineas for a new overcoat: 'I look so different to the other girls in my worn old country coat. It's a child's one really. I'll never get work dressed as I am,' she wrote and, to her surprise, a registered letter arrived a few days later containing a five-pound note. The letter said she was to study hard and return the money as soon as possible because it was only a loan. Minnie Dawes offered to help her choose the coat, but she preferred to shop on her own even if the thought of opening great glass doors and being accosted by a haughty shop assistant was a little frightening. After two afternoons spent in window shopping and a considerable amount of thought in bed at night, she chose a navy velour wrap-over coat with a grey fur collar and from her small store of money bought a pair of suède gloves. The long plaits of black hair swinging over the grey fur collar looked out of place, so she bought some hairpins on the way home and after some experimenting decided to twist the plaits into a coil at the back of her head.

When she arrived at the Academy wearing the new coat and with her hair in a great glossy coil the girls exclaimed, 'What's happened to Baby?' and, intrigued with her improved appearance, clustered round her suggesting further improvements. 'What about some lipstick?' 'Here, try mine,' and a golden lipstick-case was thrust in her hand. 'No, you fool, that's the wrong colour, too orange. Mine will suit her better,' and the gleaming lipstick was snatched away and replaced by a glowing red one in a blue enamel case. Blanche gingerly applied it to her lips while the girls shouted instructions: 'Now some powder,' and golden powder-compacts were produced and shades discussed. Blanche was backing away from a horrible black brush that someone was insisting on smearing her eyelashes with when Mrs Mostin's drawling voice called the girls and they clattered off to their lesson, stuffing beauty aids in their bags as they went. Blanche slowly followed, tasting the lipstick on her lips and blinking her stiff eyelashes. She was relieved that the beauty treatment was over because she had noticed that one of the girls had had a pair of sinister little tweezers in her hand.

When Blanche had been at the Academy for nearly a month, I wrote to tell her that I was definitely going to Holland. It was all arranged in spite of great opposition from Edward. Strangely enough, Mr Hobbs had been in favour of the plan because he had once visited Amsterdam as a young man and it had made a great impression on him. 'Something about eating huge pancakes on the Amstel, he goes on about them all the time,' I wrote. 'I now have a British passport and a Dutch second-class boat ticket and a beautiful red leather coat, very suitable for a traveller. Old Hobbs gave me twenty pounds of my money after a bit of a battle and I've kept two pounds of it so that we can have lunch together in the grandest hotel you can suggest. I expect you know them all by now.' Blanche replied, 'The Ritz is all very well but rather old-fashioned. I think the Piccadilly Hotel would suit us better.'

THREE

THE MORNING I LEFT home Mother was recovering from being poorly and she'd been sick in the vegetable basket. We didn't think it was safe for her to travel in the Ford, although it was old – the driver was rather particular. So we parted on the doorstep. I had already said goodbye to Edward in the dining room and left him staring at an underdone fried egg on his plate, muttering crossly, 'You know I hate them with their eyes open; you should have fried it both sides.' He was still annoyed with me for going to Holland and didn't even warn me against strangers.

I cried a little on the station, I can't think why. I travelled in the same carriage as a woman who was on her way to spend a winter holiday in Eastbourne. I told her casually that I was on my way to Amsterdam and stopping in London for a few hours to have luncheon in the Piccadilly Hotel and asked if she knew it. The woman flicked imaginary dust from her dark coat and answered, 'By sight, of course, but if I'm in that neighbourhood I always go to the Popular. You can't do better than the Pop, the best value in London.' Feeling snubbed, I took a guide to London from my pocket and studied the map carefully, folding it into small squares so that the woman couldn't see what I was doing – I didn't want her to think I did not know my way about London. I was planning a route from Victoria Street to Regent Street via Trafalgar Square, so that I could visit the National Gallery if my walk didn't take too long. It seemed safer to walk than travel in a bus that might take me anywhere. The thought of the taxi journey from Paddington to Victoria weighed on my mind. I'd heard of London taxi drivers taking country people miles out of their way and demanding huge fares and there was the embarrassment of tipping. How much would they expect? Mr Hobbs said he had once tipped a taxi driver a penny and he had flung it in his face. This problem was solved by my fellow-traveller who suggested we share a taxi. 'Then you could leave your bags at the left-luggage office and collect them in the evening in good time for your boat train.' She gave me a penetrating look through her rimless spectacles and said dampingly, 'I must say, you appear very young and inexperienced to be travelling alone. I only hope you'll be all right.' I hoped so too, but replied, 'Oh, I'm used to travelling,' then checked my train and boat tickets for the third time since I'd entered the train. The boat tickets were printed in Dutch *Tweede Klas Batavia Line* and I was to arrive at Rotterdam and then take a train to Amsterdam where I was to be met by Mevrouw Groningen, my future employer. The journey did not worry me as much as the thought that Mevrouw Groningen and I wouldn't recognise each other. When the most filthy backs of houses appeared on either side of the train, I realised we must be nearing London and it was time to start heaving suitcases off the rack. The fellow-traveller had already let the window down and was sticking her head out in a purposeful manner, so I left the organising to her.

We parted at Victoria Station and, still convinced that I was not a hardened traveller, she pointed out to me where the bus terminal was – it seemed a most confusing place although I did see that some of the buses had Regent Street mentioned among many other names. I turned my back on them and nervously crossed a road, and then another with a clock in the middle of it and stood outside an old-fashioned draper's, and studied my map. From it I gathered it was the easiest thing in the world to walk to Trafalgar Square and then on to Regent Street. I walked up Victoria Street, only stopping to look in the windows of the Army and Navy Stores – the first big shop I could remember seeing. The street became more and more ecclesiastical, even faintly smelling of churches and I thought it an ideal place for public funeral processions. When I reached Westminster Abbey I was not in a mood to appreciate it. I kept saying to myself, 'This is the famous Abbey and there are the Houses of Parliament and that's Big Ben,' but it didn't mean much – perhaps my feet were tired. I trudged up Whitehall, wondering why walking in London seemed so tiring although I was trying to think about walking where King Charles II had trod – I'd been in love with him for years. Then suddenly, when I reached Trafalgar Square, my tiredness left me and I felt that I really was in London. The fountains were playing and the sun shining through the water, even making a rainbow of one jet of water. There was a building I was sure was the National Gallery and, on the right, a beautiful church with slender pillars decorated with what I took to be parsley made of stone, at its top a delicate spire. I looked around me and knew that I really was on my travels, and I stopped creeping about like a snail with its house on its back. I spent a confused hour in the National Gallery and almost staggered down the steps trying to digest what I had seen, so much beauty, so much flesh, colour, boring detail, fascinating detail and above all El Greco.

I saw Blanche standing outside the Piccadilly Hotel gazing across the road at some pigeons on a sunny windowsill, her dreamy face even more lovely than I'd remembered. Then we were madly talking, interrupting each other and laughing, and it was some minutes before we calmed down enough to enter the hotel. I can't remember much about the lunch except that the waiter was kind and helped us order a suitable meal and gravely thanked me for a sixpenny tip – the woman in the ladies room refused to take a penny and demanded a shilling.

Blanche took me home to Minnie Dawes for tea because she wanted to show me her room and 'a real London house'. 'There's an honourable in one room, but he never comes out, and a fortune-teller on the third floor – he's like a slug, all white and flabby. He told me my fortune for nothing although I had to let him hold my hand in his while he did it. It was such an awful hand, but the fortune was worth it. Plenty of money and two husbands – there are some hard times to go through as well. Oh, and I'm to beware of a man whose name begins with an R for some reason, and if ever I start a baby a bottle of Beecham's Pills will do the trick. What trick? I didn't like to ask.'

We returned to Piccadilly and said our goodbyes outside Swan and Edgar's. Blanche did not feel like walking to Victoria in her new high-heeled shoes and we considered it risky to chance an unknown bus with only an hour to go before my boat train left. I rushed along bumping into pale office workers and found hundreds more of them milling about Victoria Station. I retrieved my luggage and followed a porter to an almost deserted platform and into a dark train which looked as if it would never move again. I sat in my corner seat alone at first and was then joined by dim figures wearing what I imagined were foreign-looking clothes – fur-collared coats, square spectacles or Cossack hats. When the lights came on, I saw one very fat man with thick blue lips, who may have been Dutch, and two young men, both wearing depressing navy raincoats, both reading the *Evening News*; one had ratty teeth and the other a nose drip which he kept attending to with a sodden handkerchief. Just as the train was leaving, another fat man joined us. He really did look foreign, with his short fur-collared coat, and, as soon as he lit a small cigar, the railway carriage began to be abroad. It was then I noticed that the windows had 'Smoking' written on them and that was why I was the only woman, and I began to panic in case I had to share a cabin with these men. When we reached Gravesend I noticed a large girl who was travelling on her own and I kept as near to her as possible. Actually we were put in the same cabin and my fears were groundless. I could not have had a better travelling companion. She was a year or two older than me, plain and heavy, but kind and friendly. She had been living with a family in London for a year to improve her English and said I'd find Dutch family life terribly stuffy after England. The houses were stuffy, the food greasy and stuffy, and everyone too fat; all the same she was delighted to be going home. We walked up and down the deck together, the Dutch girl telling me about the sort of life I was about to live in Holland, making it sound rather dull but safe and a good place for an inexperienced traveller to start with. As we talked, the banks of the estuary grew further and further apart and the lights fewer, and then the boat started to lurch about and we were on the sea and could see the lights of other ships passing on the horizon.

Lying in my bunk I thought I was happier than I had ever been. The pitching of the boat, the sound of heavy footsteps overhead, voices shouting in an unknown language. I'd made up my mind to go abroad, and now I really was doing it. I suppose I must have slept because I can remember being disturbed by shouts and the boat seemed to stop and, thinking we were about to be wrecked, I called out to the Dutch girl, and she muttered something in Dutch, then English, about a pilot and after that the boat moved steadily and I felt that the night was almost over. I quietly dressed and went up to the deserted deck and there was Holland faintly showing. I could make out the forms of cows grazing in the flat fields, and later on I saw that the black and white cows wore overcoats. When it was light my new friend joined me and we went together to drink coffee and eat bread with thin slices of gingerbread on top and slices of delicious cheese. Then we went down to our cabin and exchanged addresses and I gave her a small bronze ladybird to remember me by. When we had disembarked and got through the customs, she was met by a large, darkly dressed family and I felt very much alone. I was horrified by the red-faced porters rushing about, all doubled up under heavy luggage as if they were slaves, and hardly liked to trust my suitcases to them they looked so savage. Somehow I found myself in a train heading for Amsterdam; but I was so afraid I can't remember how I got there. I looked out of the windows and was reassured by the homely view: more overcoated cows, and cheap villas with bedclothes pouring from their windows, square churches looking as if they had been built with children's bricks, more flat fields, an occasional gasworks – and hardly any windmills. When I reached Amsterdam another slave-like porter loaded himself with my cases and tried to force me to follow him; then I was rescued by a tall thin woman wearing a sealskin coat. She had the face of a greyhound and was Mevrouw Groningen. Although I found her appearance repulsive, I was impressed with her almost perfect English. We took a taxi to another station and from the windows I saw the lettering over the shops was square. Mevrouw Groningen felt my leather coat between her fingers and said it was good; then she put her fingers on my face and said something in Dutch that I later knew meant dirty. I was wearing face powder. Her face was pale and shiny like a stale candle. We got into a little train with a bell clanking to warn people not to walk in front of it. Later I heard the bell clanking day and night and it became a symbol of my misery.

We reached a bleak suburban station and walked on a dried mud road with a man following behind pushing my luggage on a barrow; we passed shoddy little houses with flat fronts and huge lampshades near the windows. I caught a glimpse of a flat little park with an arched bridge over an ornamental pond; then we came to a house exactly like the others except that the windows were dirty. A plump little German maid opened the door and we walked into a narrow passage and I was in the Groningen home. Dirty newspapers covered the bare boards of the floor and there were some newspapers falling down the stairs like a crazy carpet. We entered a sitting room and I saw dirty, stuffy curtains hanging over the windows. A dusty serge cover was draped over the table and the room was dominated by an organ-like sideboard which took up an entire wall and was loaded with tarnished silver-plated cups. An ugly stove gave out a faint warmth and there were a few chairs upholstered in brown American cloth with velvet cushions hanging on their backs. The maid was the only cheerful thing I saw in that house and she left a few days after I arrived. Mevrouw Groningen and I drank a cup of stewed tea together; then I was taken up to my bedroom and told to write to my family. The bedroom was tiny, with a collapsible iron bed which hung from a wall, but it was cleaner than the rest of the house. Sadly I stood by the window and saw a yard full of barking bull terriers, my future charges. I wrote to Blanche and Mother, they were quite cheerful letters; but I did tell them about the dirt and in each letter included a portrait of Mevrouw Groningen's terrible face. When she took off her hat I saw she had bald patches in her scant red hair.

I wrote my letters and unpacked. My hands were numb with cold and I was trying to summon enough courage to go downstairs when Mevrouw entered the room. She took my letters away and said her husband would post them, it wasn't safe to post them locally.

She took me outside to meet the Hounds of Pleasure in their wire cages and they were the most miserable dogs I have ever seen. There was something wrong with most of them. One had the ears of a bat and another, called Albert, had a dreadful broken tail that lay flat on his back – I've never seen a tail like it. One had lost an eye in a fight and another was deaf, and a poor bitch had had a paw bitten off in a fight. They were such savage fighters they had to be taken out singly unless they were different sexes. There were five dogs and three bitches living in separate cages and there was another bitch with puppies living in what should have been the drawing room. My first job was to give each of the six puppies a separate saucer of food. As soon as I entered the room, the mother flew at me madly barking, then bit my leg and tore my stocking. It wasn't a bad bite, more of a graze, only I was sorry about the stocking. Then the puppies clawed the other to pieces. It wasn't only my stockings that were destroyed, but the entire room. Dogs had eaten holes through the walls and gnawed away at the floor boards, and the grey wallpaper hung down in shreds, dog-high.

In the evening Mijnheer Groningen returned from the insurance company where he worked, and again I was surprised. He was a fair, rosy-faced man, quite good-looking in a tubby way, but years younger than his wife and spotlessly clean in his well-pressed black and white speckled suit. He could speak English, but not so well as his wife, and on the whole was a silent man. For dinner we ate almost raw steak fried in margarine with sauerkraut, followed by stewed tea. Before I went to bed I was presented with an alarm clock set to ring at six in the morning and was instructed in my duties. First the puppies were to be fed; then the dogs had to be taken out one by one on leads. I protested that it was still dark at that time, but was given a lantern and shown how to use it. Looking back I can't think why I wasn't given an electric torch.

I seemed to have hardly pulled my hard bed down from the wall before I was woken by the alarm shrilling in my ears. I stumbled out of bed and splashed some cold water on my face, dragged my clothes on any way and, without even brushing my hair, went down to meet the fearful dogs. The yelping, tearing puppies were bad enough at that time in the morning; but there is something horribly depressing about walking the roads with a bad-tempered dog and a lantern before dawn. It was bitterly cold and I could feel the corners of my mouth drooping with misery. Sometimes in the darkness groups of early workers would clump past in their clogs and, except when it was just a boy and girl, their voices sounded angry. When the dog work was finished, I breakfasted in the kitchen with the German maid – bread and cheese and more stewed tea. The pot stayed on the stove stewing all day. Although we could not understand a word the other said, the maid and I managed to have the most terrific conversations, and during the three days we were together I learnt all her history and most of the Groningens'. Apparently Mevrouw Groningen had been married to an elderly German in her youth and later had been divorced from him and her present husband had been the co-respondent. The maid said he couldn't escape, that he was trapped, and she laughed and laughed, showing her pretty teeth. They had only been married two years. Later in the dogs' drawing room I found a stack of silver-and-white invitations to their wedding. They must have been printed and never used.

When the German maid had gone Mevrouw Groningen said I was to take on the housework as well as the dogs. I didn't object to the washing up and was ready to attack simple cooking, and the cooking was extraordinarily simple in that house – steak eaten almost raw, sauerkraut, pickled herrings, smoked eels, dried fish with rice and, of course, slices of cheese. I couldn't bear most of the food and often longed for roast lamb followed by apple pie, but I knew that if I wanted to be a traveller, I must put up with queer food. It was the dogs and housework that bewildered me. I didn't know where to start, it was all so hopeless and dirty. Like most dirty women Mevrouw Groningen kept emphasising how clean she was, so houseproud and particular. She told me to scrub all the floors, so I lifted the newspapers and scrubbed away on all-fours: but the wood was so dirty the water turned to a sort of paste. A hose might have cleared it. Another day it was washing. A large wooden tub appeared in the kitchen and into it were thrown sheets, shirts, towels and socks and various underclothes. I added a few of my own clothes but unfortunately there was a sordid pair of dark blue bloomers in the water and for some reason they turned everything purple. Mevrouw Groningen was lying down while the washing was in progress and screamed when she came downstairs and saw the mauve and purple laundry dripping over the kennels in the yard. That was the only time any clothes were washed during my stay with the Groningens. I had the same sheets on my bed for nearly three months. I soon became filthy because the bathroom was unusable. There was a bath and geyser, which only Mijnheer Groningen was allowed to light; but no hot water came out of it the only time I tried to have a bath. Before I had it I had to spend ages emptying the bath, which contained soiled clothes, a dog's travelling box and heaps of old books that no one read. I found one English one among them and read it in my dirty bed.

I had one free evening a week, which I looked forward to all the other days. I would clean myself as well as I could with cold water and put on my least dog-damaged clothes, a decent pair of shoes and my red leather coat, and feel almost normal. At the station I'd powder my face and use the lipstick Blanche had recommended me to buy. I had to remember to wipe it off before I returned – I didn't want Mevrouw Groningen to point and say *vies*. For the first few weeks I was allowed out on Sunday afternoons. That soon ended; but while it lasted it gave me a chance to explore Amsterdam, which was all I had hoped 'abroad' would be. I used to pass restaurants and, as people came out, the revolving doors made a hissing sound because there was some kind of brush at the top. There was a wonderful smell of coffee and cigars and sometimes the sound of music, too, when there was a notice in the window saying 'Concert'. Sometimes I went to cinemas which I found surprisingly cheap, even the luxurious ones. There was one that was filled with oriental carpets, hanging from the walls and draped round brass pots containing ferns. It had a Russian name, perhaps Tuschinski; it was the grandest place I had ever imagined. In those silent days the films were easy to follow although I could not read the captions. As I wandered round the streets and quays men often came up and spoke to me and because I was so dark they were always convinced I came from the East Indies. It made me feel so lost and lonely. I went to the Rijksmuseum several times and although I enjoyed looking at the paintings I longed to be with some knowledgeable companion and some of the paintings made me afraid, the corpse in Dr Deyman's anatomy lesson and the beautiful and nightmarish Hieronymus Bosch.

Sometimes I stood by a clock tower in the centre of the city and, watching the trams whizzing past with bells ringing and lights flashing, I'd think, 'This is it, this is abroad.' Then the exhilaration would wear off and I'd feel lonely again and remember Mevrouw Groningen and the terrible dogs and the alarm going off in the darkness. I think the times I really enjoyed were when I walked by the canals in the residential areas, the tall warm-bricked houses reflected in the water and the peacefulness. Once I was sent to buy horsemeat in the port area. I was glad to get out even if it was only to buy horsemeat. I found the shop without difficulty, but was appalled when I went inside and saw skinned horses' heads with furry ears hanging from the walls, some with eyes and some without, some with slices of meat hanging from them. I managed to ask for the meat, then my upper lip became all damp and my ears were singing. A laughing woman led me outside, and the butcher also laughing came out with the meat saying, 'I speak English. Gee Gee, Gee Gee,' and made clicking noises with his tongue. I hurried away and found myself in a street of small houses with women sitting like fat birds in the windows, quite still. It was late when I returned and Mevrouw Groningen shouted at me in Dutch for about ten minutes; fortunately she was partly drowned by a German band playing outside. They sometimes came down our road and the people who liked the noise they made gave them money. Nearly every day an enormous dog pulling a cart filled with herrings would pass down the road. He belonged to a bad-tempered old man with a cigar always between his lips and a cap with earflaps on his head. Mevrouw Groningen said he was a bad man who spoke with double meanings, but she bought herrings from him most days.

I found that the letters I gave Mijnheer Groningen to post for me hardly ever reached England, so I guessed he must open them and read all the horrible things I said about his wife, the unlovable dogs and dirt. By a nearby blue-painted windmill I had seen a door with a letterbox cut in it, so for a time I posted my letters there; no one received them and later I discovered it wasn't a real letterbox, just one belonging to the deserted windmill. After that I gave up writing letters because there was only misery to write about.

It was a bitterly cold winter even for Holland. The canals became frozen and the children skated to school. There was a great chugging in the canals caused by icebreakers fighting the ice, which froze over almost as soon as it was cleared away. On Sundays the people from the surrounding countryside flocked to Amsterdam to skate on the main canals, the women looking wonderful in their national costumes, with their arms bare from the elbow. Although they were not elegant skaters, they skated with great gusto and the scene was exactly like the paintings I had seen in the Rijksmuseum. The man who served in the local butcher's shop was always asking me to go skating with him. He had his bulging eye on me and used to offer me bits of raw fat on the end of his carving knife.

Often during the night I would wake to hear the Groningens quarrelling and once Mevrouw Groningen ran out into the yard screaming in a horrible way into the darkness. She stayed in bed the next day, but her husband was the same as usual, quiet and rosy-faced. Sometimes, just for a day or two, Mevrouw Groningen would be kinder to me; then something would go wrong, usually a bloody dog fight and one of the dogs would get damaged. If they were in the house, they would eat their way through the walls until their heads met. She was always at her worst after one of these fights. It was my job to separate them, which meant that I was covered in bites and my clothes were torn to shreds. A hysterical bitch called Mavis had puppies in the Groningen bed and the entire litter was born dead. There were tears and scenes over the poor little bodies and she took to her bed for a week. When she recovered I found another very smelly puppy entangled in the bedclothes. I kept quiet about it. The dogs all had English names, but not the sort of names English people call their dogs. There was a Charley and an Edgar and, of course, Albert of the broken tail, and the bitches had names like Gladys and Veronica.

I remember there was a lull about the time of St Nicholas, which lasted until a day or two after Christmas. Once they gave me a slice off an enormous pastry letter filled with marzipan and one particularly cold evening, when I was shivering, a glass of Bols with hot water. When the bottle was empty I used it as a hot-water bottle. It was made of stone. A thing that added to my worries was that they only paid me for the first month. The following month nothing was said about money until I mentioned it, when Mevrouw Groningen said she was saving my salary to send to my mother. I told her Mother wasn't as poor as all that, so she said she would save it until the January sales when we could buy sensible clothes together; but when January came, she brought a great roll of black and grey check material and a dressmaker came to live in the house while she sewed it up into the queer straight dresses with short sleeves that Mevrouw Groningen always wore.

I only dared mention the money once more because it made her hate me so much. Nothing I did was right after that and she gave me the most humiliating work to do. I told her I wanted to leave and she laughed and shrugged her straight and narrow shoulders because she knew I couldn't return to England without the money for the fare. Some people who came to buy the puppies noticed how wretched I appeared and offered me a job as nursery governess to their small children. I took the visiting card they slipped into my hand behind Mevrouw Groningen's back; but, although they were pleasant enough, I felt ashamed of my torn and dirty clothes. I longed to be home and have a deep bath and start life again. I felt degraded, and when I curled up in bed at night I thought my unwashed knees smelt of roast chicken.

I dared not spend my last silver guilder. Although it was not worth much, I did not want to be completely without money like a tramp.

When my free evening came round there was nothing I could do except wander round the frozen roads in the darkness. There was a row of shops, but they were small and there was nothing to look at in their windows; so I looked in private people's windows and saw families sitting in the glow of a centre light almost as large as a cart wheel. They were usually eating. The last evening out I took was really one of the saddest times I can remember, not tragic but so desolate. I broke into my last guilder and bought a small bag of monkey nuts and, lying down on a felled tree in a frozen field, slowly munched them as tears of misery and cold ran down my cheeks. I was so tired I had to lie down somewhere. When I returned I met Mevrouw Groningen in the hall and she told me that she had once had a very bad servant that she disliked as much as she disliked me, and, while she was out, she had called the police and, when her boxes were searched, stolen linen was found among her things. She said this in the most threatening way and I thought she would put things in my suitcases if I left the house again, so I gave up my free evenings.

I had one more outing, though. I think it was a Sunday or public holiday and, when I returned with my lantern from exercising the dogs, I found both the Groningens up and dressed and several dog boxes in the hall. I hoped some of the dogs were going to be sold or sent away before they told me that we were all going to the Hague for something called a Dog Match. There was a wild two hours of grooming dogs and preparing food for animals and humans. At about eight o'clock we drove off in a small motor van which must have belonged to a greengrocer because the floor was strewn with broken vegetables. The Groningens sat in front with the driver and I sat on one of the dog boxes in the back facing a flapping curtain. As soon as it became light, I parted it a little so that I could see the landscape we were leaving behind. It was bitterly cold and rather sickening watching the roads narrowing and the trees flashing past. We seemed to be travelling much faster than we were. The imprisoned dogs scratched and whined in their boxes and once we stopped so that Mevrouw Groningen could be excused; otherwise the journey was uneventful and I was half asleep when we entered The Hague. I heard singing and saw a row of young men all arm-in-arm and their voices sounded beautiful in the frosty air. It must have still been early because the wide streets were almost deserted and the houses looked as if they were resting. I hoped I would be able to wander about the streets later on because I liked the few glimpses I had had of the town. The Match was held in a large hall; but it was not at all like an English dog show: no benches to display the dogs, a tremendous amount of talking and not much judging. It was the most cold and boring day and the Hounds of Pleasure didn't do well. There were some bitter feelings among the exhibitors and a certain amount of hard words. The Hounds of Pleasure were so depressed that I was able to lead two about at once without a fight; they had completely lost their spirit and one even licked my hand. By the late afternoon the Match appeared to be over and people started to leave the hall; but Mevrouw Groningen, to my amazement, went into a corner and started undressing. From a sack filled with dogs' travelling coats appeared a pink shining dress, very short and straight. She wriggled into it and dragged a comb through her scanty red hair and told me they were going dancing and I was to return alone. The van would call for me in an hour or two. Eventually I was the last person left in that dreary hall except for an old man in a fur cap who was waiting to lock up; but I suppose the van did eventually return for me otherwise I'd still be there.

The backs of my heels became all sore and chapped and Mevrouw Groningen laughed and said I had got 'winter heels'. Then the dog called Charley bit one of my fingers, the middle one on the right hand, and it became infected and the dirty work I had to do made it worse. It became so painful I used to chew my soiled sheets at night. Mevrouw Groningen made me put my finger in a cup and poured boiling water and soda on it and the nail fell off in the cup. The following morning she showed me a huge earthenware bowl filled with horse's dirty bowels and told me I was to wash them thoroughly and boil them for the dogs. Demoralised as I had become, I could not bring myself to touch those disgusting bloated tubes and backing away from them muttered, 'No, no.' Mevrouw

Groningen went mad after that and beat me about the head and then rubbed a great lump of raw meat in my face, screaming and shouting, beating and slapping, with her eyes bolting out of her head; but I had become so low I didn't hit her back. Suddenly she collapsed and bent over the sink and I escaped to my room. I couldn't lock the door and there wasn't even a chair I could put against it. Then I heard the welcome sound of the doorbell and Mevrouw Groningen answering it and talking to someone in a perfectly normal voice. They went into the sitting room and closed the door. Shuddering I saw my bloody face in the tiny looking-glass, not my blood, but some poor horse's. After I had washed my face, I changed into a dark woollen dress that had not been damaged too much and, with wet hands, tried to stroke off the dogs' hairs. I tidied myself as much as I could and pulled the cases from under my bed. With my septic hand I knew I would not be able to carry all my belongings, yet I could not bear to leave my books behind – some contained reproductions of paintings I loved and there were a number of old *Studios* that someone had once given me. There were my painting materials, which had never been unpacked, and my only evening dress, which I had never worn. There were so many things I could not leave behind and soon both the cases were full and I was stuffing toilet things into an overnight case. A silver-backed brush and mirror, the brush rather dirty, and a small silver box which may have been intended to hold sweets. These things might be worth something, but never enough to get me home. There was another book in my top drawer, one I couldn't remember owning; it was small and dark blue, with a gold design on it, and still very new and bright. My passport. I opened it and read on the first page 'to afford the bearer such assistance and protection as may be necessary'. I could go to the consul and show him what was written in the passport and he would have to send me home. Why hadn't I thought of it before? I crept downstairs with the heavy case containing books and heard a reassuring natter natter in Dutch coming through the sitting-room door. The dog Albert appeared from nowhere and followed me in quite a friendly manner. As soon as I started dragging down the second case he gave excited barks. I bashed him with the small case I was holding in my bad hand, but he thought it a game and barked even more and I couldn't quieten him. The natter in the sitting room ceased and Mevrouw Groningen's terrible profile appeared through the door, also a flurry of white and the most fearful dogfight started. One dog had the other by the throat and Mevrouw Groningen stood there screaming and holding her own throat as if it was being torn as well. My one idea was to get the cases safely out of the house and, leaving the front door open, I left the house for ever. I had to drag my cases one by one to the station, and once I looked back and saw Mevrouw Groningen standing in the frozen street in her short-sleeved dress. When she saw me turn, she shook her skinny fist and shouted something about police. It was dark by the time I reached the station and there was nearly an hour to wait for the train, so I hid in the lavatory in case Mevrouw Groningen with an army of police came searching for me. As soon as I got into the train with its clanking bell, I felt drunk with relief. I found myself gasping out little Dutch sentences to my neighbours. Some of them could speak a little English and we were all soon laughing and talking and, to my relief, one of the young men carried my cases to the left-luggage office and I was saved the expense of a porter. I had my silver, my magic passport and the equivalent of eightpence in Dutch money. I felt wonderfully hopeful.

A friendly-looking policeman told me the address of the consulate, but added that it was too late to call there; I'd have to wait until the morning. I thanked him and walked away not very downcast because I knew my bits of silver would bring me enough money to pay for a night at a cheap hotel. I had never stayed in one and began to look forward to the experience. I imagined hotels were rather wicked places, filled with haughty women wearing evening dress and slightly drunk men smoking cigars as they played cards.

I had no watch, but I saw by the clock that had all the trams clanking and ringing round it that it was later than I thought, and then I saw that although the shop windows were brightly lit many of them were already closed. I hurried down a nearby arcade where I had noticed a jeweller's shop; it was already closed and, in any case, looked so expensive I could not imagine they would be interested in my battered silver. I started to run towards the poorer streets of the city, banging my case into people as I ran. I couldn't last the night on only eightpence. Eventually I found a small jeweller's which was in the process of closing. I rushed in and opening my case displayed the brush, the mirror and the little silver box. I had given the silver a quick rub with Frau Mevrouw Groningen's bedcover, but the bristles of the brush were dirty. The old jeweller put down the wooden shutter he was holding and gave one glance at my silver and, shaking his head, placed the things back in my case, carefully arranging my sponge-bag over the looking-glass. I shut the case and slowly walked away; neither of us had spoken a word. I made my way back to a more familiar part of the city although it did not matter if I got lost. I had all night to find my way in. The cold was intense and my hands felt dead in my leather gloves and my face had become all numb.

I wandered aimlessly by a frozen canal and walked into a tree because I was so numb – the pain, when it came, was worse. Then I saw the windows of a restaurant shining through the bare branches of a tree and there was a large painted sign of a teapot which somehow reminded me of the Cheshire Cat, and it appeared to be vanishing and becoming bright again. I went upstairs and ordered a pot of tea. There were only a few people in the restaurant, mostly men sitting at tables near the windows eating proper meals. I felt embarrassed only ordering tea, so went to the back of the room where no one would notice me. Every now and then waves of wonderful smell came my way, perhaps jugged hare, and I thought that if I sniffed it for long enough it would be almost the same as eating it. I heaped sugar into my tea because I knew it was sustaining. I sat over it as long as I could and it must have been after ten when I left my table. I paid for the tea, but there was not enough money to tip the waitress, and in my hurry to escape before she found out I left my wretched case behind. An elderly man with a clipped moustache hurried after me with it and, when I thanked him in English, he replied in such perfect English I looked at him hopefully. Then I saw his face was Dutch, and went away without daring to ask his help.

After that there was a nightmare time of walking and walking. My poisoned hand had become so painful I couldn't bear to wear my glove. I had cut off one of its fingers because of the bandage, now my whole hand was becoming swollen. I had to walk quickly to try and keep warm and to look purposeful, otherwise men came and walked beside me, even taking my arm. I hit one in the face with my case and he slunk off. As usual, most of them asked if I was from the East Indies. The men were worse in the quiet streets where I hoped I would find somewhere to sit down. I so longed for somewhere quiet where I could hide until morning and I realised it was better to be a stray dog than a stray human because they are not so noticeable.

I tried sitting on my case for a few minutes, but it was too small, and, when I got up and started my aimless walking, it suddenly flew open and its contents spread over the icy pavement. This was more than I could bear and I knelt among the scattered objects crying hopelessly. A man was peering at me and I thought, 'Oh, God, not another!' He bent down and picked up my hand mirror and it was not broken. He said kindly, 'My dear child, what are you doing at this time of night?' It was the man who had spoken to me in the restaurant. For a moment I thought he had been following me all this time; then I realised I'd been walking more or less in a circle and was near the restaurant, only its sign was not lit now. I got up and leant against a wall while this man picked up my things and I was glad the light was dim and he wouldn't see how dirty my hairbrush was. He went on questioning me, so I told him about the consulate being shut and having no money and nowhere to go and, when everything was back in the case, we walked away together to his house. I thought, 'Well, if he rapes me, things can't be worse than they are and at least there'll be a warm bed.' We came to his house, tall and dark on the edge of a canal, and, when he opened the front door, I saw a great brown and white marble staircase. There was an oriental air about the place: Persian carpets and dark carved wood and tall ferns in oriental pots. We walked up these great stairs and I thought, 'Are we going to bed already without anything to eat first?' The room he took me to was not a bedroom; it may have been a morning-room, a hot and over-furnished morning-room. As the cold in me melted, I felt as if I was throbbing. The questions went on and I answered them as well as I could: then he went away for a time and I was glad to be alone. When he returned, he was carrying a silver tray with tea things arranged on it and sweet biscuits. I did not like to take too many and give a greedy impression although I was feeling hungry and sleepy in alternate waves. Through the waves I listened to my rescuer talking in his flattish voice and came to the conclusion that I wasn't to be raped at all, he didn't have a raper's face. It was a plump, precise businessman's face, very clean and pink, with this grey clipped moustache and a smile below which showed square teeth but was not a real smile. His hair was silver-grey and the short parts at the back stuck out straight, but he managed to smooth the top part down. He told me that he had English blood in his veins, far back but flowing strongly; he even had an English name, Herbert Crump. It suited him very well. He lived alone except for a housekeeper. His family had lived in the same house for three generations and now he was the only surviving member and this seemed to worry him. There had been a younger brother but he had died of meningitis as a boy and, when he spoke about his death, even after all these years, his voice shook. After he had been talking for some time he noticed me emerging from one of my waves of sleep and started worrying about where my sleep was to take place: he obviously wasn't keen on me doing it in his house. Then he remembered a friend who owned a hotel and went to his study to telephone him. I would have been happy to sleep in my plush armchair, the thought of facing the cold again was so repellent; but at least I was not going to be raped and I would see the inside of a hotel at night.

Mr Crump held my arm in the deserted street until we came to the Amstel. It was not frozen and

I could see the water very dark. I was so tired I could see nothing of the hotel when we reached it and only had a vague impression of Mr Crump talking to a tall thin man who resembled Hans Andersen; then I was in my bedroom. It was the most beautiful room I had ever seen, with paintings on the ceiling and a huge four-poster bed.

The next morning the landlord, who I now saw had a better nose than Hans Andersen, bathed my septic hand in the gentlest way. I was served with a luxurious breakfast, cheese and ham and several kinds of bread and the most heavenly coffee. I was finishing my third cup when a grave young man with a shining face appeared at my table and said he was Mr Crump's secretary and he had come to take me to the consulate. Mr Crump had been in touch with them and they were expecting me. When I arrived there, I was immediately taken to the consul's office. I had my passport open on the first page, but it wasn't necessary. He was the most helpful and charming man, wearing an impressive overcoat with an astrakhan collar. This was the first Englishman I had talked to for over three months and I talked away as if he were a near relation. He told me he had been to the South Pole among other places and that was where his beautiful coat had come from. He asked about my family and what my future plans were and I told him I was determined to study art and I was going to force Mr Hobbs to give me my money. I had been eighteen for over six months and had hardly had a penny so far. That brought us round to money and he offered to lend me some for the journey home, not the Government's money, but from his own pocket. It was less complicated that way. Someone was sent out to buy my train and boat tickets to get me as far as London and I was given money to cover the rest of the journey and the odd meal on the way. He even sent a telegram to Mother so that she would be expecting me. When I left the consulate, I found the young secretary still waiting for me; he was a pleasant boy but had not the glamour of the consul.

Mr Crump's elderly housekeeper told me that he was not returning for luncheon and that I was to sit in the study. She served me a cold meal there and I felt she had a disapproving air and was relieved when she cleared it away and I would not see her any more. I longed to explore the house, but knew that would be unpopular. It was enormous for a single man; he had told me that there were disused warehouses on the top. The air in the study was stupefying, as if it had been breathed over and over again by very old people, and the furniture was mostly made of brown, cracked leather. The books looked as if they had not been read for years and gave the impression that they were collected sermons. I did eventually find two books printed in English – Foxe's *Book of Martyrs* and a Victorian book on famous witches. I chose the book on witches, but it turned out to be rather disgusting.

Soon after six, when I was almost in a coma through boredom, Herbert Crump returned in a brisk and lively mood. He said he was going to take me out for an early dinner and then put me on the boat train. I showed him my tickets in case he would like to check on the time, but he waved them aside and said he had done so already.

We went to a very large restaurant near the station, most likely the dining room of a hotel. There was hardly anyone there, just masses of waiters. Mr Crump ordered an excellent dinner and we drank wine with it. We talked about the English blood flowing strongly in his veins and about boats. He owned a small yacht and was devoted to sailing and said he hoped to take me sailing when the summer came. I said I'd love to, although my one idea was never to set foot in Holland again. Then we walked to the station arm-in-arm and collected my luggage, which I was allowed to have in my compartment because the train was not crowded. Mr Crump gave me a kiss and called me his dear little friend, and soon I was rattling through the night on my way home.

FOUR

WHEN I REACHED THE port at Rotterdam, I had a shock. My boat had already sailed and I would have to wait until the following evening. Mr Crump had made a mistake. A taxi driver who spoke English was really sorry for me, particularly when I told him I had hardly any money left. He took me to a clean cheap hotel, the sort of place that only does bed and breakfast, and he refused my tip. It was extraordinary how many kind people I was meeting now I was leaving Holland.

Although the guests were expected to leave the hotel early in the morning, I sat over breakfast as long as I could because I did not want to spend hours walking the streets. One of the disadvantages of being almost penniless is that one is so cut off from lavatories. I know there are free ones but they never come my way.

Again I was plodding through the streets with my little case and I felt ashamed, as if I had let the consul and Herbert Crump down after their help. In spite of the cold I enjoyed the first hour or two exploring Rotterdam. I tried to find a museum where I could keep warm; but instead found the largest post office I have ever seen. It was beautifully warm inside and, although I did not like to hang about indefinitely, I went there from time to time and wrote telegrams, standing in the booth as if in deep thought. Years later, when Rotterdam was bombed, I remembered that friendly post office and hoped it was spared. I bought a roll of bread and ate it in a frozen park and still had a small silver coin in my bag as well as an English pound note that the consul had given me. I thought I could afford a coffee in a cheap restaurant, but while I was searching for one in a narrow street, found something better – a small cheap cinema. The seats were only wooden ones but it was wonderful to have somewhere to sit. I could hardly see the film because I was so close to the screen, which did not matter much because it was a gangster one and I never cared for them. I stayed there for hours listening to the tinny piano and thinking of other things.

It was dark when I collected my cases from the depot where the taxi driver had left them. My hand was so much better I was able to carry them both at once and in the darkness I managed to escape the porters. Everything was still and there was a white boat gleaming on the dark water. I saw it had the right name on it and, as I walked up the gangplank I felt so moved I could hardly control my tears. I dumped my luggage on deck and looked round. The ship seemed to be deserted until a tall young man, who I later learnt was a steward called Frans, appeared. He told me that passengers were not allowed to board the boat for another hour. He spoke English fluently and, when he heard my tale of misfortune, he took me to the first-class lounge and we talked to each other there. He would have been good-looking except that one of his front teeth was decayed, which hurt me every time I looked at him. Although he knew I had no money to pay for a meal, he brought me some sandwiches and fruit and, what I was longing for, a cup of coffee. He sat gazing at me while I ate, telling me from time to time that I was the prettiest girl he had ever seen. I didn't feel pretty because I had a horrible suspicion that a stye was coming on one of my eyes.

Frans left me when we heard the sound of other passengers arriving. There were very few travelling that night and I had my cabin to myself. I lay on my bunk reading my old *Studios* and studying the advertisements, particularly the ones advertising art schools.

There was one called Wracker's that advertised itself as a Parisian School in London, which seemed to mean that you could start to draw from the nude straight away and not waste years studying from the antique. I knew I had not enough money to start at the bottom; far better to start at the top and work down if necessary. I knew nothing about grants, which was perhaps just as well, because they were not plentiful in those days and were usually given to established art students. I made a note of Wracker's address and hoped I'd have time to call there on my way through London.

The sea was rough that night and I woke up once feeling as if my stomach were up in the ceiling. The boat was lurching about and creaking and groaning, but I was so tired I went to sleep again until I was awakened by a gentle knocking at the door and Frans appeared with my breakfast. He dumped it down on the opposite bunk and tried to kiss me as I lay under the blankets. I felt his hand sliding underneath and sat up quickly and was relieved I was wearing a strange garment consisting of knickers and petticoat all in one. Frans produced a postcard showing a small Rotterdam hotel which he said belonged to his parents. He lived there between boats. He wrote his name on the back and asked me to write to him there. He wanted my address and I told him I would let him have it when I was settled. I was planning to live in London. Then he became quite desperate and cried out that he didn't want to lose me, that he wanted to marry me. While I ate my breakfast, he stared at me with his brown eyes and told me the sort of life I would lead living with his parents and perhaps helping in the hotel. It sounded ghastly, but I smiled at him when I wasn't eating and let him hold my hand because I was so grateful for his kindness. It was a relief when the boat came to life, bells ringing and the usual clumping about overhead. He had to go away then and I was able to dress. He had told me to wait for him on the first-class deck and he would bring up my luggage.

It was becoming light when the boat berthed at Gravesend and the parting from Frans was not too embarrassing because we were surrounded by first-class passengers wearing heavy overcoats. I was disappointed to see that Gravesend seemed very like Holland and I had no real feeling of homecoming until I reached Victoria Station and saw newspaper placards about King George's illness. I had seen headlines about it in the Dutch papers, but I had only been able to make out a few words. Now I could read everything I saw – Platform 2, This Way Out, Ladies, Underground – the magazines on the bookstalls had familiar faces; *Punch* and *The Tatler* looking exactly the same as they had looked all my life; and there was the green *Lady* where our governesses had come from.

I had now lost my fear of public transport and, after I had disposed of my luggage, took a bus to Oxford Street to hunt for Wracker's which the advertisement had said was behind Selfridge's. I found the right building, although it did not look much like an art school, with its large window displaying trusses and other surgical appliances. There were some pincers and forceps which could have been used for sculpture, but that was all. Then I noticed a side entrance with a lot of names painted on the wall. Wracker's was fairly high up and I had to use the lift to get there. I had imagined a huge building with picturesque art students pouring through its doors; all I found was a single door slightly open, so I pushed it a little more and crept in feeling horribly nervous. A dim little woman shot out of an office and I asked if this really was Wracker's Art School and she said it was, only it closed on Saturdays. I was surprised it was Saturday; I had lost count of the days long before. Then Mr Wracker appeared in person and stood smiling in the doorway and the place became alive. He had a white fringe of beard round his chin and perched on his head was a small black beret which he used to say he wore to keep the flies off his bald head. I told him that I had seen his advertisement in *The Studio*. 'Oh, we advertise, do we? I never know what Miss Dunn is up to,' he said vaguely and Miss Dunn gave a prim little laugh. 'Well, come along, my dear, I'll show you the school, it isn't very large you know, but individual, not another school like it in London.' The school consisted of a large life room, a painting room and a students' sitting room. It was very small and someone had painted the furniture scarlet. Then there was the office and Mr Wracker's own studio, where we ended up to have a little talk. There were a few unframed paintings that looked as if they had been painted long ago, not badly painted, but dead. On an easel there was an unfinished painting of a nude wearing a turban on her head and, when I looked closely, I saw it had been painted years ago: the white parts of the canvas had gone yellow with age. In the middle of the room there was a seesaw made of polished wood with carved seats; it looked Victorian or perhaps earlier. 'Sit down, dear, sit down,' indicating the seesaw with a chubby hand. Gingerly I sat on one of the seats and Mr Wracker climbed onto the other. 'Now tell me, child, why do you want to study art?' We talked for about twenty minutes; sometimes we went up and down, but most of the time I was suspended in the air because Mr Wracker was heavier than me. When I asked about the fees he said, 'I know nothing about that. Miss Dunn looks after all that sort of thing.' So I went back to Miss Dunn and she gave me a prospectus and made a note of my name and address. Then I hurried off to catch a train home. I had been away exactly three months.

FIVE

ABOUT A MONTH BEFORE my flight from Holland, I had received a letter from Blanche telling me that she was home again because the Mannequin Academy had been unable to find any work for her or many of the other girls for that matter. She was fearfully depressed about it and said home seemed even worse than usual now she had had a glimpse of London. That was the last letter I had received from home, but during that month there had been several changes. The main one was that Mr Hobbs had died of a stroke, so there was no one left to look after our money, unless one counted Edward. He had become more human while I had been away, perhaps because he had a girlfriend called Sylvia, who had pink cheeks and a soft expression although her eyes were a bit slitty. She was a secretary and lived with her parents in a village about ten miles away. Edward had met her on the train but I cannot imagine how he came to speak to her without a formal introduction – perhaps she dropped her gloves or fainted. Mother tolerated her. She still slaved away with Marcella Murphy cleaning the house and was hardly ever poorly because it interfered with the housework. Blanche and I were back at our old job of sweeping carpets and in spite of the carpets I was glad to be home after the horrors of the Groningen establishment. One of the first things I did, of course, was to write to the Amsterdam consul and return the money I had borrowed from him. I hoped we would start a correspondence. I never heard from him again. Herbert Crump on the contrary showered me with formal letters, written in neat, spiky writing. It was nice to receive letters from abroad although they gave me a feeling of guilt. I was afraid I would have to marry him out of gratitude. I never wrote to poor Frans.

I stayed at home for three weeks and during that time made arrangements to become an art student. At last I had my own money and a cheque book and was able to pay a term's fees to Wracker's school. The two hundred pounds had dwindled alarmingly because of the money I had already spent and the fifty pounds

Blanche owed me. Poor Blanche, I couldn't go off and leave her at home waiting to become eighteen. She would pore over the advertisements in *The Times* and *Telegraph* and was always seeing things that might suit her: 'It needn't be mannequin work. I'm willing to do anything, even be one of those women who sit in lavatories and collect tips, or a shop girl or one of those girls who demonstrate things in big stores. It is making a start that's so difficult.'

Our lives depended on advertisements in those days; we were so cut off, we had to do everything through them. In some paper I discovered that a girl could live in a hostel in the centre of London with meals included for as little as a pound a week. The prices of hostels varied considerably and some of them must have been subsidised in some way. I found one just off Baker Street, very near Wracker's, and I arranged for the two of us to go there. I think we had to provide a clergyman's reference, which pleased Edward. He had been against Blanche going to London until Sylvia said that two girls are less likely to get into trouble than one on her own. I don't know how she came to that conclusion, but Mother and Edward both fell for it. This time there wasn't anything particularly emotional about our departure and the only tears were shed by Marcella Murphy. We just went away one morning and never returned.

As we had never been to boarding school, the hostel was a shock to us; nothing like it had come our way before. As soon as we entered the hall, we saw a pale girl with eyes red from crying, running down the stairs and she snarled at us, 'You'll be fools if you come here. It's worse than prison.' Then she shot through the front door with her cardboard suitcases. We looked at our heavy luggage and wondered if we should follow her example and escape while there was still time and were whispering agitatedly together when a woman who resembled a hippopotamus appeared. She had not the charm of a hippopotamus and there were stiff white whiskers growing on her chin. This hippo-woman was called Miss Bowles and she was in charge of the hostel. She took us to her little cubby-hole of an office – there was scarcely room for the three of us – and gave us a talk about the rules of the hostel. We were to be in by ten every evening unless we had special permission. We were not allowed to wash clothes, even stockings, on Sunday. No gentlemen visitors were allowed further than the hall. We were expected to go to church, preferably with a group on Sunday morning, and also to attend missionary lectures which took place in the hostel fairly frequently. There were Saturday afternoon rambles too. There were a lot of other rules and restrictions written up in our dormitory. We had never seen one before and this one had sixteen beds and only two windows one end. We did have curtains we could pull round our beds to give us some privacy; but with all this white rag hanging about and the windows only open a chink, it was horribly claustrophobic at night. We were given adjoining cubicles. Blanche found a black crutch trimmed with brown leather by her bed and it frightened her.

In the morning we were woken by clanging bells. Then a battle for the two washbasins started and later there was the clatter of about eighty girls on the stone stairs. The dining room was a huge place with texts all over the walls – the house was stiff with them, these texts, all miserable ones. We had to stand at our long tables while Miss Bowles said prayers and grace. The prayers she mostly made up as she went on, rather personal ones, asking for forgiveness for girls who behaved badly. That first morning it was a prayer for the girl who had spoken to us when we arrived. She had been sent away for washing stockings on Sunday and there were prayers for girls who were out of work or ill and for ungrateful girls. This went on for ages while our porridge cooled. The hostel food was the kind you eat to keep alive. Even then it gave you boils; the girls were covered in them.

That first morning I was feeling apprehensive about going to the art school, the thing I had been longing to do for years. It was the thought of facing all those students and drawing in public, perhaps at an easel, and on the way there I remembered that there were at least three art masters to be faced as well. Blanche and I stood outside the building watching the people who entered and wondering which were on their way to Wracker's. Blanche had a *Times* and a *Telegraph* under her arm and was bravely going off in her search for work. I was the cowardly one. Fortunately I met old Wracker in the passage and he took me to the office and told me all the things I would need – drawing paper, charcoal, a portfolio, an extraordinary sort of rubber which seemed to be made of plasticine, and a small piece of shammy-leather. There was also a book on anatomy that all the students had to buy and that was another fifteen shillings. It was stolen before I even had time to put my name in it. Wracker took me into the life room with all my equipment and introduced me to the art master; but I hardly noticed him because I was so arrested by the model posing on a platform. She was a slim, young girl, the colour of an unripe peach and seemed to be almost floating above the forest of easels. I had thought of 'life' meaning alive, not naked. There was something extraordinarily moving in seeing this girl so still and remote, apparently unconscious of all the eyes peering at her.

I stood in the overheated room with a huge piece of drawing paper facing me and a stick of charcoal in my hand. I tried to copy the student directly in front's drawing, but all that came on my paper was something small and mean and smudgy and I hastily flapped it off with my shammy-leather and started again, this time looking at the model. The result was no better. Then the art master was standing behind me and my hand shook so much the charcoal broke. He helped himself to a new piece and drew over my smudgy drawing, lovely easy lines with a swing to them, and I began to grasp what it was all about. He was an excellent teacher and I learnt a lot from him, although the method was wrong, probably an idea of old Wracker's left over from his youth. We did these large drawings in charcoal, obtaining highlights with the plastic rubber so that the breasts stood out like apples and smudging the darker places with our fingers or the shammy-leather. When you got the knack of it it was most effective, just a trick really. We were supposed to make a drawing last a week, but we usually became bored with our overworked drawings after three days and started another from a different angle. There was a painting room for the more advanced students. My money ran out before I got there.

The students were mostly girls wearing overalls, often with charcoal drawings on the back. Only about half of the girls were serious students, but the young men were all hard-working. Perhaps they were paying their own fees. There wasn't a handsome one among them; they were all inclined to be pasty faced and squat and wore businessmen's suits. Later on a young man from Arizona appeared and he was handsome, only so conceited no one could bear him. He was always dressed in riding breeches and boots that looked as if they had never been near a horse. He must have known about horses because he never drew anything else if he could help it, even the models were often given horses' heads and legs. There was a tall girl called Vi who was the life and soul of the school. She had a group of followers and they used to crowd into the little scarlet room and play records on a portable gramophone. If anyone else had gone into this room they would have been made to feel pretty uncomfortable. There were a few middle-aged women wearing flowered overalls and one took a liking to me when I first came. I asked her why the model had been changed in the middle of the week before we had finished our drawings and she said, 'Oh, my dear, she was menstruating all over the throne.' I said, 'Menstruating, what on earth do you mean?' She looked surprised: 'Surely you menstruate, child?' and I looked at her angrily because from her expression I was sure she meant something disgusting and replied,

'No. I don't,' and we avoided each other after that. On the whole the students were friendly. One or two even asked me home and eventually one helped me to get my first job. Only there was this feeling that they all came from such safe backgrounds, and Blanche and I were so alone. Sometimes I was afraid and thought how easily we could fall off the world.

The girls in the hostel were very different. I call them girls though there were a few elderly council-school teachers with home-dyed black hair. You could see it was home-dyed because their scalps were dyed as well. Some of the girls were cripples and sewed in the workrooms of dress shops, often in the basements. Many of them were shop assistants. Some worked in wholesale houses and a few in offices. One or two were foreign. Without exception they were all exceedingly kind to us, giving us the best places in front of the fire and showing us how to knit and sew and how to cut out sleeves and collars and even how to sew on buttons – you sew the button first. They also gave Blanche advice about finding work. Hardly any of them had boyfriends, in London, anyway. The early hours of the hostel made it difficult and they had so little to spend on dress and make-up; also most of them had a wan look and, of course, there were the boils. In spite of the girls' kindness, we were wretched. Miss Bowles was the worst thing about the place, or it may have been the food.

Luncheon sausage and veal loaf, watery cornflower shape and dried-up rice pudding; sometimes there was a small kipper for high tea, only they were not like the kippers at home and did not go well with cocoa. There were some nice kitchens down in the basement and a terrible place where we were supposed to wash and dry our clothes. My only attempt at laundry work had been at the Groningens' and that hadn't been a great success. We had no idea of what kind of soap to buy and how different materials should be treated and we had never come across hard water before. Frightful black specks came on our underclothes and one morning, when we had the dormitory to ourselves, we took our mirrors to the window and saw that we were dirty too, sort of grey looking. I think we were only allowed baths at weekends. I bought some tins of theatrical make-up remover and we cleaned ourselves with that. It took us months to get used to the insidiousness of London grime and the hard water.

On the first Sunday at the hostel we were taken to church by Miss Bowles, a whole group of us, with Miss Bowles and one of the elderly schoolteachers walking behind. We went to an imposing-looking church with pillars; but the service was not the same as in the church at home, perhaps it was some kind of chapel. It was an interesting experience but we decided we wouldn't do it again because we had to wear borrowed hats which came low over our brows. In the afternoon we went to a Lyons Corner House in Oxford Street and sat over fourpenny ice-creams listening to the band. We vaguely fell in love with the leader, a violinist we called Byron because we thought he had a mad, bad face. There was a large family party sitting at the table next to us, chattering away in some strange language although at times they spoke English; later we realised they must have been talking in Yiddish. We used the Corner House as an escape from the hostel and must have sat longer and spent less than any other customer. Indians wearing turbans, some accompanied by exotic women in saris, swarmed in and out. Black and yellow faces (and a great many pasty-pink ones) and all this lush music hypnotised us. Then we would return to the hostel for high tea in the basement surrounded by texts.

I think it must have been our second Sunday at the hostel that Violet Scoby came to visit us. We had missed the high tea when we returned and were worried about the ice-cream having to last us until the next morning. Then a girl came to tell us that a woman was waiting for us in the hall, 'Ever so smart, with a big hat,' and, wondering, we went downstairs and there was Violet Scoby, one of the Scoby family that Mother often mentioned. I think Violet must have been a fifth cousin or something like that. She certainly was rather elegant, very tall and wearing a black wrap-over coat trimmed with fur, and a three-cornered hat. She told us who she was and asked if there was anywhere we could talk. There wasn't anywhere private, only the big sitting room with all these poor girls with boils milling around. I suggested the ABC over the way and we went out with her without putting on our coats; we felt like dogs being taken an unexpected walk. She ordered coffee and the waitress suggested 'pastries'. We hated cakes being called such a ridiculous name and shook our heads. Then Blanche asked, 'Would it be awful if we had buttered toast? It's a long time to last, until morning.' We sat there stuffing away and answering Violet's questions between mouthfuls, we felt so cheered that we were even making jokes about the hostel – we had only been able to cry about it before. Violet said that what we needed was a bed-sitting room; she didn't think the hostel quite suitable for us in spite of being so central and cheap. She also said she might be able to get Blanche work as a mannequin; several friends of hers had exclusive dress shops. She asked us for luncheon at her parents' house in St John's Wood for the following Sunday. She was bristling with plans for our future.

The Scobys lived in a large mid-Victorian house in a road which ran down to Maida Vale. The interior smelt of expensive food, tobacco, furniture polish and good soap and the kitchen contained at least three servants and a huge Eagle range similar to the one we had in the kitchen at home. The drawing-room walls were hung with dim watercolours that old Mr Scoby thought valuable and, as an art student, I had to admire them every time I came to the house. He hoped that one was a Boucher and another a Cotman; but the only one that might have been authentic was a Birket Foster. Violet had a bedroom and her own white sitting room upstairs and we used to sit there after luncheon, burning our faces in front of the electric fire fitted into a panel in the modern fireplace. We sat on cushions on the floor eating chocolates and listening to Violet planning our lives. I remember the first time we went to the Scobys' we ate all the roast potatoes. We piled our plates with them although we could feel the parlour maid was trying to take the dish away. After hostel meals we couldn't resist them and hardly realised what we had done until we saw there were not enough left to go round and Mrs Scoby's surprised face.

Violet must have been about thirty when she first came into our lives. She owned a half share in a Sloane Street hat shop and was inclined to wear embarrassing hats herself. She wore a different one every time we saw her and we were convinced she tried out all the hats in the shop. She was a tall, handsome girl who had been engaged to be married twice, though for some reason both the engagements had been broken off. Perhaps she was too self-sufficient and managing – or it could have been the embarrassing hats.

Within ten days of our meeting Violet she had provided each of us with a hat which we never wore; recommended a furnished flat which we did not take because it was too expensive; and found Blanche a job as a mannequin which only lasted a week because her underclothes were so bulky. In those days she wore a woollen vest, something called a liberty bodice which also held up her stockings, and pink Celanese bloomers. The woman who owned the shop did not consider these things worn under the dresses she displayed improved the look of them. Actually those lumpy underclothes saved Blanche from some sinister fate soon afterwards; but we never knew what the sinister fate could have been. It was connected with an advertisement for a free film test that Blanche saw when she was combing through the papers trying to find work. We were both intrigued with the idea of a film test and on a Saturday morning, when Wracker's was closed, we put deep red lipstick on our lips and, coating our faces in powder, went off to Charing Cross Road, where the 'studio' was situated. It turned out to be a wretched place and the director a seedy-looking individual – a dark gentleman with deeply pitted skin. He may have had Arab blood. The film test consisted of us walking in turn to the window and pushing up the sash, then turning round and giving a big smile. I think he wanted to have a good look at our legs from behind. As we self-consciously walked, he turned the handle of a rickety camera on a stand, shouting instructions as he did so. But the funny thing was that there were no lights and no film in the camera. Before we left he took our address and told us he would let us know the result of the test. We went away feeling strangely cheated.

A day or two later a square, dark young man called on us. He had got our address from the bogus film director, only he didn't call him bogus. He said that he had heard that we were very beautiful and wondered if we would be willing to sit for some photographs that could be used for commercial purposes, in the evening because he was a copywriter during the day. We enthusiastically agreed. We were about to move to a bed-sitting room and would be free to stay out at night as much as we liked. So it was arranged that Blanche would pose the following Monday, and I was to pose later on. He obviously preferred Blanche.

On Monday evening Blanche went off after spending hours over her appearance. She was nervous, but happy to be earning money at last. The address she had been given was somewhere off Fleet Street in a block of offices and she arrived there promptly at eight to find the place deserted and the lift not working. She had to climb the stone stairs to the top floor and felt more and more depressed as she went up. When she reached the photographer's door, he opened it before she had time to ring the bell and welcomed her into an untidy room which was partly office and partly sitting room. There was an unexpected divan in it. After some easy chatter he asked Blanche to pose on the divan while he did a drawing of her head. He seemed to have forgotten about the photographs. When they were getting on quite happily he suddenly asked her to pose in her underclothes. It was for some advertisement and he thought it the most natural thing in the world for a girl to start undressing in a deserted building at eight-thirty in the evening; so Blanche, not wanting to appear prudish, pulled her dress over her head and asked him how he would like her to pose. The unnerving thing was that a strange clicking sound came in the room. He said it was due to illuminated signs on the building, but it made Blanche feel uneasy. The young man seemed uneasy too and it wasn't due to the clicking noise; it was the underclothes. He suggested she take off the Liberty bodice; but she told him she couldn't do that because there would be nothing to keep her stockings up and she didn't want to show her vest because it had gone a funny colour. The young man made a pretence of drawing her; but all the heart seemed to have gone from his work and after a few minutes he said he wasn't in the mood and she could go home if she liked. He left the room for a few minutes while she dressed and she could hear him talking to someone. We both felt something fishy went on and he only gave her five shillings.

The hippo-woman was very put out when we told her we were leaving and said she forbade us to go. We were too young to live on our own; it would be the ruination of us. So we lied and said we were taking a room in a relation's house and we gave the Scobys' address. Actually we had found a room in Mornington Crescent on the border of Somers Town. On Saturday nights we frequently saw the most terrifying fights taking place, the worst between women with their hair falling down their backs. Crowds used to collect to watch these fights and the police kept out of the way. Our bed-sitting room was in a large Victorian house in quite a pleasant square with a garden in the centre where lime trees grew. Our room was on the hall floor and was painted a brilliant orange and blue, even the cheap china was orange and blue. The divan cover was a large damask tablecloth dyed black. We thought it a wonderful room with its gas fire and ring with a little tin kettle on it. There were even a few books on a shelf. The toilet arrangements were crude, consisting of an enamel basin and jug standing on a painted packing case behind a curtain, and water had to be fetched from the bathroom. The room had been advertised on a card in a shop window as 'a complete home in miniature' and it was in a way, except that it depended on what you meant by home. Behind a large blue wardrobe there were double doors which led to another room and every morning at about five an alarm went off and we heard a man grumbling and groaning to himself as he dressed and quietly left the house without even a cup of tea. We mentioned this to the landlady and she said we must be mistaken because the room next to ours was occupied by a single woman, the manageress of a stocking shop. One day she returned from managing her stockings and found her big fat sister in the arms of her lover, and then most horrible snarling-screaming sounds came through the communicating doors and into the hall. I think both women set on the man in the end and the landlady had to come up from the basement to deal with it. The next day we heard the poor manageress telling a woman friend that her lover must have been attracted to her sister's large breasts.

We did our shopping in Camden Town on Saturday afternoons. Although we were not as poor as we were to become later on, we had to shop very carefully. We used to buy grim little oranges for two a penny, which must have been dyed because the inside of the peel was almost the same colour as the outside, and there were broken biscuits that only cost 4d. a pound, and cut-price sweetshops and grocer's shops that had prices chalked all over the windows. There were jellied eels and live eels for sale and faggots and black puddings, and on Saturday nights the butchers used to auction off their remaining joints. The only meat or fish we bought were sausages and kippers, which were easy to cook on a gas ring, and sometimes we shared a ready-cooked Scotch egg. Once we felt guilty because we never ate cabbage and bought a giant one, which we kept in the wardrobe because that was the only place to keep food. After living on cabbage for a couple of days we forgot about it and a most pungent smell began to pervade our clothes and room and it was some time before we tracked it down to rotting cabbage. We never got round to buying a basket and used to return from our Saturday shopping loaded with cheap paper bags that were always bursting and carrier bags about to give at the handles. Often Blanche would suddenly hurl all the bags into my arms and, saying she had grit in her eye, run off home. There was a lot of grit blowing about those streets and it was some time before I realised that all this grit in her eyes was Blanche's excuse to avoid being seen carrying all these sordid parcels of food, sometimes even wrapped in newspaper. She minded that kind of thing more than I did and would never go in a grocer's shop that hadn't a bacon-cutter. We used to have our shoes mended by a shoemaker called B. E. Wellshod, who would mend your heels while you waited.

Living in a blue and orange 'complete home in miniature' began to affect us in various ways. For one thing, everything I painted became blue and orange and it also got into our clothes. We bought some vivid blue and orange shantung and I made an orange dress trimmed with blue and Blanche a blue dress trimmed with orange. We cut the necks too large and the collars would not sit properly. We wore these shining dresses for the first time on a sunny spring day when we were lunching with the Scobys and, as we walked down the hill that led to their house, we felt people staring at us and we heard someone say, 'Spaniards, I suppose.' We looked at our dresses with the sun on them and they were so bright they seemed to be beating.

We were wearing the same blue and orange dresses when we engaged a bedroom for Mother in a small Bloomsbury hotel and the startled landlady asked us if we were wearing our national costume. We wore them in bed as nightdresses after that. The thought of our mother's visit to London worried us at first; we couldn't imagine her there. But it turned out to be a great success. She was not shocked to find us living in Camden Town because it was romantically associated with Dickens – Mr Micawber and Tommy Traddles had lived near the Veterinary College and she had some idea that Edgar Wallace used to deliver milk in that area. She was amused by the jellied-eel stalls too. Before visiting the Scobys she bought herself a complete new outfit, visited a hairdresser, and had her poor hands put into some kind of order. She appeared to be in far better health than she had been for years. Her eyes were clearer, her mind seemed more alert, and her face had lost its blurred, vague look. She stayed for a week and it must have been the happiest week she had had since Father died. She saw Marie Tempest in a play, also her first talking film – they had only been going for a few months – and she went to her first cocktail party, given by the Scobys. She went home determined to sell Grandfather's house and live in London permanently.

A few days after Mother left, Blanche got a job demonstrating oil stoves. She was still only sixteen, so she added two years to her age and told a few other small lies, and they said she was just the girl they had been looking for. It wasn't a well-established firm and one of her jobs was to trim the edges of the director's frayed cuffs. She was paid two pounds a week, which seemed a large sum to us and took a weight off my mind because, although I never dared check the stubs of my cheque book, I had a depressing feeling that if I did I would have a horrible shock. The shock came about six weeks later.

SIX

WE HAD BEEN LIVING in London for about six months when the bank sent a letter saying I had spent all my money and had a small overdraft. I frantically checked the stumps of my cheque book and it was true. We had felt so secure and happy since Blanche had been working and at last we were really enjoying London. We discovered the parks and used to row on the lakes in hired rowing boats, and one of the girls at the art school introduced us to museums, which we visited over and over again. For me the most wonderful place of all was the Tate – and all these places were free. I developed an urge to learn and regretted my feeble education. I joined the free library and read rather old-fashioned biographies of famous artists and, remembering my urge to travel, read everything I could about modern Russia, for and against. That led to the Russian novelists, whom I first read like a greedy child eating sweets, afterwards slowly re-reading them and incurring fines from the library.

My money coming to an end was a fearful blow because it meant I would have to leave Wracker's, where I had hoped to stay for at least two years. I must have had a crazy idea about the value of money, expecting it to last all that time, but it was the first time I had had any. From studying paintings in galleries I knew I would never be a serious painter myself, although I had a chance as a commercial artist. My line was good and I was clever at arranging black, grey and white; only there was so much to learn. I took one of the more serious girls into my confidence and she thought I might be able to get work in one of the smaller commercial studios although as a learner I could not be paid much. Her father was a printer and in touch with several of these commercial places, which were usually situated in the Fleet Street area, and it was arranged that she would ask his advice. After our talk I felt all shaky inside and had to leave the school before the morning's work was over because I couldn't concentrate. There were only a few more days of the term left and it seemed a pity not to make the most of them; but I was in such a state my charcoal kept breaking.

Feeling rather guilty I walked among the trees of Regent's Park and ended up at the Zoo. I often went there to draw the animals, only this time I hardly saw them. They were just vague smells and noises, and I was surprised to find myself in the parrot house surrounded by lonely birds all calling for my attention. I scratched the head of an ancient cockatoo who had once been beautiful; he had lemon and white feathers, only most of them had gone now. A fat man wearing a peaked cap waddled up to a chair with 'Keeper' painted on the back and sat down to read the evening paper. I asked him timidly if the Zoo needed any girl assistants and he looked up from his paper to say, 'It's boys we need, boys,' and he spoke in such a way it sounded as if he ate them. I left the parrots and walked back to Mornington Crescent. The lime trees in the square were in flower and smelt so sweet, it reminded me of the garden at home. I borrowed the landlady's key and sat under the limes, sniffing their scent and thinking of the future.

The immediate future turned out to be a job in a commercial studio – a very small one on the first floor of a grimy house in Pimlico. The firm consisted of two men, one of whom had a bed without sheets in the room that was used as an office. The larger room was a makeshift studio, with an easel by the window and a kitchen table in the middle of the bare floor, which was littered with trimmings of white cardboard and paper making a crazy pattern. I went to the studio straight from the art school, carrying my portfolio and a note of introduction from my friend's printer father, and was interviewed by the elder of the partners, the one who did not sleep in the office. He looked like an ugly bird who had been given beautiful dog's eyes by mistake and disconcerted me by asking questions in a brisk, impatient way, dismissing the contents of my portfolio with, 'That kind of thing is useless here. What about lettering?' I admitted I knew nothing about lettering. Then it was typing. Could I type? I lied about that because it was no good saying 'no' to everything. There was the telephone as well and a petty cash book I had to look after. It did not seem as if I was going to do much painting except washes on backgrounds, and there was something about blocks: 'I suppose you know the difference between a halftone and line block?' I said, 'Oh, yes,' although I had no idea what a block was unless it meant blocking-in. He told me that they really wanted a boy apprentice, but they would try me for a month at a salary of one pound a week. They couldn't afford to pay more so I could take it or leave it. I took it.

I started work the following Monday after a week-end of typing on the landlady's typewriter. She had a small office in the basement, an animal charity, I think, because we used to come home sometimes and find a dying pigeon or cat in our room and the paper in the lavatory was usually pamphlets with sad pictures of animals on them. The men who owned the studio were called Javier and Gray; Javier was the ugly one who had interviewed me and was the brains behind Gray's painting hand. Recently Javier had discovered he owned a remote Spanish ancestor and now insisted on his name being pronounced in the Spanish way. When I answered the phone, I had to say 'Harvier and Gray', which I found embarrassing at first. Few people could bring themselves to call him 'Harvier' – even his wife shied from it.

I soon learnt what blocks were because I was always carrying them to and from the City. Sometimes I had to take taxis to remote parts of the East End to deliver folders that had been ordered. Besides being a commercial studio Javier and Gray acted as an agency for printers and in return these printers used to give us small jobs to do, covers for catalogues and folders and that sort of thing. The work that really kept the firm going was posters and there was a great happiness in the studio when Mr Javier landed an order for a poster. Often I was sent to draw something in a museum or park, strange little parks miles away in Tramland, and my drawings were used on the tram maps. I loved the travelling part of my work, particularly if I was allowed to go overground and see the places I was passing through. Mr Javier was an Underground fan and used to map out my journeys for me, and he always knew if I cheated because it took longer.

I worked a five-and-a-half-day week from nine to six and used to travel by bus from Mornington Crescent to Victoria for three-pence – twopence-half-penny if I managed to catch a pirate bus. I often got off at Whitehall and walked through St James's Park so that I could feed the ducks on the lake with bread left over from breakfast. My hours were longer than Blanche's and she was still in bed when I left the house. On Sunday mornings we used to have break-fast in bed, taking turns to make the toast and tea. We had no tray, so used a floppy cardboard-box lid, which sometimes resulted in the entire breakfast spilling in the bed, a catastrophe if we had our favourite breakfast of kippers and had to spend the rest of the week with kipper-flavoured sheets.

We made friends with a girl who had a room upstairs, a chubby blonde called Fanny, who had been a dispenser but had given it up to become a dancer, she said, though we never saw her dance. She had a number of student friends, mostly Indians, and took us to an Overseas Student Club in Russell Square, where we became friendly with students of all nations. I don't know how they behaved with Fanny, but their relations with us were most honourable. They gave us meals at Poggioli's, in Charlotte Street, and occasionally drinks in the Fitzroy, where we saw battered celebrities becoming drunk under the paper streamers that hung from the ceiling. One young Indian took me to see a display of dancing given by coloured students. I was expecting strange African dances, but it turned out to be English Folk Dancing and it was so unexpected to see these dark faces appearing out of poke bonnets. All the dancers were men. Blanche and I were like children and had no anti-racial feelings; we thought foreigners fascinating. The thing that did shock us was that it was always the older, well-established men who behaved badly towards us, men we expected to be reliable. Mr Javier used to send me to some of the firms we dealt with to collect orders; in fact I became a sort of commercial traveller. Some of the men I visited used to send their secretaries out of the office and say we were not to be disturbed, then start giving me awful sucking kisses, and I dared not be too rude to them in case it resulted in my losing my job. There was a horrible sleeping partner of Javier and Gray's who used to turn up at the studio in his lunchtime, and, if the other partners were out, he used to pester me. Although he was not really old, he had a bald head and hardly any front teeth and was a most unattractive perky little man; but again I dared not hit him on his bald head with the paperweight as I often longed to. During our first months in London the only man Blanche and I were seriously attracted to was an exceedingly handsome young priest whom we called the Pope. He worked in a nearby mission and our day was made if we met him in the street.

Towards the end of the summer the cuffs of the director of the heating place where Blanche worked became so frayed that Blanche's daily trimming could disguise them no longer and the firm faded away and she was workless again. Our rent was twenty-five shillings a week and we only had my pound a week coming in. There was the terrible gas meter screaming for shillings and, when it was empty, our light went out as well as the gas ring. I pawned my portable gramophone, one of my early extravagances, and a gold ring and a tiger's claw set in gold went the same way. To avoid spending shillings we used candles; but it was a slow way to cook – about twenty minutes to get an egg to boil. For some reason porridge responded best to candle-light cooking. With the help of the Camden Town pawn shop we were still able to pay our rent; but the landlady must have noticed the candles or something because she started pressing soup on us. It was composed of an egg dropped into the water the dog's meat had been boiled in and the egg turned into a sinister bird's nest of yellow streaks. We mostly lived on cocoa, thin-shelled stale eggs, and bread and cheap cheese which had maggots in it, big ones descended from flies.

We became afraid and noticed things that had meant little to us before – Welsh miners standing in circles, cupping one ear and singing 'Men of Harlech', and ex-servicemen begging or selling writing paper from door to door; once one burst into our room and said he had been sent by the Prince of Wales, but we did not believe him. There were long queues of grey-faced people shuffling outside labour exchanges and terrible Dickensian streets with spilling dustbins outside the filthy houses and children playing in the litter, poor rickety children with knowing, jeering faces. In Somers Town coalmen wouldn't deliver bags of coal unless the women showed them their money first. They were often reduced to burning old tyres under their coppers and the stench used to drown all the other smells of that neighbourhood.

Blanche said we must marry for money and forget the Pope, it was only a matter of good clothes and meeting the right people. She thought that perhaps Violet Scoby might find us suitable husbands. Looking back on it, I think she might have, only we were too shy to ask her. She did find Blanche some rather pleasant work sitting for a woman portrait painter, seven-and-six for the morning and lunch included. Before the painting was finished an elderly artist who lived in the same block of studios caught her leg as she was running up the stairs and asked her to sit for him in the afternoons and for a time our money troubles receded. The artists Blanche posed for were middle-aged, well established ones, the men mostly married, so there was no chance of finding a rich husband among them. The money she earned enabled her to buy a few clothes and I was surprised to see how well chosen they were, no more bulky underclothes and blue and orange horrors. She was growing more and more beautiful in spite of a certain big-eyed frailness due to the lack of nourishing food. There was not enough money for clothes as well as food and sometimes there was a dearth of sittings, partly because she relied on recommendations from one artist to another and was too timid to ring strangers' doorbells and ask for work. Once she fainted while she was sitting for a Strand-on-the-Green sculptor and, when she came to, the artist and his wife were bending over her with worried expressions on their kind faces. They asked if she would like a drink of water or perhaps wine, but she shook her head and asked if there was a piece of cake in the house, she was so hungry. After that they fed her on steaks and mutton chops. Poor girl, she was only seventeen, still growing and almost always hungry.

We realised from our reading that we were hand-icapped because we did not know how to dance. We gathered that dances were one of the best places to find husbands and it was sad to be young and unable to dance. Again Violet came to our aid and gave us a few simple instructions in her room although she wasn't a dancing sort of woman. Then she got a pert little friend to give us a few lessons and we danced in the Scoby drawing room to an old-fashioned gramo-phone with a horn. We could have asked Fanny to teach us only she had left the house. There had been some trouble with the landlady and, as they both gave us different versions of what happened, it was not very clear. She did visit us one evening when she knew the landlady was out and we both complimented her on how pretty she was looking. She appeared to be glowing with health and had lost pounds in weight; but she told us she was being treated for tapeworm.

SEVEN

WHEN WE HAD BEEN living in London for a little over a year our mother died in her sleep. It must have been a terrible shock for Marcella Murphy finding her unexpectedly dead the day after she had been sweeping the walls with a long broom. They said the blood had become clotted in her heart and she died painlessly. We did not go to the funeral, but Edward came to see us a few days afterwards wearing a black tie and we wondered if he had broken the glasses the undertakers had drunk from. It was his first visit to London and he was shocked at the neighbourhood where we lived although he did not see it at its worst. We thought our square a pleasant place with its lime trees and church at one end. He said there might be bugs, but we never saw any, only mice. Once I had woken up to find a mouse entangled in my nightgown. Edward gave us Mother's rings, one each and our christening mugs and told us that he was going to marry Sylvia – the girl with the slanting eyes – as soon as the house was sold. It had been left to him. Marcella was looking after him and he planned to take her into his new home although he couldn't bear her having only one nostril to her nose. He only spent one day in London and we took the day off to show him Buckingham Palace, Westminster Abbey, the House of Commons, St Paul's, Piccadilly Circus and Prince Monolulu whom we came across in Regent Street. He bowed low to us and we said he was a friend. We did not consider Edward had been in London long enough to appreciate the restaurants in Charlotte Street, so we suggested the Russell Hotel. We had often passed it on our way through Russell Square and imagined the satisfying meals that were going on inside. Blanche did not tell him that she was working as an artists' model because she knew he would imagine all sorts of horrors. As it was he thought we had good steady jobs and was impressed with the way we dressed, particularly Blanche, who managed to look wonderfully prosperous.

When we had first heard of our mother's death we were shocked, but not deeply unhappy; the sadness came afterwards when we talked together. Years before

I had found an old letter she had written to her mother when she was staying with some of her Scoby relations. It was all about skinning shrimps for a dinner party and a great-aunt who kept her jam in articles because they were easier to transport by train than the usual jam jars and how was her little dog Scrap? Reading that letter had depressed me for days because of the lonely, wasted life that had come afterwards, years and years of it. Many women are widowed and left with little money and several children and they live normal lives, often marrying again; but something must have been lacking in Mother that caused her to take to drink and then fierce housework. We felt worried in case we went the same way if our lives became too difficult. Blanche had developed a habit of standing by the door and crying into a towel that hung there every time she lost her job or if we had no money. She would stand there for an hour or more with this towel draped round her head, and sometimes when I returned from work I wouldn't be able to open the door because she was using it as a wailing wall. We decided we must practise fortitude. It was a word I had recently discovered and when things became too depressing we kept saying the word 'Fortitude' to each other and Blanche almost gave up crying into a towel, which was a good thing because it made such a mess of her eyes.

I thought it might be wicked to sell Mother's rings but Blanche insisted on selling them so that we could buy evening dresses with the money. She said it would be almost impossible to find husbands unless we had evening dresses and Mother had always been going on at us about getting married. After a lot of discussion we pawned the rings in the hope that we would marry in time to reclaim them. I only had my lunch hour to shop in so left Blanche to choose the dresses because her afternoons were often free. She combed the shops for days before she found what she wanted and I was beginning to think we would eat the money before she found anything; already 37/6 had gone on food. The dresses she eventually found were expensive for those days, round about ten guineas each, which left just enough to buy fine stockings and evening shoes. I was delighted with her choice for me – emerald green, shaped to the hips and then flaring out; and it rustled. Blanche's dress was a severe black. I could hardly believe it when I saw this narrow black thing coming out of its box, but when she put it on, she looked marvellous. We had been brought up in the tradition that only old women and widows wore black, but after seeing Blanche in that black chiffon dress I believed that seventeen was the perfect age for black. There is something about a defenceless young neck rising up from black that is terribly touching.

A day or two after we had bought the dresses I was asked to a Master Printers' Ball by the son of one of the printers my firm dealt with. Blanche said it must have been Mother's ghost who had given her the message to pawn the rings and buy evening dresses. I told her I couldn't possibly marry this printer. He was short with a large square head and pale eyes. She laughed and said there couldn't be a ball without at least one handsome, rich man there and he would be bound to want to dance with me all the evening. 'You must be ruthless and dish little Squarehead,' she said firmly. 'If you fail to find a husband this year you never will, because your dress will be out of fashion and you won't be able to afford another.'

I didn't feel at all confident as I drove off to my first ball with little Squarehead. Even his car was a square little box and he said a terrible thing: 'All the nobs will be there, but we'll enjoy ourselves in our own little way, won't we?' The Printers' Ball was given in a large hotel and there was a dinner with a cabaret afterwards and, with the exception of my partner, it was all I had imagined a ball to be. There were advertising men there as well as printers; but everyone was in a private group and the only other men I danced with were ones I had already met through my work. None of my partners danced very well, mostly what Blanche and I later called 'the old one-two'. After having my toes squashed fairly frequently I soon learnt to step back further and enjoyed myself. Squarehead was a bore, but at least he didn't give me sucking kisses when he brought me home, just a clumsy peck.

Suddenly it was summer again and, when we were in Camden Town shopping, we noticed boxes of pansies and daisies were displayed on the stalls. Men were pushing barrows filled with cherries, and ice-cream men were ringing their bells. It seemed to us that there was no spring in our part of London, just winter and this sudden summer. Even the gardens in Somers Town had a few limp flowers growing in the sour soil and we sometimes came across a dusty lilac-bush in flower. The flowers coming to London seemed to make the artists Blanche sat for get all excited about landscapes. Some of them went abroad on painting holidays and others joined artists' colonies in Cornwall and one or two went to the Lake District. Within a few weeks of the Academy opening they had all gone and Blanche was without work again.

With all the artists going away, eating had become even more of a problem than usual and we had to return to candle cooking. We came to loathe flabby broken biscuits that cost fourpence a pound and cocoa without milk and those stale thin-shelled eggs. I remember one Sunday when all the tulips were out in Hyde Park. We were feeling all soft with hunger as we leant over the bridge watching well-fed girls with their skirts spread out being rowed up and down the Serpentine. We were nearly crying and I was saying 'Fortitude' over and over again. Blanche stopped me with 'Damn fortitude! The only thing I want is roast beef with roast potatoes and Yorkshire pudding.' I told her to stop talking about things like that because it made me feel my stomach was just a hole. We turned away from the water and there were cars slowly gliding past driven by young men accompanied by more well-fed girls. Often when we walked in the parks men in cars stopped and asked if we would like to go for a drive. Although we encouraged the handsome ones in open cars until they spoke to us, we never dared accept their invitations and we were terrified of middle-aged men in saloons with curtains. This Sunday two boys in a commonplace car that obviously belonged to their father stopped and spoke to us and they were so cheerful and young we found we were talking to them as if they were our friends. They were not handsome or anything, but they made us feel happier. After we had been talking for a few minutes they suggested that we lunched with them. We said, 'Did you say lunch?' and they laughed and said, 'Don't you eat?' We quickly got into the car and within half an hour were sitting in a small restaurant on the edge of Hampstead Heath eating roast beef and Yorkshire pudding. We felt as if we had rubbed a magic ring and a couple of genii had appeared. After lunch we drove about for a little and ended up at the boys' home in some distant suburb. There was a large cabinet gramophone in the drawing room and they played records and after a time we danced. It was the first time Blanche had danced with a man and, as she had always taken the man's part when we danced together, she did the same with the boys. They thought we were mad anyway because we told them we cooked on candles, that we were descended from Shakespeare and that our grandfather had been excommunicated because he had smoked a pipe in church. Once an elderly man with a newspaper in his hand came sliding through the door and, giving us a disapproving look, slid away again. He was the only member of the family we saw except the boys. We were not even sure that they were brothers.

We never saw them again, those pick-up boys, but we always remembered them kindly because of the roast beef. Since Fanny had left the house we had rather lost touch with the students of all nations except for a tall and gentle South American who was studying how to make matches. We called him the Little Matchmaker. His parents had rented a large house in Eaton Square and we met his great black-eyed sisters who played the guitar and sang sad Spanish songs, I also had a spotty-faced son of a clergyman as an admirer. He used to take me for walks on Hampstead Heath and feed me on baked beans afterwards. I tolerated him for a time because he was quite harmless even if he did wear a raincoat instead of an overcoat, but gave him up after he showed me a feeble little book which was supposed to be sexy – nursery rhymes with words missing and you had to put rude ones in their place. He kept reading these rhymes and going 'Umpity, umpity, ump' in the spaces and giving me arch glances over his spectacles. I couldn't bear him after that. Later I met a medical student who said he made a practice of sleeping with nurses with their uniforms on. I noticed that it was always the unattractive men with absolutely no sex appeal who said things like that and thought they were getting ready to turn into Dirty Old Men.

The dog-eyed senior partner where I worked increased my salary to thirty shillings a week and told me I could have a week's holiday in August because I was looking 'white about the gills'. I was grateful although it only left me five shillings for food and bus fares. It was at about this time that we started getting boils.

Although the lack of nourishing food seemed to affect Blanche more than me, I was the first to get a boil. It came right in the middle of my forehead like a unicorn's horn. It may have been a carbuncle. I dared not stay away from work now I had been given a rise, but I felt so miserable and ashamed of appearing with this dreadful thing growing out of me. I begged Dog's Eyes not to send me on my rounds with this disfigurement. The pain made me want to hide in a dark place; it was like a nail being driven into my head. Dog's Eyes could be pretty hard sometimes and sent me off with some drawings to the block makers in Holborn Viaduct, also telling me to call at a nearby printer's to collect an order, and of course it was the one that belonged to the man who had taken me to the Printers' Ball. Although I didn't care what he thought of me, I felt so ashamed of his seeing me with this humiliating thing on my face. If I had had more self-confidence I would have refused to go; as it was I went there praying he would be out. But there he was, and jumping up from his ponderous desk and taking me by the hand, he flashed his rather good teeth at me. When he saw this revolting thing that had come on me, his smile went and he asked how it happened. I told him the first lie that came into my aching head and said I'd fallen down a flight of steps. He peered at my forehead with his pale eyes and said, 'It looks more like a boil to me. Have you been squeezing it?' The humiliation lasted long after the scar had disappeared.

Blanche fainted when she got out of bed one morning. Then she started boils too, one of them right in the middle of her lip so that she appeared to have a beak. These boils were always symmetrical and it added to their grotesqueness. Although I continued to pay the rent, the landlady saw that something was wrong and started pressing the water the dog's meat had been boiled in on us again, and tied stale milk up in a handkerchief and gave it to us to eat instead of cheese. A postcard came from the Scobys saying that they were on a cruise and Anna May Wong was on the same boat. It seemed as if they had been away for weeks and they were the only people we had to turn to. We didn't want to worry Edward with the big house on his hands and only a small salary to run it on. He said he was having difficulty in selling it because it was in a state of bad repair and the garden was so neglected. He was longing to get rid of the poor old house so that he would have enough money to marry on.

On a wet Friday evening, when we were taking turns to hold a saucepan of water over a candle, we heard voices in the hall, then a quick knock on the door and in came Violet Scoby, wearing a strange wet hat. She saw the boils, the candle and two cups containing meat cubes and our thin faces and began to organise us immediately. She hunted in her bag and produced shillings for the gas meter, then rushed us out into the rain to the nearest restaurant, a charming little Italian place we had never noticed before. I felt guilty about her putting money into the meter when we had wasted so much on clothes and hoped she would not open our wardrobe when we returned to our room. Fortunately she only stayed a few minutes because she wanted to go home to do some telephoning. I heard her talking to the landlady before she left the house.

Saturday was my half-day and, when I returned at lunchtime, I found a beaming Blanche and a large box of groceries on the table. Blanche said the landlady had bought them with money that Violet had given her. There was a luxurious smell of freshly ground coffee in the room as we put the groceries away together; all those shining tins and exciting packets, we felt as if we were playing shops as we loved to do as children. The landlady was very kind to us after her talk with Violet and told us that if we ran out of shillings again we were to come to her. She also gave Blanche a glass of hot cabbage-water to drink because she was constipated; she said it was an infallible cure. It resulted in the poor girl making the most dreadful smells all night and I found it impossible to share the same bed. I remember sitting on a little stool crying most of the night, fortitude all forgotten.

A few evenings later Violet appeared wearing another hat, a white straw one with a fringe round the edge that she had picked up on her travels. She had been doing a great deal of organising since she had last seen us and had found a job for Blanche. When she first told us about it we were horrified because it was to look after an old madwoman in Letchworth, take her for walks and have meals with her and see that she did not fall down the stairs or wander away. We immediately imagined an old woman like Rochester's wife and liable to dance about the roof after setting the house on fire. Violet said she had only lost her mind in recent years and was very sweet and harmless. Blanche asked with a tremble in her voice, 'Will I have to bath her?' Violet laughed reassuringly, 'No, no. The district nurse looks after that side of it. You're to be a companion to the old lady. I have never met her but have heard she is a dear old soul.' She rushed Blanche into accepting this job, which I don't think she would have taken if she had had more time to consider it. When Violet had gone Blanche kept saying, 'It was only a matter of hanging on until the middle of September. I hate the thought of this old woman and living with strangers. If only I could stay here.'

It was when Blanche said 'If only I could stay here' that I realised I would still have to pay twenty-five shillings a week when I was on my own. I ran down to the landlady to tell her I could not keep the room on any longer. She was in the middle of stuffing pillows with the combings from her dog's coat and appeared to be enjoying herself. We often wondered why our pillows smelt queer. She didn't mind about us giving up the room; she seemed glad to be rid of the responsibility of her two starving young lodgers. She said she knew of a room across the square that would just suit me, a tiny room with a rent of only twelve shillings a week, and she very kindly reminded me that I had paid a week's rent in advance when we first came to the house so there was no more rent to pay.

I went across the square to see this slip of a room, just a narrow camp bed and a bamboo chest of drawers with an enamel jug and basin on top, one bentwood chair and on the floor, linoleum decorated with swastikas. The one thing that pleased me about the room was the window, which looked onto a large plane tree with the afternoon sun shimmering through its leaves. This little room was far lighter than the ground-floor one we had been living in. I had taken it for granted that all London rooms were dark and now I would have this lovely faintly green light.

Within a week of Violet arriving in her big wet hat to organise our lives, Blanche was collected in a car driven by the madwoman's niece – a Mrs Buller. We had expected her to be a monster of a woman for some reason; actually she was rather nice in her brisk way. She was small, with close-cropped dark hair just turning grey, and all her movements were neat and quick. She only stayed in our room for about five minutes, her eyes flicking round like a hen's, then she bustled Blanche out into an open Lancia with a big black retriever curled up in the back seat. The landlady and charwoman came bumping down the front-doorsteps with Blanche's trunk, and a coalman who had been tipping coal down a hole in the pavement heaved it into the car beside the retriever; then Blanche and I stood looking at each other for a miserable moment before she turned away and stepped into the car and was driven away by Mrs Buller.

EIGHT

THEN I MOVED ACROSS the square and was surrounded by new sounds and new people. There was someone above who used to play a gramophone and I could hear the thin songs of popular musical comedies coming through the ceiling, and there was a baby somewhere that cried at night. In the front room that led from the hall there was a man who looked like an opera singer who wore a florid dressing-gown all day and quarrelled with his thin-faced wife, who used to wander about the house with bare feet with a Pekinese clasped to her chest. Every night at eleven o'clock the landlord would stump up the stairs to turn all the lights off and the first sound I heard in the morning was the tenants' newspapers coming through the letterbox. On Sunday mornings when the tenants slept late, I used to creep down and borrow some of the papers, reading them with care, before returning them to the hall floor. When my window was open I could hear the lions in the Zoo roaring at feeding time and the short sharp barks of the seals.

Blanche's letters were inclined to be abrupt, but not unhappy. The main trouble with Mrs Buller's mad aunt seemed to be a loss of memory combined with a tendency to wander and disgusting table habits. She was put to bed at an early hour in the evening and Blanche had her dinner with Mrs Buller. 'Heavenly food and a manservant to serve it' and 'Mrs Buller is a widow and on lots of committees. She is nicer than we expected and quite witty sometimes.' So at least Blanche was well fed and living a civilised life. At first I was unutterably miserable on my own. Then I saw a film called A *Student of Prague* with Conrad Veidt as the student and fell in love with him. He took the place of the Pope for a week or two, and then I really did fall in love with a black-haired art student.

We met in the Tate in front of Degas's *La Plage*. I was mentally comparing it to Steer's painting of the *Beach at Walberswick* and wondering which was the better painting, they both seemed perfect to me. I was so absorbed I hardly noticed that someone was standing behind me until I heard the floor faintly creaking and turned and saw a gaunt young man standing there. He followed me round the gallery and when I stopped to look at a painting, there he was standing behind me. At first I thought our tastes were similar and he admired Picasso and Modigliani too; then I tried stopping in front of Holman Hunt which I was sure he would not like and there he was like a shadow. It made me nervous and I hoped the seams of my stockings were straight. Suddenly I panicked and hurried through the galleries towards the entrance hall, but I knew he was still behind me and by the time I reached the postcard stall he was walking beside me as if we were friends. He walked with one hand in the pocket of his short dark coat, so short it was almost a jacket. He said gruffly, 'Let's have some tea or coffee or something downstairs,' and, taking my arm, steered me to the restaurant. I had never seen it before and the Rex Whistler murals were such a pleasant surprise that, when I had finished examining them, the first difficult moments were passed. We were discussing paintings quite happily until I mentioned Reynolds and he almost hit me and said his paintings were *merde*. Sargent was a bad painter but 'he definitely had something'. He was a great admirer of Cézanne and I dared not say that he usually left me feeling rather cold and I thought his paintings looked as if he lived on sour apples. He talked enthusiastically about Léger and artists I had never heard of, an Italian called Carlo Carrà and a Japanese called Foujita who drew cats. The names of artists came pouring out of his desperate mouth and, as he described paintings, he made suggestive shapes with his beautiful long hands, so sensitive they slightly trembled. His hair fell in a short black fringe over his forehead and gave the impression that it all came sprouting from a hole in the middle of his head. I once had a Japanese doll with hair like that. His dead white skin was rather coarse, almost pitted; I've noticed a lot of young artists have skins like that, even the women. He smoked in a furious sort of way, holding the cigarette with his fingers close to his lips and flicking his ash about the floor. He told me that he was a student at the Royal College of Art and was living on a grant of three pounds a week. This seemed like affluence to me, particularly when he added that his father allowed him another pound a week although they were not on speaking terms. He didn't ask me many questions about myself, but was impressed when I told him that I was already working in a studio. I did not mention that I spent most of my time being a commercial traveller and typing letters.

We left the Tate and walked up Millbank together and all the way I was hoping he would arrange for us to meet again. We passed the Houses of Parliament and still nothing had been said, although we were getting close to my 24 bus-stop. I always tried to travel on a 24 because it was a pirate bus and cheaper than the red ones. He was saying he could kick himself because he liked baroque, particularly in churches. I was hardly listening because my bus was turning out of Victoria Street and I was too proud not to board it. Just as the bus drew up he demanded my telephone number in his desperate way and I gave him the studio one; then, when I was standing on the platform he shouted, 'Your name. Who am I to ask for?' and I shouted back, 'Victoria Green,' and he shouted 'Sounds like a station,' and suddenly he was laughing and he was just a happy young man and not desperate at all.

After this first meeting we were soon spending all our free time together and there was my wonderful week's holiday which we shared in a sort of dream. This art student that I was soon to love so much was called Eugene Reeve and was the son of an eccentric solicitor from Harrogate. His French mother had died some years earlier and for a time he had lived with her family in France. He had been very happy until his father sent for him; then he had three miserable years in Harrogate as a day boy at a school he hated, then another miserable year in his father's office. It ended in his quietly leaving home with a few pounds in his pocket and a suitcase full of drawings. When he first arrived in London, he worked in a bookshop during the day and attended the St Martin's School of Art at night; and then he was given this grant and sent to the Royal College and I couldn't help thinking how well he had managed compared to me. I was so much in love with him that I couldn't walk straight when we walked in the streets together. If he held my arm it was as if we were floating and in the evenings we would sit together in his Charlotte Street room, leaning close together with our arms entwined, talking or listening to the gramophone playing *The Three-Cornered Hat*. Sometimes Gene drew me and I painted a weak little portrait of him which I framed and hung in my room so that it was the first thing I saw in the morning. Although we were so much in love, we were not lovers and I always spent the night in my slip of a room. At that time marriage never entered our minds; we lived in the perfect present and, looking back, I know it was the happiest period of my life.

When the holiday was over I returned to the Pimlico studio and somehow managed to drift through my work. Several times I cut my fingers when I was trimming layouts and I got into trouble when I had to draw a blindfolded woman holding scales. I think she is called Justice; but I made the scales crooked when they should have been straight. I took some blocks to the wrong engravers and hit the sleeping partner when he tried to give me one of his sucking kisses, so that he became my enemy. Sometimes at the end of the day Gene would be waiting for me outside the studio and sometimes we met at South Kensington Underground station. There he would be, very black and white and his long, long legs in their narrow trousers, looking so wonderfully different from everyone else.

With five pounds ten a week to spend, we had no money worries. There was plenty for all we wanted to do. We used to eat in the cheaper Charlotte Street restaurants two or three times a week and other days we ate in Gene's room, snacks from Schmidt's or an omelette or anything easy to cook on a gas ring. On Saturday evenings we used to drink in the Fitzroy or Wheatsheaf or go further to the Café Royal. We were neither of us fond of drink, but we liked to watch people. I remember Dylan Thomas gently kissing me in the Wheatsheaf and his face was soft like a balloon and there was a black mark under his skin as if coal were there. Augustus John sometimes came there and he stood at the bar like an elderly Viking, breathing heavily. It was the ambition of all the arty girls of that period to be painted by John or sculpted by Epstein. Epstein did once say he would like to do a head of me, but nothing came of it and, although I met John several times, he never showed the slightest interest in my appearance. At that time I began to dress in an arty way. Blanche's good advice about clothes passed from my mind. I wore heavy gold earrings in my ears and my shoulder-length hair was parted in the centre and pushed behind my ears in a great dark bush which made me look like an ancient Egyptian.

Blanche came to London for the day towards the end of November and she had changed as much as I had. Her beautiful hair had been cut off and was now curly and chrysanthemum-like and she looked more like other girls, only she was more beautiful. She had lost her wan and mysterious air, but had gained other airs, sex appeal and assurance among them. She was wearing a light grey coat and skirt that Mrs Buller had had made for her at her own tailor's and it was very becoming, not at all mannish like Mrs Buller's own clothes. We could only spend my lunch hour together so we sat talking in an enormous ABC near Victoria station. There was so much to say, but actually nothing much was said. I had mentioned Gene in my letters, but now we were together, I could not bring myself to say much about him while we ate buck rabbit. It seemed as if we were almost strangers until we went to the wash place and Blanche showed me the crêpe de Chine knickers trimmed with real lace that she had made. She said Mrs Buller only wore hand-made underclothes, or if she did buy any ready-made, she took them to pieces and resewed them herself. 'Real people feel almost ill if they have a machine stitch anywhere near them, not only hems, tucks and embroidery, but everything,' she said with awe. She walked with me to the dirty street where I worked and everyone turned to look at her as she passed; it was as if a beautiful tall rose had come walking through the streets.

NINE

JUST BEFORE CHRISTMAS Edward wrote to say that at last the house had been sold and he was about to get married. He said that he had not got a very good price, just enough to buy a modernised cottage. He was furnishing the cottage with the best things from the old house and selling the rest. He added that, although the house and its contents had been left to him, he felt that Blanche and I should have something and he enclosed a cheque for twenty-five pounds and Blanche was to have the same amount. It was several days before I could cash the cheque and, while I was waiting for the money, an idea more than once crossed my mind and, although I never mentioned it to Gene, it somehow entered his mind.

Another coincidence was that the flat at the top of the house where Gene lived fell vacant at this time and he immediately arranged to move there. It was completely self-contained, with a tiny bathroom and kitchen and one long room with French windows which led onto a flat roof with a fascinating view. I remember there was a small toy factory almost opposite and they used to dry the painted wooden toys on their balcony – horses and red trains mostly, and, one Christmas, wooden fir trees.

Gene seemed to take it for granted that I was to share the flat with him and spend the twenty-five pounds on furnishing it, but did not say anything about getting married although I was longing for him to. On the first evening he moved upstairs we were sitting on the camp bed, the only piece of furniture in the flat except for a bookcase and easel, making out a list of what we needed when he suddenly leapt to his feet and started striding up and down the room. He went on and on about how he disapproved of marriage, calling it a *petit bourgeois* institution, a pandering to respectability, a life sentence – H. G. Wells and someone called Godwin came into it. This must have gone on for at least half an hour while I sat on the horrid little canvas bed feeling miserable. Suddenly he stood still for a few minutes without saying anything, then he sat down beside me again and leaning his face against my shoulder said, 'All the same I think we had better get married, don't you?'

We were married in a registry office three weeks later with two student friends as witnesses. We had lunch together afterwards at Bertorelli's, and later bought a few bottles of Médoc, salted peanuts and olives and gave our first party in the new flat. It must have been a noisy one because an Italian in a nightshirt came up and complained. Gene did not tell the College that he was now a married man in case it interfered with his grant, but he wrote to his father because he was intrigued to know what his response would be. It might mean that the allowance would abruptly end; on the other hand his father was such an unpredictable man he might even double it. Actually there was no comment and a registered envelope containing four pound notes continued to arrive every time there was a new moon.

I found it difficult to write to Blanche to tell her I was married to Gene and was now Mrs Reeve. I knew she would be hurt that I had not mentioned it or invited her to the wedding, but, if I had told her, she would have tried to talk me out of it. She had developed a horror of poverty after living in Mornington Crescent and would consider marrying an art student with no prospects a crazy thing to do. Eventually I telephoned her and her reactions were just what I had expected. 'Oh, no!' she wailed over the telephone wires. 'I knew you'd get all arty on your own. Have you forgotten how our stockings had hardly any feet, the cabbage in the wardrobe and cooking over a candle, and that wretched enamel bowl behind the curtain that we had to wash ourselves and the dishes in. Oh, and the boils. I know you'll both get boils!' I reassured her as well as I could, boasting about our bathroom and not mentioning that dead bugs came out of the geyser. Besides there was Gene's allowance and the grant. 'You'll go on working, I know you will, at least until you start having hundreds of babies. Artists always do.' At the second lot of pips I hastily gave our address and rang off, although I had had the fore-sight to reverse the charges, hoping that Mrs Buller would not notice when the bill came in. I wrote to Edward and told him that I had married an artist with private means and that we had a self-contained studio and excellent prospects. He replied that he did not approve of my marrying in such a hole-in-the-corner way and hoped there was no special reason for it. Later a most extraordinary present arrived from him – a set of embroidered cushion covers which must have been an unpopular wedding present of his own. I had hoped the parcel contained sheets, coloured ones perhaps, but it was these horrible cushion covers which I was so ashamed for Gene to see. They were the kind of thing that made him get all worked up. He liked things to be stark and functional and I was not allowed to paint the hardwood furniture we had bought and it looked so famished against the whitewashed walls. The floorboards were so discoloured I stained them black, but he didn't like it, nor did I. I longed for some rugs, even woven grass ones would have been better than nothing. We hung some of Gene's paintings on the walls; but, as they were rather sombre abstracts, they did not add much colour to the room. The only bright thing we had was a crimson linen divan cover, which Gene took off when he was painting because it kept catching his eye. He preferred the grey army blankets underneath. He wanted our room to look like Cézanne's studio at Aix.

When we had been married for about a fortnight, Blanche came to visit us. Fortunately I had known she was coming and had made the place look a little brighter, with flowers and a large bowl of fruit from Berwick Market. She arrived breathless because a Cypriot from the street had chased her up the stairs, and we revived her with a glass of wine. By the time she had drunk the wine she was talking to Gene as if he had been in the family for years. When we were washing up together after lunch she said, 'I'm sorry I was so discouraging over the phone, but it was such a shock. I can see why you fell in love with

Gene, though, he isn't like anyone else. Perhaps he's a genius or something.' She absent-mindedly rolled our only teacloth into a damp ball and added, 'I think someone wants to marry me, at least Mrs Buller thinks so, although he hasn't said anything. He's very formal, almost a stick in fact.' I was all against her marrying a formal stick and she smiled vaguely and said she didn't think she would, and no more was said about him that day.

I didn't tell the people I worked for that I was married because I felt they might resent it for some reason, although it made no difference to my work and I was still dashing about collecting printing orders and blocks and painting flat backgrounds. I had become quite a good typist, even managing statements and estimates with columns of neat figures. It was while I was typing for Javier that he started fixing his dog's eyes on my left hand. He was standing behind me, waiting impatiently to sign the letter I was typing and was making me feel on edge. It was a monster of an old-fashioned typewriter that one had to thump away on, not at all like the ones I saw in the offices I visited where the typists' hands flew over the light keys. When I finished the letter Javier snatched it and read it while I thumped away at the envelope, then signing it and neatly folding it into three, said, 'That ring you are wearing. Is it a wedding ring?' I said it was and that

I had been married exactly seventeen days, less two hours. He then proceeded to give me a lecture about being deceitful and made a thing about my insurance cards being all wrong. I hoped that would be the end of it. A few days later Javier returned to the subject and said he had been talking it over with his partners and they did not approve of married women working and I was to take a week's notice. I was sure it was the sleeping partner's fault because the grey young partner who slept in the office only thought about his work and had no ideas about married women working or anything else. He lived for commercial art and sometimes I used to see him wandering round stations gazing at posters as if he were in an art gallery.

When I left, Dog's Eyes gave me an extra two pounds besides my salary and said he would miss me. He also said he was sorry that he had sometimes been bad-tempered. We stood there shaking hands and smiling at each other, and by the time we finally said goodbye and I had reached the street, I was crying. I walked up towards Victoria Street and had a last look at a new cinema that I had been watching being built; I had grown to have a proprietary interest in it. It was white and resembled a great boat and I admired it intensely. When I saw it a few years later, dirty and with queues of darkly dressed people waiting outside, I thought I must have been mad.

I found it difficult to get work in another studio. The jobs advertised always seemed to be for men and there were so many young men clutching their portfolios that I hadn't a chance. The lifts and stairs and waiting rooms were full of them and they nearly all had the same strained expression on their faces. Some of their lips slightly moved, and I guessed they were rehearsing their interview. I wondered if Gene would look the same in a few months' time. He only had one more term at the College, then his grant would end.

I had a very happy fortnight at home practising cooking, cleaning the flat and using Gene's paints when he was out. I kept my paintings under the divan because I did not want him to see them in case he thought them *merde*. They were the first oil paintings I had attempted and there was something rather primitive about them and the colours were intense. I laughed sometimes in the night thinking of Gene peacefully sleeping above all these little horrors. In time they mounted up and there must have been at least thirty lying there wrapped in newspaper.

As soon as I had put the breakfast on the table, I used to run down Charlotte Street to the shop where they sold Continental newspapers and buy the *Telegraph* so that I could study the advertisements while we munched our toast. Gene kept saying, 'Don't bother, we'll manage,' and we would kiss each other with toasty lips and I'd forget about work until he'd gone. I applied for all kinds of jobs. Many of them were unsuitable, but I felt crushed just the same when I was turned down. One windy morning I answered an advertisement for an assistant in a jewellery shop, one of those glittering places that sell imitation jewellery. I never expected them to engage me because I knew nothing about jewellery, real or imitation; but, to my surprise, they took me on at a salary of thirty shillings a week plus a very small commission on the things I sold. Afterwards I heard that I was engaged because the owner liked my voice. The only qualifications I appeared to need were a black dress and a pair of high-heeled shoes. I can still remember the relief of kicking off our shoes as soon as the shop closed and the heaven of walking about in our stockinged feet after hours of standing. There was a chair in the shop, I think by law, but we would have been shot if we'd been caught sitting on it.

As I knew nothing about the ethics of being a shop assistant I mishandled things the first day and put the other girls' backs up. Someone called the first sales lady, who was also the manageress, handed me a red book to write my invoices in and told me I was to be the fifth sales lady. This meant nothing to me; all the same I was pleased to see that another new girl was the sixth. We had to dust the shop together and polish the counters with a damp shammy-leather. Everything

146

had to glitter and the counters were illuminated show-cases lined with red velvet. The jewellery displayed in the window cost only five shillings but there was some quite expensive jewellery inside. There were wrist-watches bristling with diamonds stuck in with glue, and one of my jobs after the shop closed was to stick in any stones that had fallen out. There were pearl necklaces from five shillings to ten pounds and real silver animal brooches decorated with chips of crystal which had to be polished once a week. With the exception of the things in the window nothing had a fixed price, although they had tiny code labels attached. On that first morning while we did the dusting the manageress adjusted the window and the other sales girls talked about their weekend. I gathered that one was already married and didn't care for her husband and the other was having difficulty in getting married because her boyfriend was trying to back out after a long engagement. All the girls were pretty and although I did not realise it at first, most of them were Jewesses. The owner of the shop was partly Indian, very dark and slightly sinister, but handsome.

As soon as the first customer entered the shop I beamed on her because I was dying to sell some-thing and earn some commission, and seeing my wel-coming smile, she came straight to me and said she wanted to buy a pendant and some earrings to match.

I was heading towards the window with the woman following expectantly when the first sales lady caught me by the wrist and told me I wasn't allowed to touch the window; I was to wait in the lavatory until she had time to speak to me. It was an excuse to sit down, but I was very frightened. After about ten minutes she appeared at the door, straight and stiff like a ruler in her shining black dress. She asked what I meant by poaching her customers when I was only a fifth sales; I was not to go near a customer until the sales ladies above me were serving. I tearfully explained that I had never worked in a shop before; but to her it seemed almost impossible that I'd lived for twenty years and didn't know about shop procedure. Later in the morning the owner of the shop appeared and gave me a lecture on how to be a sales lady and explained the code. He told me to concentrate on selling the more expensive jewellery, watches in particular. The higher the price the more commission I would earn.

I had never been good at mental arithmetic and the code was a shock as well as a surprise. It consisted of the unlikely words – 'King Alfred' and the K stood for one and so on. 1/6 was K/l, 12/9 – KI/E and £2.3.8 – I/N/R. Fortunately two code letters were more usual and some things cost as little as /G. These prices were what the firm had paid for the jewellery and we were expected to make as high a profit as possible, with the exception of the things marked in the window. We had to know the window pretty thoroughly or we might make the mistake of asking seven and sixpence for something that was glittering away in the window for only five shillings. For the first week I used to be counting with my fingers on the counter every time I made a sale, then I suddenly got the hang of it and found being a fifth sales lady was not so difficult after all. I had the beginner's luck of selling a watch my first day when my terrifying new boss was standing beside me scowling as I tapped away with my fingers translating K/N/E to £1.3.9. I daringly asked £3.3.0 for the watch and got it. I only sold two other watches while I was there, but plenty of pearl necklaces. People did not mind how much they paid for them. At first I worried about charging too much for this junky jewellery. Then I realised that the shop's outgoings must be pretty heavy, with six sales ladies eating their heads off and the rent of a shop in the West End – and it must have cost quite a lot to keep that air of artificial brilliancy going. Then I began to worry about the time I was wasting selling artificial jewels to silly women. I earned a little over two pounds a week.

Gene hated my working in the shop. On Monday evenings I didn't get home until after nine because we had to stay late to change the window, polish silver and brush all the velvet objects the jewellery was displayed on. We used to work in our stockinged feet and a considerable amount of sexy talk used to go on, mostly old wives' tales about young brides who had had their nightgowns torn to shreds on their wedding night, childbirth and abortions, monster babies and the almost mystic horrors of the change of life. All these things they spoke about were new to me and they called me naïve, making it rhyme with 'rave', and thought up fresh horrors I should know – hermaphrodites, VD and falling wombs. I did not believe half they told me, but it was depressing.

I was wonderfully happy at home, though. Being married to Gene was all I had hoped it would be. Everything about him fascinated me, the way he moved and spoke, his husky voice with its faint French accent, his dark, shining eyes contrasting with his white face, and even his savage impatience. The thing that did unnerve me slightly was the way he suddenly became worked up about things that did not matter much, like pink may and stucco on houses – both things that I rather admired, ugly furniture in shop windows and any sort of fussy ugliness. Once a friend took us for a drive in his father's car and Gene got so worked up about the houses on the Hendon By-pass that we had to return another way at dusk.

One evening, soon after I returned home there was a loud knocking at our door which was at the bottom of a few steps that led directly from our living room. The door opened straight onto them, or rather it opened onto the landing, bumping into anyone standing on the other side and causing a certain amount of confusion. This evening the door bumped into two tall people wearing evening dress, a man and woman. I thought they were strangers for a moment until I recognised Blanche, draped in furs which I later learnt were borrowed from Mrs Buller. I felt a little put out because I was still wearing my black working dress and had no shoes on my feet and the visiting man fixed his steely eyes on them. Blanche introduced him as Captain Cressy, but she called him Rollo in a rather self-conscious way so I gathered that calling him by his Christian name was something new. She said they were on their way to a theatre and could only stay for a few minutes because Rollo had booked a table for dinner at the Isola Bella. I put my shoes on and offered them some wine, but Captain Cressy refused in such a way that I knew he thought it would be filth. Things were very sticky until Gene came running up the stairs clutching a long French loaf, two plucked pigeons and a lettuce to his chest. He threw the shopping down, kissed Blanche on the cheek and shook hands with Captain Cressy as if he had been longing to meet him. To my surprise, he showed him some of his paintings and, when their backs were turned,

I asked Blanche if this was the formal stick. She nodded and whispered, 'He's nicer than I thought.' I just had time to say, 'He won't do. His eyes are too cold,' before they turned round to examine a portfolio of drawings lying on the table. After a few minutes Captain Cressy said it was time they left. I walked with them down the stairs, but did not get another chance to speak to Blanche. I knew she would never be happy with Captain Cressy. He was impressive at first sight, but he had a skin like cold-boiled bacon. The red and white had set and he had a flat back to his head, not as flat as some Germans, but flat enough, and combined with the icy eyes it was not a good mixture. I found Gene all disconsolate upstairs because he had imagined Captain Cressy was a rich man Blanche had brought round to buy his paintings. I said, 'No, darling. I have a horrible suspicion that you have just met your future brother-in-law.'

Ten days later Blanche wrote to say that she was engaged to marry Captain Cressy and they were marrying immediately because his leave had almost expired and he was due to go to Singapore. She said very little about the man who was to be her husband except that he was thirty-five: 'But that isn't old, you know.' She was obviously delighted to be going abroad and about the wonderful trousseau she was to have. Rollo had given Mrs Buller a hundred and fifty pounds to spend on it and she was buying underclothes from Daphne and had already chosen two evening dresses from Harrods; at least, Rollo had chosen them while she had walked about displaying them. 'I must have tried on almost twenty dresses before he made his final choice,' she wrote enthusiastically.

I saw Blanche once more before she was married. She called for me at the shop and we had lunch together at a restaurant all done up like a German beer place and wonderfully cheap. There were masses of waiters, which gave it an expensive air; but, when you had a good look at them, you couldn't help noticing that most of them were on their last legs and their clothes were splashed with soup and gravy. We ate jugged hare and water ices, the water ices because Blanche said they were more sophisticated than the creamy ones and she was trying to cultivate a taste for them. All through the meal she talked so gaily and with such hope for the future I couldn't bring myself to say that I thought she was making a dreadful mistake. While we were having coffee she abruptly said, 'You don't like Rollo, do you?' I fiddled about with a piece of sugar before replying, 'No, not much,' then added, 'Do you?' A slow and terrible blush spread upwards from her neck and over her face so that I almost expected it to come out of the top of her head in the shape of a deep pink hat. Her eyes filled with tears as she muttered, 'I do like him, of course I like him,' and dabbed at her eyes. 'Don't make me cry, you know how my eyes stay red for hours.' Then with more confidence, 'Look. I'll tell you how it is. I admire Rollo tremendously and at parties and things I shall be so proud when I look across a room and know he's mine. Perhaps I'll fall in love with him, I don't know much about love yet. I so long to be looked after and know I'll never be poor again. You see, so much poorness came all at once – you remember Mother scrubbing floors on her knees and that ghastly time in Camden Town. You don't mind poverty as much as I do, in fact I think you almost like it. I can't bear to see dirty little shops with broken biscuits in boxes outside, dirty streets where there's always a gritty wind blowing, people with oafish faces and greasy backs to their collars, whining children with bad teeth, and feeling so dirty and degraded oneself. I detest poverty and once I'm married to Rollo I'll be safe from it.' She caught my hand in hers: 'Oh Vicky, you must like him. I do, I really do.' I was almost crying myself and mumbled, 'Of course, I'll try and like him.' We went downstairs and patched up our faces and walked back to the shop together. I felt ashamed for Blanche to see the tawdry place where I worked.

Blanche was married from Mrs Buller's house at Letchworth three days before their boat sailed, so there was not much time for a honeymoon unless you counted the voyage. Gene and I went to the wedding and I wore a new coat and skirt, new suede gloves and a small black hat perched on the back of my head. Gene wore his only suit. Unfortunately he had had it dyed green and there was no stuffing in the shoulders; but he looked very tall and narrow and completely unlike anyone else. Edward came to the wedding with his Japanesey little wife Sylvia and he was obviously delighted with Blanche's choice of a husband. Looking doubtfully at Gene, who was leaning against a wall with a faraway expression on his face, he said, 'I can't think why you couldn't have done the same.' I said teasingly, 'What! Married the same man?' He turned away crossly. 'You know perfectly well what I mean. You could have married a gentleman, not an eccentric dressed like a character out of Dickens.' Sylvia, who was a kind little woman said, 'I'm sure Vicky is very happy with Gene and he looks so clever and romantic.'

It was a small reception, only about twenty people, and most of them I had never seen before. The Scobys were there, otherwise they were Rollo's army-type friends and I found it difficult to talk to them. Blanche specially brought Rollo over to me because she so wanted me to know and like him; but the only thing we had in common was Blanche and he said over and over again, 'She is very beautiful, isn't she?' and we agreed on that. He was watching her all the time with his steely eyes and making remarks like, 'Look at old Colonel Ore making up to her, she's completely bowled him over,' or 'She is by far the most lovely woman in the room. Makes them look a bit dim, what?' All through the marriage service I had been trying to like him and he did look rather good back view. The flattish back to his head didn't show so much and he had wonderfully straight shoulders, but there seemed to be something lacking, a deadness that went with his set face. His main ambition appeared to be to own the best of everything, the best car, horse, home and now wife.

I did not see Blanche again before she left for Singapore and it was eighteen months before she returned to London to have her marriage annulled.

TEN

JUST BEFORE THE END of Gene's last term at the Royal College he sold two paintings which had been hung in a Cork Street gallery. We had been so pleased when they were accepted, but we hardly expected them to sell. To see them hanging on the walls and having Eugene Reeve in the catalogue was enough. When the gallery had taken their commission, there was still thirty pounds left for Gene. Instead of saving the money, we went off to France with it, first to Paris and then on to Orléans to visit relations of Gene's who owned a hotel there and we stayed as their guests for three weeks. It was strange to find my husband changing into a Frenchman, completely at home with this French family, teasing his young cousins and helping them with their homework. The boys had close-cropped black hair which smelt of brilliantine on Sundays and they went to school wearing queer overalls and very long socks and very short trousers. I was afraid of them at first; in fact, I was afraid of the whole family and dared not use the little French Gene had taught me; but they were so friendly I soon thawed and felt as if I belonged to the family. I enjoyed myself in the big living room behind the reception desk and taught the boys to play snap and whist and they taught me how to play chess; but whatever we played, they always beat me. Sometimes, when English guests who could speak no French came to the reception desk, Tante Madeleine would call for me if Gene was not there, and they put up a notice saying 'English spoken'.

We wandered about with our sketch books drawing old houses by the river and sat in little bars drinking wine or coffee. On Sunday evenings we used to go visiting with the family, who liked to show off their English relations. Gene was bored with the visiting. I enjoyed it in spite of my limited French; but I was surprised to see what ugly furniture French people often have in their homes. Until then I had thought the French renowned for their good taste. Most of the homes I entered were hideous, either crammed with stuffy late-Victorian furniture and huge family photographs in heavy frames, or vulgar modern style with a vase of artificial flowers in the centre of a varnished dining-table and a plaster Saint Joan on the sideboard. The kitchens were invariably the nicest rooms in the house. Almost every day I went to look at the cathedral, which I thought the most beautiful building I had ever seen, particularly from the front, with its slender columns. To me it seemed such a feminine cathedral. Gene said it was nothing compared to Chartres, which we planned to visit on our way home. We never got there because our money started to run out. Although we were living so cheaply it had somehow managed to melt away and when we returned to England we were almost penniless. It was fortunate that a new moon was due and we could expect the customary registered letter from Gene's father containing four pounds.

I had given up my work in the jewellery shop a few days before we left for France, so we both were in search of work. Gene now had ARCA after his name and he applied for teaching jobs, but without much success until one of his former art masters gave him a recommendation to a workmen's institute that needed a teacher three evenings a week, just enough to cover the rent. Fortunately the winter was over and the days were already warming and we could manage without a fire; but food was a problem. We lived on a diet of bread and over-ripe bananas which were reduced in price, very boring but quite wholesome Gene said.

His paints started to run out, one colour after another, and he had to experiment with cheap powder colours mixed with flake white and his paintings looked as if they had been painted by a ghost.

As I was walking through Percy Street, I looked through a window and saw several young people bending over desks with paintbrushes in their hands and I thought at first it must be an architect's office. Then I saw a notice saying it was a film company, and wondered if they were designing scenery or costumes. A girl with a pasty face and her hair done in a large golden bun looked up from her work for a moment and, seeing me gazing through the window so intently, smiled at me, so I smiled back and, on a sudden impulse, walked in through the side door and, following one of those old-fashioned painted hands that often point to public lavatories, I opened a door and found myself in the room I had seen from the street. There were four girls and three young men all working at roughly made deal desks with an illuminated window let into them. An elderly man with a clipped moustache seemed to be in charge. There was a long workbench and on it were drying paintings on transparent celluloid, and there were a series of drawings pinned on a wall that appeared to be illustrations for *Robinson Crusoe*. Hurriedly looking round I realised I must have come to a place where they made cartoon films. Everyone was looking at me, but I was feeling brave that day and went straight up to the elderly man and asked if they needed any extra help in the studio. The girl with golden hair murmured, 'Kathy is leaving, you know,' and the elderly man, who I later learnt was the head animator, said it wasn't his place to employ artists but if I cared to bring some specimens of my work, he'd show them to someone called Captain Chambers. I dashed home and collected the best life drawings I had done at Wracker's, some of my secret paintings I kept under the divan, also two watercolours Gene had done in Orléans. I felt guilty about this but would have taken drawings from the British Museum if I could have laid my hands on them, I so needed the work. I saw Captain Chambers the next day and he said he liked my work, particularly the French landscapes, and complimented me on being so versatile. He agreed to take me on in this girl Kathy's place, but the salary was small, only thirty shillings a week. The firm had not been going long.

I lived only a few minutes away from the studio; so there were no fares to pay and I could go home at lunchtime and eat with Gene if he was working at home. He had been commissioned to illustrate a children's book about a black kitten and he brought up one of the kittens that were always playing around our grocer's shop and used it as a model. Of course, we became so attached to it we kept it permanently and for some reason he was called Nero. This was a perfect time for me. I loved Gene, enjoyed my work and had no real money worries because two people could manage quite well on four or five pounds a week in the early 'thirties. There was one thing that made me slightly uneasy and it always came so unexpectedly. It was Gene getting so worked up about trifles. Some small thing would set him off and he would go on and on about it, particularly during the night. Once it was about a maid they had had when he was a child who pulled the golden centres out of the lilies that grew in the garden to prevent rain washing the gold onto the snowy whiteness. This maid used to prepare poultry for the table and, although it made him shudder, he couldn't help watching her tearing out bowels and slashing off heads, 'and she kept the corn from their crops to give the living hens. She was such a disgusting woman, with coarse red hair, every hair separate like twisted wire, and she enjoyed cutting up meat, you could tell she did.' I would try and comfort him in the night; but, when once they started, these outbursts might last for three or four hours and sometimes he had to get out of bed and walk up and down the room. Often it was politics and the unemployment or some Minister who should be kicked out of the Government. I can't think how he knew about these things because we only read newspapers on Sunday.

These attacks did not happen very often, perhaps once in three weeks, and, although they were a strain at the time, I soon forgot them.

Blanche in Singapore seemed to be living just the sort of life she had hankered for: parties and picnics, horses and servants, everything was wonderful, including Rollo. Then, after she had been married about four months, in the middle of a description of a dinner party she had given, she put in brackets, 'I think there is something not quite right about my marriage.' There was no more about this for a month or two, then a PS, 'I talked about my marriage to the Colonel's wife and she says there definitely is something missing.' I wrote to her asking what was missing, but she did not answer and as her letters continued to be happy, I didn't worry much. Gene said he thought she meant that Rollo was cold in bed.

When the spring came, I found I was pregnant. Except for a slight feeling of nausea and finding there were an awful lot of unpleasant smells about that I hadn't noticed before, I felt marvellous. We were both so pleased about this baby coming, although Gene never thought of it as a baby but always as 'this little boy' and I hoped he wouldn't be disappointed when a screaming little red girl arrived. I did not tell anyone at the studio where I worked that I was pregnant because I was afraid they would expect me to leave and I really enjoyed the work besides needing the money. I had progressed from painting on transparent celluloid to animating, but was still at the stage when the key figures were supplied by the head animator. He was pleased with my work in spite of the fact that I occasionally fell asleep over my desk, not from boredom, but because Gene had had one of his talking nights.

On the landing below our flat there was a single room which had become a sort of dumping ground. There was a bicycle there and mouldy trunks, stacks of newspaper and cheap religious prints in broken frames. An Italian family lived across the landing, but this room did not connect with their flat and the landlord was always saying, 'I could get good money for that room if only I had time to clear it.' He worked at night in a bakery and looked like a piece of mildewed bread and people said he was a gambler. He never interfered with his tenants although he sometimes opened his door and looked out into the hall as we passed. He usually wore a dirty woollen vest with long sleeves and his grey-green face above it wore a hopelessly melancholy air. One afternoon as we passed we felt his sad eyes on us and Gene stopped to ask if we could rent this unoccupied room, if we cleared it out ourselves. At first he dropped his paper and shuddered at the suggestion; but when we reassured him and said he needn't come near the room, all he would have to do was take extra rent, he agreed to let us have it for seven and six a week. It took us several weekends to clear and clean the room, then Gene whitewashed the walls and, to please me, painted the ceiling sky blue sprinkled with a few gold and silver stars. I bought a small chest of drawers and began to fill it with baby clothes and was able to put a few shillings each week on one side towards other furniture we would need. Every evening when I returned home I would stop for a moment before going upstairs to admire this new room and, although there was only a chest of drawers there, I always saw it as a complete nursery and sometimes there was a baby sleeping in the cot.

I had hardly missed the country all the time I had been in London, but now I longed for it. It was September and I remembered the heavy morning dew on the grass and the mist lifting over the river and ripening apples hanging from the trees. The rustling rushes by the river and the dahlias like glossy stars edging the lawns and the gardener mowing the grass in stripes of light and dark green and the smell of freshly cut grass. It was almost the smells I missed most, crushed nettles and walnut leaves, roses, newly picked fruit and the slightly muddy smell of the river. I'd close my eyes and imagine I was sniffing remembered smells, all nostalgic ones. Gene took me to Kew for the day. It was delightful, but quite different.

ELEVEN

WHEN I WAS ABOUT six months pregnant things began to go wrong, not with me, but with Gene. Our marriage was such a happy one, perhaps partly due to the fact that Gene always had his own way over everything because whatever he wanted, I wanted too, even the stark wood furniture without a shred of paint on it. When he got worked up about things being ugly or fussy, I knew he was right. Often he went out of his way to torture himself by looking at things that would upset him – furniture shops and windows filled with plaster little girls lifting up their skirts and gnomes and monks or demons twisted up in agony. These things were frightful but one could always look the other way. Gene would return home quivering with the horrors he had seen as if it had been cruelty to children or animals. I could tell by the way he walked upstairs if things were wrong. Sometimes I thought I must be insensitive that I did not worry enough about ugliness, unemployment and all the things that upset Gene; but life would have been frightful if we had both suffered so much.

I heard from Blanche and she seemed to be in some trouble too. She said she would tell me about it when she saw me and that she was returning immediately. She wanted me to take a small furnished flat for about twelve or sixteen pounds a month in Kensington or Chelsea. 'Nowhere near Charlotte Street', underlined. Somewhere she could move into as soon as she arrived because she did not want to stay in a hotel on her own. I guessed her marriage had broken up and, although I did not care for Rollo, I was sorry. I found her a small flat in a converted house in Queen's Gate Terrace and the back windows overlooked Epstein's house, which I thought amusing. At first the house agent did not want to show me over the flat, muttering something about no children allowed, and it took me some time to convince him that the flat was for my childless sister. I realised then how obvious it must be that I was about to have a child; I'd imagined that it hardly noticed and had hoped that no one at work knew. The following day I told the head animator in a loud voice that I was due to have a baby in three months and would it be all right if I stayed on as long as possible? The girls all started to laugh and said, 'We wondered when you were going to mention it and were beginning to think you didn't know yourself.' They produced a beautiful cobwebby shawl that they had bought between them, saying that they had had it for over a month but had not liked to give it to me. No one seemed to expect me to leave. This was a great relief, not only from the point of money, but because I liked the safety of the studio. I was beginning to feel uneasy at home, not all the time, but in waves.

The gallery in Cork Street sold another of Gene's paintings and were becoming interested in his work, even suggesting that they might make him a small allowance. One of the partners came to the flat and looked at all Gene's work. He was a handsome, fragile-looking man and kept saying 'Very interesting, very interesting,' with the 'very' drawn out, and we hoped this would result in great things. Gene became bored with the kitten illustrations, saying they were *merde*; but they were eventually finished and I took them to the publisher myself in case Gene was too disparaging about them. I was very pleased I did because they gave me a small book to illustrate – it was the kind of thing I could do on my head. For the first time in our married life we had a surplus of money and started a joint bank account with fifty pounds.

Blanche returned in October and, as I had feared, her marriage to Rollo had broken up, in fact it was to be annulled because it had never been consummated and was not a proper marriage at all. She said the worst part had been Rollo pleading with her not to leave him, not so much that he would miss her but because he did not want his friends to know the reason the marriage was ending. 'He'll miss me as a hostess and he was proud of me and all that sort of thing, but he had no real feeling for me. Nor, I suppose, had I for him, except a sort of gratitude because he gave me such a lovely life.' They had parted as friends and he was making her an allowance. Rollo's own lawyer was arranging the annulment, which might take some time. She felt she could make no plans for the future. Perhaps she would take up some sort of work or train for something; she didn't know. She was vague and calm and rather far away and I felt that she was keeping something back.

We went shopping together and she was alarmed when people pushed past me. She kept asking if I was all right and worried in case the baby arrived in Harrods although it was not due for another two months. She said I couldn't last much longer or I'd burst. When I saw myself in the Harrods mirrors, I could see what she meant; we had no long ones at home. She wanted to buy the baby an enchanting little cradle all trimmed with frilled muslin. I longed to accept it, but knew Gene would not approve of it; so she bought a high chair with a padded seat and rabbits painted on the back. I hoped Gene wouldn't scrape the rabbits off.

It saddened me that Blanche and I had secrets from each other because I was sure there was something she had not told me and I had kept back the fact that I was worried about Gene. He liked Blanche and was always at his best with her although she teased him about his austere ideas – a thing I had never dared to do. One Saturday afternoon Blanche and I were having tea together in front of the living-room fire, eating the first crumpets of the year. Butter was running down our chins and we were laughing and saying that we were glad Rollo couldn't see us, when we heard the door below open and then Gene's steps all heavy on the stairs, and I knew he was in one of his states. He stood on the top of the stairs leaning on the rail, ignoring Blanche, and started off on a long rigmarole about how he had finished with those swine in Cork Street; they were exhibiting the work of some degraded artist not fit to hold a brush in his hand, let alone touch a canvas. I had never heard of this artist before although he must have been someone he had been despising for some time. I tried to stop the flow of excited words and took his hand and drew him towards the fire. He shook me off and walked up and down the room almost shouting. Blanche's face had gone bluish with fright and she whispered, 'What is it, what is it?' I said it was nothing, men sometimes became nervous when their wives were expecting a baby. This did not appear to reassure her and, gathering her things, she crept away with her chin all glittering with butter.

I gathered from what Gene was shouting that he had made the most frightful scene in Cork Street, which had ended in the owners of the gallery having to push him into the street and lock the doors on him. Now he was regretting that he hadn't smashed the windows. 'But I suppose the fools would have called the police if I had,' he added in a bewildered way as he sat down on the divan and tugged at the cover with his long thin hands. He dejectedly asked if any tea was going and when he had gulped it down said, 'I know I have done a terrible thing. Do you think I'm going mad or something?'

We were both very quiet for the rest of the day and it was the first time we had been really unhappy since our marriage. The thing I had been trying to push to the back of my mind for weeks or perhaps even months had come forward and wouldn't go away again. I had to face the heartbreaking fact that there was something wrong with Gene's mind. I wondered if it really could be connected with me being pregnant and decided to ask the woman doctor who was attending me. She was young and sympathetic and I regarded her as a friend, but even so it would be difficult to discuss Gene with her.

The next time Blanche and Gene met I could see she was watching and wondering about him all the time; but fortunately Gene did not realise she had been there during his outburst, so things were not too strained. We went to the Café Royal together and amused ourselves drinking lager and watching people. After a time I saw with horror that the fragile young man from the gallery in Cork Street was sitting at a nearby table and watching us intently. I had to pretend that I was feeling faint so that we could leave quickly and made a great thing about needing fresh air. I had a crazy fit of laughing in the street. I was laughing from nerves, not from cheerfulness, but they thought the lager had been too much for my condition.

Gene's unsold paintings were returned from the gallery in Cork Street in a large van and we carried them upstairs without saying anything. A few days afterwards he started work with a firm that made those huge signs they have outside cinemas advertising films – giant women with big breasts bursting out of their clothes, prehistoric monsters or men fighting in a jungle. They are painted from squared-up photographs and are usually as ugly as a nightmare. I thought Gene must have taken up the work as a sort of penance. He went off to work all dejected and returned even more so, never saying a word about what happened in his day, hardly saying a word any time except during the night when he couldn't sleep. Sometimes strange fantasies took possession of his mind and he talked with such conviction as he walked about the room in the darkness that I believed them too. He thought that buildings varied their size from time to time, houses in particular. He said you could see it all the time – the newly built villas in the suburbs hadn't had time to grow yet, the middle-aged houses in the older suburbs were enormous compared to them – in Kensington, for instance. In old age, houses tended to shrink, although a few grew larger just as people did. He thought that this growing and shrinking of houses was something they had caught from the humans who lived in them. One night he had mistletoe on his mind and said that he had been afraid of it for years, ever since he had seen trees smothered with it in France. He had driven in a little open car with his parents and for one whole day they passed these trees still bare of leaves, but festooned with bunches of mistletoe. Some of the older trees were obviously dying as if from a malignant disease; they were covered in these sinister yellow-green growths. Some trees appeared to be free of it, but if he looked carefully there was usually one small bunch of mistletoe somewhere. He had thought he heard the trees calling out, 'I have got the mistletoes, I've got the mistletoes,' and kept urging his father to drive faster; but the car was old and slow. Often, when he found it difficult to sleep, I would wake and find him sitting quiet in a chair and in the dark I would get out of bed and sit with my arms round him, hoping that I was comforting him. We would say nothing, just sit in silence.

A month before the baby was due I reluctantly gave up my animating work. I was finding it uncomfortable to sit for eight hours a day and I felt I was a bit of an embarrassment to the people I worked with. The doctor examined me in her surgery once a week; but in spite of her being so sympathetic it took me a little time before I could bring myself to discuss the state of Gene's mind with her, partly because I didn't want to say disloyal things about him. Eventually I managed to say that he was sleeping badly and worrying a lot; but she thought that quite a normal state for a young husband whose wife was expecting her first baby. Then I added that he got into states about things that did not matter very much and that he had queer ideas in the night. She asked me what kind of queer ideas and, remembering the previous night, I told her that he thought that cats should wear little muzzles so that they could not catch birds and that he had thrown the alarm clock out of the window because it was leaking and wasting time. She said she did not consider that very serious and suddenly we were laughing and I felt as if I was making mountains out of molehills. To set my mind at rest the doctor said she would like to meet Gene; she had been meaning to come and see where I lived for some time. I had planned to have the baby at home because I didn't want to go into a public ward in a hospital and we couldn't afford a nursing home. In any case I thought I would enjoy my baby more at home. The doctor had given me a list of things I would need, rather sordid things like rubber sheeting and kidney bowls and the inevitable bed pan. The Italian woman who lived below had promised to come in to help for a few hours a day. We had become friends after I presented her with Edward's gift of embroidered cushion covers. She had sewn them all together and made a dressing-gown of them.

The doctor called on the evening of one of Gene's good days. The staff where he worked had been allowed to leave an hour or two early because there was no work for them that afternoon and he had been able to do a little painting at home – a view of chimney pots and the toy factory from our balcony. The light was exactly right for it just before dusk, so he was only able to work on it for about half an hour at a time. We were having a late tea when she arrived and she sat down and joined us, happily eating golden syrup on bread. To my amazement Gene started to tell her about painting these enormous squared-up figures that depressed him so much; but talking to her he made the work appear rather amusing and laughed at the horrors he had to paint. He told her strange stories about the men he worked with. One was a spiritualist and thought he could levitate though no one had seen him do it; another was a bigamist and proud of it; and there was a very fat man who grew mushrooms under his bed. He was always trying to press them onto his fellow workers, who refused them because they were the colour of dirty bedclothes and smelt queer. I had not heard about any of these people before although he had been working with them for a few weeks.

When we finished tea, I showed the doctor all the things I had collected for the baby and my confinement. I had planned for the birth to take place in our new room under the gold and silver stars; but the doctor said it was too far from the bathroom and kitchen, and the living room would be more practical. Then she showed me how to bake cotton wool in biscuit tins and make it sterile. When we were in the kitchen she told me that, as far as she could judge, Gene appeared to be perfectly normal except that he looked so tired. She suggested that we took a country holiday as soon as I recovered from having the baby, and added casually that she was not charging anything for her service and that the money we had from the insurance society would help pay for our holiday.

In spite of my shape I went to see the publisher of children's books and he was pleased with my illustrations and said there would be more work for me after Christmas; he needed some line drawings for a child's first reading book. I paid the cheque he had given me into our banking account and returned home feeling content but intensely tired; the stairs had never seemed so steep. It was now the middle of November and the baby was due in a few days. All my preparations were made and I could hardly believe that someone would really be wearing the little clothes waiting in the chest of drawers, that the wicker cradle would be occupied and the tiny hairbrush used on someone's hair, if they had any hair. I did not want a bald baby; I wanted one with short black hair like Gene's.

I had not long to wait because I started labour pains early the next morning. I lay by Gene all doubled up, longing for him to get dressed and leave the house before he discovered that the 'little boy' was on his way. He started work at eight in the morning and insisted on getting his own breakfast and giving me a cup of tea in bed. This morning I left the tea untouched and he saw it cold and undrinkable on the stool that served as a bedside table. 'You're not ill?' he enquired anxiously. 'You look all different and your eyes are huge.' He bent to look into my face and I caught him to me and kissed him fiercely as if I would never see him again, almost biting him as another pain started. When it passed I told him there was nothing wrong with me except tiredness and I would rest all morning. He did not appear to be reassured and went into the dark morning looking thoughtful.

I waited for five minutes in case he returned and then went down to my Italian friend and banged on her door. She took one look at me shivering in my white nightdress and took command. Her husband was sent down to the grocer's shop to telephone the doctor; my bed was made up with rubber sheeting; and water was boiling away in the kitchen. I insisted on preparing the cot and laying out the baby clothes myself and, while I was doing it, the doctor arrived, earlier than we expected. Gene had telephoned her on his way to work because he had felt uneasy. This made me so happy I hardly noticed the labour pains. As they grew worse the Italian woman became more and more excited, sometimes giving out cries herself as if she were in labour. She was wearing her dressing-gown made of cushion covers and her hair was still in curlers. Sometimes she would disappear downstairs to attend to her own family and once all her children surged into the room, some even crawling on my bed until the doctor turned them out. I discovered later that they had been stamping on tubes of paint to make the colours squirt out. When the pains were very savage I tried to comfort myself by thinking that this time next year I would be making a birthday cake and once I found myself shouting out 'Birthday cake!' After that I was given a thing like a large scent spray to press every time I felt a pain coming and it helped, although it didn't deaden all the pains. Just when I was beginning to think something had gone wrong and the baby would never be born, it arrived and I heard it cry and knew it was alive. I must have fallen asleep or become unconscious after that because the next thing I knew was that I was wearing a clean nightdress and the bed had returned to normal, the doctor's things had been cleared away and little noises were coming from the cradle. The doctor told me that the baby was an eight-pound boy and gave him to me to hold and I saw he was exactly the sort of child I had hoped for, not bald, but with glistening black hair and beautiful in every way.

Gene returned at lunchtime and everything was as usual except that I was in bed and the baby in his cradle. He stood looking down at his son for a long time and then said, 'He certainly is a very little boy, but he'll soon grow.' He kept returning to have another look at him and laughing to himself. He even laughed about the children jumping on his paints. We were so happy together the day we became parents.

TWELVE

FOR FIVE DAYS I lay in bed being looked after by Gene and the Italians and my only anxiety was the baby crying and that did not occur often, only when he was hungry and being bathed or needed changing. I broke Truby King's rigid rules and fed him during the night, and he thrived on it, not losing weight as most newborn babies do. Blanche came to see me every day bringing delicious things to eat and Violet Scoby arrived one evening wearing an outsize toque made of leopard skin. She presented me with three baby's bonnets and a basket of fruit. She sat on one of our hard chairs for over an hour, her large eyes darting round our bare room, with its uncarpeted floor and sparse deal furni-ture. I told her we were not all that poor, Gene liked it that way. Sometimes the flat was filled with Italians, even ones I had never seen before, and they all gave me good advice; one of them even suggested that the baby should wear corsets. Blanche could not bear them and said they smelt; but it was only garlic and sausage, not sweat. They had usually all departed by the time Gene came home, often leaving a tasty red stew or pasta to be warmed up for our dinner.

We decided to call the baby Paul Eugene, Paul after my father – although I could hardly remember him, the family always said he was a wonderful man and a hero. If he had lived my baby would have been his first grandchild.

Gene appeared to be extraordinarily light-hearted since Paul's birth. He would race upstairs when he returned from work and sit on my bed laughing and talking and flicking his cigarette ash over the floor. Sometimes he would break off in the middle of a sentence and start on something completely different; then he would jump up and hold the kitten Nero above his head and say he was a flying cat and I was relieved it was the kitten, not the baby. He was still a little timid of touching him, but would gently stroke his cheek with one finger as he talked to him in French so that he would be bilingual. He said he couldn't start early enough if he was to have a good accent; his mother had nearly always spoken to him in French. He was experimenting in painting by electric light and had finished a most successful painting of malevolent potatoes – sprouting potatoes he had found in the kitchen. There was something menacing, yet beautiful, in the way he had portrayed the withered brown tubers and vigorous, almost sinister purplish shoots springing out like crab's claws. Now, whenever I see sprouting potatoes, I remember that painting and see them with Gene's eyes.

The doctor advised me to stay in bed for ten days; but on the afternoon of the sixth day I felt bored and got up for a few minutes. I was surprised to find how difficult it was to walk. I seemed to have lost my balance and felt weaker than I had expected and was glad to return to bed. I must have gone to sleep because I woke with a start to hear a loud knocking on the door which was left slightly open so that friends could walk up. I shouted, 'Come in,' but there was silence for a moment except for heavy breathing, which was followed by very heavy footsteps indeed. I saw a policeman's helmet advancing up the stairs and then the policeman under it and he came into the room. He stood there looking around, not seeing me at first lying in bed with my baby beside me. When he did he said apologetically, 'I'm sorry to disturb you when you're feeling poorly,' which made me smile although I was afraid I had broken the law in some way – perhaps we had delayed in registering Paul's birth. I said in a muffled voice from the bedclothes, 'It's nothing, only a baby. Have I done something dreadful?' He shook his head and looked at me very kindly and said he had some bad news and immediately I was convinced Gene had been run over and killed. I could see him being crushed under the wheels of a great red car that wouldn't stop. The policeman said it wasn't as bad as that; it was a case of illness. Gene had been taken ill and had made a disturbance, in fact he had got over-excited; but it was nothing that a few days in hospital wouldn't put right. 'Perhaps your husband suffers from fits of excitement, ma'am?' he enquired; the notebook appeared and I was gently questioned and between questions reassured. All the same I knew Gene had gone off his head and the thing I had been dreading had happened when I was least expecting it. I kept completely calm while the policeman was with me, declining his offer of asking a neighbour to sit with me. I told him that my sister would be arriving almost immediately and he eventually went away.

As soon as his footsteps ceased I crawled out of bed and put Paul in his cradle. He was sleeping soundly and not due for another feed for over an hour. I looked round for my clothes which had been put away by kindly helpers and it took me ages to dress. I had to keep sitting down and it was like one of those dreams when one is trying to dress and never manages it and finds oneself eventually walking down a busy street in a nightgown. I knew I was too weak to carry the baby so I left him alone; but as I crept downstairs I felt I was being drawn back. Somehow I managed to walk as far as Tottenham Court Road, where I found a taxi to drive me to the hospital where Gene had been taken. I was relieved it was a hospital, not an asylum. When I got there it was the most bewildering and enormous place and I kept being mistaken for a patient and being asked to show a card. I thought they meant visiting cards at first. It was all so strange I felt like a lost foreigner who does not know the language, for instance I did not know if Gene came under the heading of casualty or the name of the ward he was in. After a time I found a sympathetic woman called an almoner who let me sit in her office while she made enquiries. It was difficult to sit when I was being drawn back to the baby all the time and I began to worry in case Nero had sat on his chest and suffocated him. I was about to run home when the almoner returned accompanied by a doctor with a tic in one cheek and I couldn't help wondering if it worked when he was asleep. They asked me questions and filled in forms until I became desperate and asked if I could see Gene immediately: 'Our six-day-old baby is left alone and I'm afraid something terrible may be happening to him.' Then the doctor told me I couldn't see Gene because he was under drugs and not to be disturbed; but I would be able to see him in the morning and I was to bring pyjamas and toilet things. The thought of bringing pyjamas was reassuring somehow. To my surprise the doctor put his hand on my arm and added, 'Don't worry, my dear, your husband does not appear to be seriously ill; we shall be able to tell you more tomorrow. There is a very famous specialist coming to see him in the morning and I'm sure we'll have good news for you.' He turned to the almoner and asked her to telephone for a taxi for me, even offering to pay my fare until I convinced him that I had remembered to bring money with me.

When I returned to Charlotte Street, I could hear the baby crying as I dragged myself up the stairs so I knew that he had not been suffocated. I found him hungry and wet but none the worse for being left alone for two hours. While I was attending to him, a few Italians appeared and I had to explain why I was dressed and where I had been. I told them that Gene had been taken to hospital with a suspected appendix, which was all I could think of in a hurry; and there they were wailing and exclaiming round me, saying that I would most likely get puerperal fever. I longed to get into bed and be quiet. When I did, one of them stayed by my bed fanning my face with a newspaper.

It was some time before I knew exactly what had happened to Gene on that terrible afternoon. Odd bits of information came from different people, even Gene himself. He could not remember much except that he had slashed blue paint all over a squared-up painting of a giant gorilla beating his chest. He said there was a lot of noise afterwards, though he wasn't sure who was making it, and he could vaguely remember being in the street and gaping faces all around. The first person to give me any idea of what really happened was the bigamist when he came to enquire how Gene was the day after he had been taken to hospital. Fortunately I was dressed; I would not have liked a bigamist to have seen me in bed, and I guessed who he was immediately. Not that he appeared sinister, but self-assured and leering and looking as if he lived on nothing but meat. After we had talked for a few minutes and he had said how sorry all the men at work were about Frenchie's breakdown (I wondered who 'Frenchie' was until I realised it was Gene), he went on to say that Frenchie was usually 'damned depressed', but on that last day he had had a 'wild manner' and had been chattering away in French until someone had told him to shut up because they couldn't stand all that *parlez vous*. The bigamist was beginning to enjoy himself and looked more than ever like a beefsteak on legs. 'Do you know what he said? "I'm not talking to

you. I'm talking to my son." Well, I thought he had
been drinking. We all exchanged glances and laughed
a bit and Frenchie turned his back on us and smoked
cigarette after cigarette non-stop until the boss told
him to get on with the job. Then he leapt up on those
long hookers of his and shouted "Right!" and started
slashing this blue paint about ruining an entire week's
work, and there was the boss yelling, "There's no call
to do that. Take your bloody cards and get out." He
didn't even wait for them, just rushed into the street
shouting about being smeared with ugliness, although
it was only paint. We thought it was funny at first, that
he was fooling or something; then a crowd gathered
and he was tearing at his clothes in a frantic way and
raving like a madman and we realised it was serious
and called the police. When they took him away his
clothes were in rags. It was extraordinary, it really was,
because your husband wasn't a man to make poppy-
cock of himself, a very reserved man, your husband.'

On the Saturday evening the man who grew mushrooms under his bed called with Gene's wages and
insurance card. I refused the money at first because
he had not worked a full week and had damaged the
gorilla, but the little man insisted the boss thought it
only right that Gene should be paid as it was a case
of illness. 'Mind you, I don't think he's keen on your
husband coming back,' he added apologetically. 'We

know he's a good painter and all that, but the work didn't suit him. He wasn't happy there. I went into the lavatory once, excuse me but you know how it is; I walked in and there was Frenchie standing facing the wall and crying like a child. I just went away and used the yard, only it gave me a turn. Poor boy, I'll never forget them struggling to get him into the van – like an animal going to the slaughterhouse.' Before he left he presented me with a bag filled with dirty mushrooms which smelt of misery. Nothing could make me sadder than I was.

They let me see Gene when I returned to the hospital with his clothes. I almost wished they hadn't because he did not appear to know who I was. He sat on a bed wearing someone else's dressing-gown, looking wretched, more like a bitter ghost than a human being. I sat beside him and took his hand and he politely took it away. Although I talked to him, he kept silent until I got up to leave. Then he looked at me for the first time with his blank black eyes and said politely, 'You are expecting a baby, aren't you?' I told him the baby was already born. 'Don't you remember we called him Paul?' I asked miserably as he turned away and muttered, 'I know nothing about it but you had better keep him away from mistletoe.' They had impressed on me that I must behave with the utmost calmness whatever he said so I left the ward and cried in the corridor. It seemed as if he would never be normal again. I saw the kind doctor with a tic on his face before I left and he told me that the specialist who had examined Gene was confident that he would recover and recommended that he should be moved to a mental hospital in the suburbs. I said, 'You mean a lunatic asylum,' and he nodded and said: 'There's nothing to worry about; he won't be certified or anything like that and will be free to walk about the grounds and go home for short periods. He may be cured in six months or even two. It depends how he reacts to treatment. It's his first breakdown and may well be his last if he avoids undue stress and strain.' This word 'breakdown' was constantly used. No one ever said that Gene had gone mad or had gone off his head; once or twice the word schizophrenia was mentioned, but that was later.

The day Gene was taken ill (I can't bring myself to call what happened to Gene by its right name either), the same day that this happened Blanche had gone to visit Mrs Buller to help her organise a charity dance and I think she was going to demonstrate the rumba among other things. She was only to be away a few days and I knew the first thing she would do when she returned would be to rush round to see how the baby was getting on. Then I'd have to tell her about Gene. I couldn't make up stories about rumbling appendixes to her. It was just as I expected; she came running up the stairs, calling, 'Vicky!' before she even reached our door. She came in wearing a Cossack hat and carrying a huge bunch of yellow chrysanthemums. 'Oh, you're up already,' she exclaimed, flinging the flowers on the table. 'I hope you've got something to put these in.' Then she hurried to the cradle to admire Paul, who had just been bathed and fed and was sleeping contentedly, with his little hands showing above the blankets. 'I am proud of being an aunt,' she whispered. Then, looking up from the baby, she noticed my worn face and asked if I was ill. We sat on the bed together and I told her what had happened. Afterwards we both cried and it was very like the days when we had lived together in Mornington Crescent – Blanche even cried into a towel hanging on the bathroom door. When she caught sight of herself in Gene's shaving mirror, she cried again because her face was in a frightful mess and she had an important lunch engagement with a man she had known in Singapore. 'I'll tell you about him another time,' she said as she bathed her eyes. 'I feel guilty to be happy when you're feeling so wretched.' Then I knew she had a lover and that was the secret I had felt between us.

Gene was removed to the asylum in the suburbs and I visited him once a week. There was a beautiful garden there; but it was too cold to walk in. From the outside the asylum looked more like an expensive school than a hospital and I never saw anyone that looked really mad; perhaps they were locked away. It saddened me to see how many young people there were there. They were always playing ping-pong, and now, whenever I hear the sound of ping-pong being played, I feel the most terrible depression. The first time I saw Gene there I think he knew who I was although he turned away from me. Then just as I was leaving words came pouring out, meaningless, incoherent, until he asked me to bring him painting materials. He stood up all the time I was there and it was a shock to see him wearing wide trousers like other men and a hideous Fair Isle pullover. Every now and then he plucked at it in a bewildered way. On my next visit he was wearing his own clothes and was in a far better state and really pleased to see me. I had brought him large sheets of drawing paper, brushes and poster paints. The hospital authorities had been afraid of oil paints entering the building, perhaps they thought the patients might eat them. Gene said many of them had filthy eating habits; that was one of the things he complained about. Now he was more normal, he had begun to worry about our financial position. He wanted to know if his father was still sending the four pounds a month, as he was paying money to the asylum for Gene's treatment. I was able to tell him that four pounds had arrived a few days ago and had been addressed to Mrs Eugene Reeve. I would have liked to have acknowledged the money, but Gene was against it. He was sure the registered letters would cease if I did. Actually we had about thirty-five pounds in the bank and there was the prospect of my having another book to illustrate. To have enough money to last us six weeks seemed to us security, so it wasn't difficult to set his poor mind at rest.

A few days before Christmas Blanche's marriage was annulled and she was free to marry her new lover – a major this time and even older than her previous husband, but a very different type of man. John Clifford Jones was small and dark, with brilliant blue eyes, very handsome in his neat way and in such perfect proportion that it was a great pleasure to look at him. His dark hair shone and so did his teeth and eyes, even his voice seemed to shine. He was one of the kindest men I have ever met and, although he was sixteen years older than Blanche, it didn't seem to matter in the least. She said young men didn't appeal to her. 'I don't want to be married to a boring young man who drives a rattling car that always breaks down and who blushes when he orders wine. I like self-assured men who can teach me how to live. I was an absolute oaf when I married Rollo and he helped me a lot. I shall always be grateful to him for that. I'm so in love with John, you know, and I don't mind him being smaller than I am; I don't want to change him in any way. Did I tell you he had been married before and his wife died when she was having a baby. Now, of course, John is afraid for me to have children; but I'll change his mind when we're married, I hope to have at least three.' She would rattle on so happily, then suddenly stop and say, 'Poor Vicky, how can I be happy when you are so miserable. Gene will be out soon, won't he?' I told her that the doctors thought he would be able to come home for a few days at Christmas and how much we were looking forward to it. Every time I thought about it I touched wood and I even went into Whitfield's Tabernacle and prayed.

Blanche went to Wales with her John to meet his mother who lived somewhere in Snowdonia. They came to see me before they started their journey and staggered up the stairs simply loaded with presents – toys for Paul and a Christmas hamper from Fortnum & Mason and a small turkey. Besides the food there was a cashmere pullover for me, the most heavenly soft thing, and a black polo-necked one for Gene. John was perfectly at ease in our stark flat and sat on our wooden-seated chairs with such an air they seemed to be wonderfully comfortable. He always made people feel at home, even in their own homes.

Gene returned on Christmas Eve and everything was as it used to be. He immediately got out his paints and started a painting of Paul asleep in his cot. In the evening friends came round and we drank some of the wine Blanche had given us and lit the candles on the Christmas tree. Although Paul was only five weeks old he loved it and smiled his first real smile, though it may have been wind. Christmas Day was a good day too. My nice doctor came to see us and we gave her the painting of menacing potatoes which we knew she admired and, soon after she left, more friends came to help us eat the turkey. No one except the doctor knew where Gene had been. Most of them seemed to think he had been on a visit to his father and it was better that way. I wanted Gene to have a normal Christmas without people being sorry for him; but I think I overdid the visitors and it should have been quieter because on Boxing Day I noticed that he wasn't quite so well as when he first came home. He kept laughing at nothing and it wasn't a jolly laugh and he said things like, 'Back to the looney bin tomorrow, Ha, Ha. I'm looking forward to seeing all my charming friends.' Once there were tears in his eyes when he asked, 'I will get better, won't I? How long do they think it will take?' We went back together on the afternoon of the 27th and we hardly spoke to each other in the train. A light snow was falling when we left the station and before going to the asylum we walked about the streets together in silence, the snow gently touching our cheeks as we watched the dull suburban streets becoming beautiful. We wandered for about an hour, the snow giving us an extraordinary feeling of lightness and unity. I don't think we were ever so close before.

Gene had a slight relapse after he returned and it was after that that they decided to give him insulin treatment. The doctors took us into their confidence, telling us that the treatment was rather alarming and unpleasant and even slightly dangerous, but 70 per cent of the cases treated with insulin recovered if they were treated in the early stages of their illness. It meant that Gene would have to be put in what they called a state of coma, but would not know much about it. He might be put in as many as fifty comas before he recovered. It sounded terrifying to me. Gene said he was willing to go through with anything, if only he could become normal again: 'Suppose I dragged on for years becoming more and more abnormal and hopeless, it would be a living death. However drastic this treatment is, it will be worth it, don't you agree, my darling?' It was not often that Gene called me 'my darling', only at times of great emotion. I agreed about the treatment, although I was afraid.

THIRTEEN

IT SNOWED FOR TWO DAYS and the roofs of the buildings in Soho stayed white although the streets were slushy. When I fed the birds that came to my balcony I liked to gaze on all this whiteness and I pretended to myself that I was in a Moorish city. I watched pigeons feeding on a lower roof, looking dark and oily against the snow, and among them were things I took for tame rabbits until I saw one of them run away with a piece of bread in its mouth and saw it was a large rat. Some of the rats were sitting up on their hind legs nibbling bread held between their front paws. They looked charming but I was relieved there were no trails of rats' feet on my balcony.

I was busy in the days immediately after Christmas illustrating another children's book about a family of kangaroos. Although the publisher had lent me some photographs of kangaroos, I found them difficult to draw at first until I suddenly found I could draw them in any position, hanging out the laundry, driving cars or rowing boats. I was drawing kangaroos on everything and became obsessed with them. Except for Paul and my Italian friends I hardly spoke to anyone. I didn't feel lonely, just dreamy and peaceful except for the day I went to the asylum to see Gene and then I was all apprehensive in case he had had a relapse and did not know me. Actually my fears were unnecessary because his condition was improving and he was fairly cheerful in spite of the horrors of his treatment. He had great faith in his complete recovery and kept saying, 'I can see an end to it at last.' The doctors were encouraging too.

Blanche returned in a state of great excitement about her marriage, which was to take place immediately, and her visit to Wales: 'We were snowed up for days, I've never seen anything like it before, beautiful but slightly frightening. We stayed in this wonderful house, almost a castle really, which belongs to John's uncle. His mother, John's mother I mean, keeps house for him. She is a dear old thing, rather frail and with large freckles on her hands. I think they came from living in India, so I must take care I don't get them.' John was being sent to India when his leave expired. They were to be married in a registry office, very quietly, but there was to be a party afterwards. They had taken a furnished house in a mews in the Queen's Gate area, a little doll's house with a yellow front door and a courtyard at the back, where bulbs were already pushing up their green leaves. I was not looking forward to the wedding party for several reasons; perhaps the main one was that I had nothing to wear, at least nothing suitable. Then I remembered seeing several dress shops where everything in the window cost only a guinea, so I bought a maize-coloured dress and when I cut all the trimmings off, it looked quite expensive.

I took Paul to the wedding party and we both enjoyed ourselves, particularly Paul, who lay in his basket being admired. Edward was not there because Blanche had not told him that her marriage to Rollo had been annulled and now thought she would wait until she had left for India. 'I feel I should be a long, long way away before I break it to him,' she laughed over her glass of champagne. 'Is it all right to drink this yet or do you think some fool will embarrass us by formally drinking our health? Two marriages in two years is rather a lot to go through when you are still under twenty-one.' They had no honeymoon, and when the party ended the hired glasses were collected, all sticky with champagne, and taken away in a van.

One day towards the end of January I was buying drawing materials in Winsor and Newton's in Rathbone Place when one of the girls from the animating studio where I used to work came in to buy poster paints. She told me that they had almost finished *Robinson Crusoe* and were about to start a new film, *The Little Mermaid*, and I immediately thought how I would enjoy animating mermaids' tails. I asked after everyone and suggested bringing Paul round to the studio so that they could see how beautiful he was. The next afternoon I wrapped him in the shawl the girls had given me and carried him to the studio where he was made a great fuss of. With the exception of one young man who was not a baby connoisseur, they all agreed that he was a fascinating and lovely child – the young man said he looked Chinese. Some of them who had met Gene asked if he was doing well with his paintings and if he was going to have an exhibition. This was a painful question so I muttered something about him being in hospital with a faulty liver, as a change from a rumbling appendix. I found it difficult inventing illnesses on the spur of the moment. The head animator, the man who had trained me, asked how long Gene expected to stay in hospital and I answered truthfully that he might have to have treatment for another five months. He looked thoughtful, then asked if I would like to return to work.

I thanked him and said I would think it over for a few days although I had already made up my mind to return to the studio, if I could find someone reliable to look after Paul. The Italians were always willing to mind him when I went out and I used to give them a little money from time to time because they were almost as hard up as we were. All the same, I didn't want to leave my baby with them day after day. Their ideas on how to look after babies were very different from mine and once I returned to find Paul with a dirty brown dummy stuck in his mouth.

That evening Blanche and John arrived with a cold chicken, a Russian salad and a bottle of wine and we had a meal together. After drinking the wine I had an inspiration. Why not borrow Marcella Murphy for a few months? She was clean and kind and her nose only having one nostril wouldn't notice; there were so many strange-looking people in the London streets. Blanche thought it a good idea too, although she was amused at the thought of Marcella clumping round London in her heavy high boots. 'She may start a new fashion, you know, like Russian boots,' she laughed as she collected her things, and I laughed, too, although a horrible thought had just crossed my mind: how was I going to pay her?

I wrote to Edward asking if I could borrow Marcella and enclosed a letter to her saying that I was in trouble and needed someone to help with the baby. I didn't think she would need much persuasion because I knew she longed to see Blanche and me again. She didn't get on with Edward very well because he always turned away when he spoke to her. The money question I left in abeyance; it was the next thing to be faced.

Within a week Marcella was hanging out nappies on my balcony and I was animating mermaids' tails. As I returned home for lunch, I saw quite a lot of Paul and in the evening I was always home in time to give him his six o'clock bottle and to put him to bed. I didn't want him not to depend on me. Marcella was blissfully happy in London; for one thing there was plenty of dirt to attack, but the thing she enjoyed most was looking in shop windows in Oxford Street and travelling in Selfridge's lifts. She refused to take any wages from me; she said it was a holiday and she should be paying me money for her keep. She had over two hundred pounds in the post office, her life's savings, and she would have willingly handed it over to me if I had let her. I felt unhappy about the wages and hoped we would be in a position to give her a present when she left.

Blanche and John left for India at the end of February and I felt very alone after they had gone. I saw Gene in the hospital every Sunday and he appeared to be entirely normal; but the doctors said he must continue the insulin treatment. I was afraid of it, because it meant that he was put into a deep coma and only restored to life by a glucose solution injected into a vein. Gene said it wasn't as bad as it sounded and every coma was one less to go through; many of the patients became so used to their treatment that they made jokes about it. To pass the time he had written and illustrated a book for Paul. It was about a timid lion who took up roller skating and became a champion, winning massive cups. A nurse typed the story and it looked almost like a real book when it was bound.

Violet Scoby had asked me so many questions about Gene's illness and which hospital he was in that she was too much for me and I admitted the truth. It wasn't that I was ashamed of Gene being in an asylum; it was that I felt that the fewer people who knew about it, the better it would be for him when he recovered. Most people tend to think that anyone who has had mental treatment is a lunatic for life and they watch them carefully, talking to them in a patronisingly soothing manner. I have noticed that incurable lunatics always wear queer hats, particularly the men. Perhaps it is the way they put them on their heads, poor things.

The spring came and the barrows in Berwick Market were golden with early daffodils and I bought several bunches although they were still very expensive. When I took them home I almost wished I hadn't, because they made me nostalgic for the country and the garden at home. I felt sorry that the only garden Paul would know was a gritty London balcony, where an occasional dusty geranium or daisy grew in a sugar crate. He had a collapsible pram now that we could carry up and down the stairs and Marcella took him shopping in it, sometimes even pushing him in her beloved Oxford Street. I hadn't the heart to tell her I disapproved when I returned in the evening and she told me the wonders they had seen – mock auctions, Eastern princes, masked men giving away five-pound notes and Woolworths. Fortunately she was afraid of pickpockets and left her purse at home.

The shock of Gene's illness was gradually wearing off and life had taken on a rhythm, the days flowing past, all very much the same with the exception of Sunday. Small worries – would Paul's rubber knickers last until I was paid on Saturday? or would the milkman mind waiting for his money for another week when there would be a new moon? How I looked forward to the new moon, when the registered letter arrived. Occasionally I went out in the evenings, but usually went to bed early and read Victorian novels in bed, Dickens, Trollope and Wilkie Collins. On Saturday afternoons I had a standing invitation to visit the Scobys and they liked me to bring Paul. I did not go very often, in spite of the fact that they gave me presents, sometimes clothes that had belonged to other babies or other women and food in tins.

It was lunchtime and I could smell Marcella's Irish stew all the way up the stairs, like a magnet drawing me up. Paul was lying on the divan kicking his feet into the air and the spring sun was making patterns on the bare floor. Marcella stood at the kitchen door stirring something in a saucepan. She said, 'There's a telegram for you dear, it only arrived a few minutes ago.' She spoke brightly although I could see she was worried. 'It's Master Edward, perhaps,' she added, her eyes flicking nervously. I held the unopened telegram in my hand, feeling sure that once I had read it, I would never be the same again, always lost. I went to the balcony, shutting the glass door after me to read it in private. The message was brief, only three words: 'Please come immediately', and was signed by Dr Rees, one of the doctors at the asylum who had become almost a friend. I stood there looking over the jagged roofs and found I was saying a muddled prayer; then I went inside and handed Marcella the telegram. She slowly read the three words out loud, adding, 'It may not be as bad as you think, it says so little.' Then, dramatically, 'He may have escaped!' I picked up my bag and turned towards the stairs and, as I ran down, I could hear her calling, 'Come back. You can't go without eating. Come back, such a lovely stew!'

FOURTEEN

THEY BURIED GENE in a graveyard at a place called Fortune Green. His father, the doctor who had become almost a friend and I were the only mourners. Although Dr Rees spoke to us both, the father did not speak to me. He stood about with an angry expression on his face, pulling at the knuckles of his fingers under the dark leather gloves. First one hand, then the other. There was only one wreath to lie on the coffin, a primrose one I had ordered, and already it was wilting. The single wreath added to the loneliness. When we turned to leave the cemetery, the doctor offered to drive me home in his car and I was glad to accept because I hardly knew where I was. I looked at Gene's father's irritable face and, after several false starts, asked him to come back with me to see his grandson. Before he could refuse Dr Rees said, 'Quite so. That's an excellent idea,' and rushed us into his car, which was waiting outside a stonemason's yard. Then we were bowling down the ugly hill. Every now and then Mr Reeve leant forward in the car and raised his clenched fists above his head in a sort of Biblical gesture. I made one attempt to speak, but it wasn't any good.

When we reached Charlotte Street Dr Rees got out of the car and gently steered Mr Reeve into the house and then I had to get him up the stairs. When we passed through the door that led to the living room, I closed it firmly so that he couldn't escape. Paul was propped up in the high chair and Marcella was spooning something into his mouth. She took one look at the grandfather and vanished into the kitchen, leaving the bowl and spoon in my hands. Paul lost interest in his food and gazed at his grandfather. They looked at each other for some time; then the old man said, 'So that's the lad; extraordinary likeness to my boy at that age. Well, I hope he will take up a sensible profession.' He turned to me and barked, 'How are you off for funds? Of course I'll pay for the interment; but I'm not a rich man, far from it and this illness has cost me a considerable amount, considerable amount.' I told him that I was working, adding that the money he sent was a great help. He fiercely demanded, 'What money?

I know nothing about any money,' and I wished I had kept quiet about it. To change the subject I asked him to stay and have a meal although I knew there was little enough in the house. He refused and said he would eat on the train. 'Yes, I must leave for the north immediately, but before I leave I would like to see the boy's birth certificate, just a legal formality, you know.' It was easy to find because there were so few places to put anything in our home; but I felt hurt because it was obvious that he thought Paul might be illegitimate. I found the certificate and pushed it in front of his eyes, almost knocking off his spectacles. He took it from me and read it through carefully, then wrote down Paul's names and date of birth in a notebook. When he finished, he laid the certificate on the table while he thoughtfully returned his notebook to his breast pocket. He turned to me and something happened to his face that may have been a smile and he jerked out, 'You're a good girl, look after the little lad.' He shook me by the hand and rushed away. When he had gone I saw there was something else on the table besides the certificate. It was white money that I did not recognise at first because it was five-pound notes, six of them.

People were kind to me, but they got on my nerves with their kindness. I longed to be completely alone in the dark with a heavy blanket over my head and stay like that for weeks, months or perhaps the rest of my life. They kept saying, 'Your baby must be such a consolation.' Actually he wasn't, he was just someone else to make an effort for. When I met the Italian mother, she said she was burning candles and praying for Gene. Returning to work after the funeral needed an enormous amount of courage, and they all tried to be tactful, which made it worse. They treated me as an invalid and I was not included in any conversation and, when they could bring themselves to speak to me, they looked away as if they could not bear the misery on my face. We used to spit on the celluloid to help the poster paint to stick, now I found tears worked just as well. Sometimes the misery lifted for a few minutes and my attention would be taken by something, an incident in the streets perhaps, or Paul would do something for the first time and I'd think, 'I must tell Gene on Sunday.' Then it would be all dark and hopeless again.

One evening Dr Rees came to see me and we sat together hardly speaking a word for over an hour. He was one of the few people I could bear to be with because he was almost as unhappy as I was. Gene was the only patient of his to die from the insulin treatment and, although he had always known there was a risk of death, he had become confident over the years and thought of it as a thing that could never happen to one of his patients, particularly Gene who had responded so well to treatment. He said over and over again, 'I was confident that he would make a complete recovery, that is what makes it so tragic.' He desperately wanted to do something to help, and it quite worried me that I could think of nothing he could do. Eventually he arranged for Paul and me to stay with his sister, who lived in a cottage in Suffolk. I was glad to accept his offer for Paul's sake, although I dreaded being polite to a woman I had never met. She might expect me to dress for dinner or be a compulsive talker, although her brother was quiet enough.

I left Marcella with Nero for company and set off in a Green Line bus on an April morning. Miss Rees met us at Sudbury and drove us to her pink-washed cottage a few miles away and, as soon as I got out of the car clutching a very wet Paul, I felt at home. Miss Rees was as quiet as her brother and spent a considerable amount of the day shut in her library writing and illustrating a book on gardening. Her own garden was delightful and filled with spring flowers. I had lived in London for so long I had forgotten the everyday things of country life, the delicate smell of primroses and the difference between pear and apple blossom. It was the same with the birds, I recognised their song, but couldn't remember which bird it belonged to. When I went to my bedroom at night, there was the lingering smell of the wallflowers that grew around the house and I would lean on the windowsill and breathe the soft air and feel that I was being made wonderfully clean and renewed inside.

We usually ate our meals in a sheltered corner of the garden and at breakfast and teatime there was always a comb of honey on the table. The bread was homemade and so was the wine, made from the grapes that grew on a large vine which climbed up the southern wall of the cottage. The house seemed to run itself. There was a married couple to do the work, but one hardly ever came across them except at mealtimes, and although I never heard any cleaning going on, when I came down in the mornings the house was shining with cleanness. On fine evenings, and they usually were fine, Miss Rees and I would take long walks together, she carrying a basket containing a trowel on her arm so that she could dig up any wild plant she found particularly interesting. She had a special bed in the garden where only wild flowers grew.

That month with Miss Rees was exactly what I needed. I returned to London feeling brave and healthy and the difference in Paul was enormous. He could sit up by himself and crawl a little and was firm and plump and brown all over from rolling about the garden with nothing on. I felt I could face anything. Actually I did not have much to face except loneliness.

I felt numbed most of the time, but can remember being tremendously impressed with the Surrealist Exhibition at the Burlington Galleries. Someone had given me a free pass and I visited it over and over again and it was as if I had been given an extra eye to see with and ordinary objects took on new shapes. Another thing which pleased me very much was that Blanche wrote to say she was expecting a baby and would most likely return for its birth. It gave me something to look forward to. I made a garden on Gene's grave. It had been Miss Rees's suggestion and on Saturday afternoons, feeling very like her, I used to set off with a basket containing a trowel and miniature watering-can to attend to it. Gene's grave became quite unlike any of the other graves, it was a brilliant jumble of flowers with nasturtiums trailing off onto other graves. In the autumn I planted bulbs and after that there was little I could do except keep it tidy. A few days before Christmas I went to see if any of the early flowering bulbs were already showing; but all I saw was a staring white cross with Gene's name engraved on it in horrible black letters and a proverb from the Bible underneath: 'My son, if thine heart be wise, my heart shall rejoice, even mine.' Gene's grave was ruined. The hideous cross was exactly the kind of thing that made him get in his states and I knew he would have called it *merde*. I never went there again.

FIFTEEN

BLANCHE RETURNED THREE WEEKS before her son was born. The confinement took place in a Harley Street nursing home and she spent her waiting weeks there because she had nowhere else to stay. In the evenings we often went to the cinema together and now it was my turn to be apprehensive and I kept interrupting the films to ask how she felt. Then, in the middle of a Fred Astaire and Ginger Rogers film, when I was so engrossed I had forgotten her condition, she suddenly let out a yelp and said, 'It's started.' With my eyes still fixed on the screen, I said, 'Hush, can't you wait until the end?' I thought she wanted to go to the lavatory and was astonished when she shouted, 'Don't be a bloody fool. Of course I can't wait,' and, leaping from her seat, charged like a tank through the people who were sitting in our row. I followed to an accompaniment of angry whispers: 'Oh, my foot! Have you no manners? Complain to the manager.' I caught Blanche by the arm and rushed her towards an exit; by this time terrible things had started to happen and she doubled up every few minutes. I had to leave her for a little time while I searched for a taxi and it was a relief to see she was still standing when I returned. It was only a few minutes' drive to the nursing home, but it seemed like hours and all the time Blanche was saying, 'John will never forgive me if his son is born in a taxi.' Actually the baby was respectably born in bed about three hours after we reached the nursing home.

Blanche called her son Stephen, and, when he was a month old, she took him to Wales to stay with John's mother, who had arranged a great family party for the christening. Before she left she bought new clothes suitable for Welsh mountains, good shoes and a soft tweed suit, also a beautiful draped dress and romantic hat for the christening. Then she insisted on buying clothes for me: a light grey coat and skirt and two cashmere pullovers, a pure silk blouse, gloves, stockings and three pairs of shoes. She said the shoes I wore always made her want to cry and I could see what she meant. We went to a hairdressers and, while Blanche had a permanent wave, I had my thick black hair cut short, with a suggestion of a fringe, and for the first time in my life had my hands manicured.

It may have been the new clothes or perhaps the spring that made me feel restless and bored. For the first time since Gene had died I wanted to enjoy myself. I longed to go out at night. I wanted to see what a nightclub was like and to dine in a smart restaurant and to drive in a fast open car, white for preference. I wanted to own a fitted dressing-case like Blanche's; in fact, although I loved her, I felt slightly jealous. My poverty began to depress me and things that had not mattered before, like an occasional cockroach in the hall, sickened me. Feeling disloyal to Gene, I made a few improvements in the flat. I bought some cheap Scandinavian rugs for the floor and painted the bare pine furniture ice blue. In a junk shop I found two small Victorian chairs upholstered in crimson velvet and a circular tip-up table made of oak which Marcella polished until it glowed. Poor thing, she had been longing for something to polish.

Miss Rees wrote asking us to stay with her again and the invitation came at a time when there was not much work in the studio where I worked and they did not mind my taking a month off. It was arranged with Edward that Marcella was to stay with him while I was away because his wife was about to have a serious operation, what kind of operation he did not say, but no doubt Marcella would on her return. Although I had some money in the bank, she refused to take any before she left, so eventually I bought her a wristwatch and had both our names engraved on the back. She was so touched when I gave it to her that tears ran down her poor misshapen cheeks. I don't think she had ever had a present before. It was a relief to get Paul away from the flat, because he was running about now and needed constant supervision to keep him from falling down the stairs that led from the living room, and it was impossible to have him on the balcony because the wall was less than two feet high and his main idea was to climb over it. He was only safe there strapped in his pram; even then we dared not leave him alone. As there was no one to leave Nero with, I took Nero to Suffolk with us in a borrowed cat basket and he added to the complication of the journey. He was an uninvited guest and I was afraid Miss Rees would look on him as a potential eater of birds. She met us in her pram-like car and appeared to be delighted to see us, the cat included.

Everything at Miss Rees's cottage was exactly as it had been before – the jugs of cream and honey-combs and the smell of spring flowers. Paul used to follow her about the garden and in spite of the fact that he only had a vocabulary of ten words they seemed to have serious discussions together about gardening.

Sometimes he would lead me by the hand to the cold frames and, pointing to the boxes of brown earth with their tiny sprigs of green, would say with pride 'seeds'. She had borrowed a pushchair for him and they used to take long walks together, each with a trowel. The gardening book was finished now and I was helping with the typing of the manuscript and was pleased to do something in return for all the kindness I had received.

My peaceful holiday was shattered by a letter from Edward saying that they would need Marcella for some time to come, perhaps until the autumn. He seemed annoyed that she preferred London to the Midlands and accused me of spoiling her. He enclosed a letter from Marcella written in capitals. It was regretful and extremely short and ill spelt; she had learnt to read when she was an adult so that she could spell out the lettering on films and, now that talking films had come in, felt that her study was wasted. Without Marcella to look after Paul I would have to give up my work and I couldn't afford to do that. The Italians would have been happy to look after him; but their flat was so untidy and airless, with dripping laundry slung across the windows, and their children often suffered from worms, a terrible contrast to life at Miss Rees's. I sat under the pear tree with the letter in my hand, watching Paul picking up the fallen blossom and carefully arranging it in a little cart made of wood that Miss

Rees had had when she was a child. The day was warm and he was wearing red cotton trousers and nothing else and his fine skin had such a wonderful sheen of health. I had never seen him looking so well and, watching him, I realised what a tremendous responsibility he was. He needed so much – good food, fresh air, clothes, education – there was no end to it and all I had to offer was love. Even if he was capable of earning his own living when he was eighteen, that left me with sixteen years of constant struggle and I'd be an old woman of nearly forty by then. I picked Paul up from the grass and leant against the tree hugging him and saying over and over again, 'Of course, you are worth it, my darling,' and the panic receded. I carried him into the house for his rest and sat by his cot until he fell asleep with his thumb in his mouth. I didn't care what the baby books said and always let him go to sleep like that. When I came downstairs, I told Miss Rees my news and to my surprise she suggested that Paul should spend the entire summer with her, 'That is, if you can trust me, dear,' she added almost apologetically. This was a perfect solution to my problem, but I hesitated to accept it at first because I thought Miss Rees did not realise what she was taking on and it would be too much for her. I didn't care for the idea of parting from Paul for twelve weeks; it was a long time in a baby's life and I didn't want him to forget me.

We talked the plan over for several days; at least, I did most of the talking because Miss Rees was inclined to be quiet. For one day she looked after Paul entirely by herself and said it was as easy as falling off a log, with the maid to prepare his food and do the laundry. So it was arranged that I was to leave him behind. Nero could have stayed, too, but I didn't want to be completely alone in Charlotte Street. He was the most companionable cat and Gene had been fond of him.

I returned to a month's gritty dust and the smell of people's meals that had seeped through the floor-boards. Cockroaches had come, too, one dead and two alive. Although I was tired and dusk had nearly come, I dragged everything movable onto the balcony and beat the mattress and pillows, then scrubbed the floors with Jeyes fluid and banged the books together. I worked non-stop for three hours, then lay in the bath reading *The Diary of a Nobody*, which I had borrowed from Miss Rees.

I returned to work the next day and took one of the girls home for the evening because I could not face the empty flat. She was a large dumb brunette, who lived with a Russian singer she was not married to. Every now and then she got into a state because she thought she was pregnant and she'd spend her lunchtime in Jack's Snack Bar drinking scalding coffee topped with castor oil, which she considered an infallible way of getting rid of babies. Years later I tried it but it didn't work. In her case it must have because she never produced a baby; but I sometimes thought she imagined her pregnancies.

Blanche and her baby, Stephen, spent a week with me while she was waiting for a boat to take her to India. I loved having them, although it was a bit of a strain. I felt ashamed of the simple and slightly sordid way I lived – the bag wash for instance that I had to collect all un-ironed and the rough white china which wasn't china. It looked as if it was made of cement under its coating of white and my silver had a metallic taste, the forks with very sharp prongs. At least no more cockroaches appeared. Another embarrassment was the Norland nurse Blanche had engaged to take back to India with her. She was still living in her home in Ealing, but was always appearing to ask about suitable clothes to take to India. Should she take silk or cotton underclothes and what about a topee? Blanche used to sigh and say, 'What have I saddled myself with? She'll wreck my marriage.' She needn't have worried because within four months of putting her foot on Indian dust she married a sergeant and was off her hands.

They sailed on the last day of May and I was alone again. The first evening I went to Jack's Snack Bar and sat over a ham sandwich and coffee watching the other customers. Some of them were eating slimy steak-and-kidney pudding and having trouble chewing the rubbery meat and making jokes about Jack's dog, who had died of old age a few days before. There was a group of people who looked like existentialists huddled in a corner, and when I felt I had looked at them long enough I left to buy toothpaste. I went to a nearby dirty chemist because he kept open late; also his shop fascinated me. The windows had not been cleaned for years and behind the filthy glass were cartons that had become so bleached with age and sun, the print on them had disappeared. There were a few jars of stuff that looked like malt extract covered in dead flies. The flies must have been an inch deep, so dry and old they resembled spilt tea leaves. The shop was kept by a sad man with a drooping moustache who looked like a dirty H. G. Wells and there were many stories about him, the most common being that he had taken an oath never to touch the window after his wife's death many years before. I should think it unlikely that there was another chemist's shop like it in Europe.

There was an old grey car parked outside the Scala Theatre; it was often there and that evening there was someone sitting on the running board, a man with light gold hair rumpled over his forehead and his head hanging down. There was some sick belonging to him on the pavement and I guessed that he was drunk. People laughed as they passed him and others crossed to the other side of the road, muttering about trouble with the police. Although I was afraid of drunks, I couldn't help feeling sorry for this man, he looked so utterly wretched and vulnerable, with his expensive suit all creased and his head in his hands. As I watched him, he unexpectedly staggered to his feet and stood holding on to a wing of the car, swaying slightly and obviously trying to make the effort to walk. I turned away but he called after me, 'Don't go. I know I'm a disgusting sight. The police . . . I don't want to be taken by the police and spend the night in a cell. Oh, God, I feel as if I'd been drinking poison.' Then he was violently sick again. He stared down at the filthy mess and observed dreamily, 'I wonder why public vomit always has carrot in it.'

I said, 'There's Jack's Bar just behind us.' He stood swaying in the twilight murmuring something about 'no more bars'. There was a policeman coming from the Fitzroy Square direction and I knew my poor drunk would be taken into custody if I didn't get him out of the way immediately. I said, 'Quick, there's a policeman coming. Put your hand on my shoulder and we'll cross the street.' As he leant on me heavily he said, 'Christ, you're thin.' It was a struggle to get him into the narrow hall of the house where I lived and we both sank onto the bottom step of the stairs.

It was more or less dark there and no one was about although I could hear the landlord's tinny wireless playing Harry Roy's 'Tiger Rag' and knew he would open the door if he heard us talking. I whispered, 'You'll be all right if you're quiet, but don't stay long.' I crept upstairs, leaving him slumped at the bottom with the cockroaches and black beetles. I suddenly felt overwhelmingly tired. I opened the door and switched on the light and picked up Nero, who was waiting for me. I held him in my arms as I went down the steps to close the door and it was then that I heard the sound of dragging steps and deep breathing and knew the drunk had followed me. For a moment I was afraid and thought of slamming the door in his handsome, wrecked face; but, when he actually stood facing me, I wasn't afraid of him any more, I only felt pity. He said, 'I'm sorry to be such a pest, it was horrible down there in that cellar. I'll only stay a few minutes, though; you can see I'm recovering rapidly, awfully rapidly.' He lurched into the living room and looked round with astonishment as he asked, 'How did I get into this boat?' He flopped onto the divan and started pulling pound notes out of his pocket, masses of crumpled notes. He held out a handful to me, 'You've been so kind, I'd like you to have these to buy new sails for the boat.' The money dropped to the floor and I saw he had fallen asleep sitting hunched forward. I arranged him in a more comfortable position; he had gone all floppy and was easy to move. Then I picked up the pound notes, there must have been at least twenty of them and I didn't like to stuff them in his pockets again, so put them on a stool by the divan, weighed down with the carton of toothpaste. I went into the kitchen to make strong coffee because I had heard it was the thing for sobering drunks although I couldn't remember my mother drinking it for that purpose. I drank a cup of coffee and did a few odd jobs in the kitchen, banging about more than usual in the hope of waking my visitor; but he slept on, and when I became too tired to stay up any longer I went to the lower room and curled up on Marcella's bed. Before I left I remembered to shut the French window in case he staggered out onto the balcony and fell to his death. I also left the front door on the latch because I did not want the Italians to hear him leave at some unusual hour.

During the night I heard him bumping about over-head and thought, 'Good, he's going home. I hope he finds his money.' I was really too tired to bother about him and went to sleep again. I was awake earlier than usual and was in good time to have a bath and leisurely breakfast – a thing that seldom happened since I had been on my own. I entered the living room feeling a little apprehensive and the first thing

I noticed when I opened the door was a stale smell of drink. I have noticed that the breath of men who have drunk too much smells either of fermenting raspberries or hard-boiled eggs, both equally unpleasant. As I opened the window, I heard a voice say, 'What a hellish draught,' and turned to see my drunken visitor lying comfortably between the sheets of the divan with his clothes piled on a nearby chair. I said crossly, 'I thought you'd gone,' and as he pulled the bedclothes over his head he mumbled something which could have been 'Don't nag'. I thought the only thing to do was ignore him; so I lit the water heater and enjoyed my bath as if I were alone and, when I was dressed made myself tea and toast and carried it in on to the balcony. As I passed the divan I heard a pathetic voice say, 'I suppose there isn't a cup of tea going for me, I've got a terrible thirst.' I poured him out a large mug of unsweetened tea and enjoyed my breakfast with my back turned to him. When I left for work he appeared to be asleep again.

It was a Saturday morning and things were slack at the studio because the head animator had taken the morning off. One of the girls asked me if I would like to have lunch at her parents' house in Highgate. Normally I would have been glad to have gone, but this morning I felt drawn to my flat. I wasn't sure if I wanted my uninvited visitor to be there or not. It had been a shock to find him still there in the morning. Now I was becoming curious about him, wondering what he was like when he was sober and what he was called. I remembered the pound notes and thought he might be a millionaire until I remembered reading somewhere that rich men seldom carry real money, only cheque books.

I usually did my main shopping for the week on my way home on Saturday mornings, but this morning they served so slowly in the shops that I went home with very little, just bread, eggs and lettuce. When I reached the living room, I saw the bed was empty, with the clothes strewn about the floor, and that the visitor had left. There wasn't even a note thanking me. I dumped the shopping on the kitchen table with such force I broke some of the eggs. I scooped them into a bowl with the yokes still intact and considered making an omelette, only it didn't seem worth the trouble. Through the partitioned wall there was the sound of running water and I thought, 'He's even left the tap running.' Then there was a splashing sound and I knew he was still in the flat and having a bath. I hurriedly made the bed and tidied the room while the splashing continued, then prepared a salad for two with a hint of garlic, as Gene used to like it. I hunted out a clean tablecloth with matching napkins and was about to lay the table for two when I suddenly felt terrified of this strange man coming out of the bathroom all sober and clean. Somehow the idea of his being sober was more alarming than his being drunk. I was making a bolt for the balcony when the rickety bathroom door opened and he appeared wearing an Aertex vest and badly creased trousers; he was carrying a crumpled shirt. He said, 'Oh good, I thought I heard you come in. I suppose you haven't such a thing as a clean shirt in the house. This is unwearable.' He seemed completely at home. I said, 'There's a French fisherman's shirt, but it's a bit arty and faded.' I had given most of Gene's clothes away except for the ones that reminded me of him so much that I couldn't part with them. The shirt was hanging behind a curtain with my clothes and I handed it to him and watched while he slipped his long arms into the sleeves. Laughing, he said, 'I could have sworn I was on a boat last night and now I'm dressed as a fisherman. It's marvellous. I have no idea who you are or where I am. I remember doing a certain amount of drinking in Long Acre and think I was chucked out of a pub in Tottenham Court Road; but that may have been another evening.' He walked out onto the balcony and examined the soot-darkened houses. 'No, I can't recognise a thing. Perhaps I'm in Sheffield.' He held a hand over his large and rather bloodshot eyes: 'God, the sun's bright,' he said, and returned to the living room. He picked up his shirt from the floor and asked if there was anyone in the house who could wash it. I said, 'I'll do it,' and took it into the bathroom. It was a long time since I had washed a man's shirt. I loved washing it and felt ashamed of loving it.

The visitor didn't eat much of the omelette, but enjoyed the salad and coffee, and when I'd cleared the meal away we talked, facing each other as we sat on the crimson velvet chairs. Sometimes he seemed to have gone to sleep, then he'd be awake and asking more questions or telling me about his life. His name was Anthony Ferris and he was a writer, not a millionaire. He had had several novels published and he reviewed for an expensive monthly. He said that although he was fairly successful, he couldn't live on what he earned. Fortunately he had an income of five hundred a year which made life comparatively easy. I asked if he was married and he said, 'Yes and no.' His wife had left him for another man. 'I don't blame her, we quarrelled like hell and she didn't like my habits.'

'You mean drink?' I asked.

'Yes, drink and writing.'

'Are you a drunkard, I mean alcoholic?'

'I don't consider myself one. I can go for weeks without a drink; then something sets me off.'

'Why do you do it, drink, I mean?'

'God knows. Why do I breathe?'

'Will your wife return?'

'I think it most unlikely. I was celebrating our decree nisi yesterday.' And so it went on, we questioned each other for hours.

In the evening he took me to dine at a Spanish restaurant that had recently opened. A friend of his, a journalist, came to our table and spoke to Anthony Ferris for a few minutes and I felt that the private world that we had made was ending. This journalist was polite to me, only there was an amused, rather catty expression on his face, particularly when he said, 'Tony, I saw in the *Standard* yesterday that your decree nisi had gone through. Beware of the King's Proctor, old man.'

We walked together through small streets where the shops sold buttons or chef's clothes, and when we came to Charlotte Street and the house where I lived the door was open as it always was. I was expecting to say goodnight there, but Tony came upstairs with me, his hand lightly on my elbow. I jerked the lights on in the living room and went into the kitchen to needlessly bang pots and pans about. I filled the kettle with water and nervously rattled cups and saucers. Tony called, 'Are you making tea? I adore it in the middle of the night, it's the only time to drink it.' I remained in the kitchen until the kettle boiled. When I took the tray of tea things into the living room, Tony was sitting in the red velvet chair he had occupied during the afternoon, completely at home, reading my Everyman edition of Turgenev's *Fathers and Sons*. I said firmly, 'You must go when you have drunk this tea,' and blushed for using the word 'drunk'. He continued to read.

Soon after twelve I kicked my shoes off and went to sleep on the divan and woke in the dark and Tony was lying beside me. He said, 'Take your clothes off and get into bed properly, you silly girl.' I uncurled myself sleepily and got up from the divan muttering, 'I can't go to bed with you here, go away.' He held me by the arm and I felt as if my bones were melting. He said, 'I won't hurt you, I promise, I won't hurt you, but I can't be alone.' Then I knew he had the same fearful loneliness that I had and told him he could stay 'Only if you keep your socks on, I'll be safe if you keep your socks on.'

I woke when the first signs of morning were showing in the room. Tony had one arm round me and it was wonderful to be close to someone again. The socks hadn't worked as I had intended and I was glad they hadn't. I can't think why I had such faith in them.

SIXTEEN

TONY GAVE UP HIS third share of a Bloomsbury flat and moved in with me. I was afraid of the King's Proctor and locked the door firmly at night, although Tony said he was most likely a myth. I told the people in the house that Tony was my cousin and he soon became known as Mr Cousin. It reminded me of the story about Turner when he lived in the Isle of Thanet and, looking for somewhere to live, knocked on a cottage door which was opened by a woman he had not seen before. He asked her name and when she said Mrs Booth, he said, 'And I'm Mr Booth,' and moved in and lived with her for many years, eventually becoming known as Pugface or Puggy Booth by the local inhabitants. I preferred Mr Cousin to

Pugface. I did not want Tony to live permanently in the flat because there wouldn't be room for all of us when Paul and Marcella returned. When I explained that he could only stay a few weeks, he suggested that we move to a larger place. Some friends of his who had a house near the Boltons were about to go abroad and we could rent their house while they were away. I felt that I would be deserting Gene if I left Charlotte Street; then I remembered how difficult it had been with Paul running about and the dangers of the stairs and balcony and said I would think about it. Nine weeks was a long time away.

When Tony's things arrived, the living room, which had always been so bare and empty, became almost overpopulated. Two long white bookcases crammed with books and a magnificent Dutch marquetry desk with a matching chair appeared and there was a French gilt mirror, very beautiful but out of place over the gas fire with its broken flue. The famished old floor boards were almost covered by a huge Indian carpet, white and fluffy and much appreciated by Nero, who sharpened his claws on it. Tony was not the sort of man who would be happy hanging his suits behind a cotton curtain; so we bought a massive late Victorian wardrobe, which I painted white, then decorated it with climbing morning glories. Tony was tremendously impressed, pointing it out as a work of art to any of his friends who came to the flat. Actually very few came, because even Tony could see that it was better to behave with some shreds of discretion until the divorce was through.

Life with Tony was mostly pleasant although there were drawbacks, drink being the main one. His income was paid once a quarter, and I came to dread quarter days because they nearly always coincided with a bout of drinking, often resulting in Tony disappearing for a couple of days and returning in a horrible state. If he went out without me in the evenings he often returned far from sober, capable of talking fairly reasonably although unsteady on his feet and holding on to door frames. Sometimes he would sit at the table to type and become all entangled in the machine, swearing something was wrong with it. He was never bad-tempered with me when he had been drinking, though he hurt me by talking wildly about his ex-wife. In spite of his bitterness towards her, I knew she still meant a lot to him. When he was sober, he seldom mentioned her.

We dined out about twice a week, the dinner sandwiched between visits to pubs. Sometimes we ended up at a nightclub. The Nest and the Bag o' Nails were favourites of his. Often we drank near-beer; but as soon as Tony bought a bottle of whisky our table was besieged by long-lost friends. At first I was fascinated by these people and thought from the way they talked that they were budding or unrecognised geniuses; but I very soon recognised them for the hangers-on they were. There were a few exceptions. I remember a young film-script writer who did very well in later years, but at that time was living on the proceeds of collecting for a hospital. He spent a few hours each day rattling a collecting box at people in the street or pubs, then took the box home to the privacy of his home and took out about half of the coins with the aid of a knife blade. He justified this by saying that the hospital he collected for had refused to take his girlfriend in when she was having a baby because she wasn't married. He was extremely bitter towards a man who went around with a poodle with a collecting box strapped on its back. 'Perfectly revolting being kept by a dog.'

With Tony in the flat my money worries ceased. He paid the rent and bought the more expensive food. I was always finding rump steaks bleeding in the kitchen. During the morning while I was working, Tony sat at his Dutch desk writing his novel or reviewing other people's and in the afternoon he usually typed what he had written on Gene's old painting table. It looked out of place now, but I wouldn't part with it. He reviewed about eight novels a month and, if I read any of them, he insisted that I keep them clean so that he could sell them before the day of publication. He said that they paid for his drinks on a sober week. It worked well, my being out most of the day, because it gave Tony the peace and privacy he needed for his writing and there was so much to talk about in the evening when we weren't together all the day. At first he wouldn't discuss his books with me, but later he even let me read his first rough drafts and, as time went on, I did most of his typing and became more or less his secretary – but that was after we left Charlotte Street.

One Sunday in July Tony borrowed a car and we drove to Suffolk to see Paul and Miss Rees. I particularly wanted to see how Paul and Tony reacted to each other before finally deciding to give up the Charlotte Street flat. I had wired Miss Rees and she was expecting us, in fact she was standing at the gate with Paul when we arrived. For the few hours we were there I could not bear to let Paul out of my sight; he even had his rest in my lap, clutching a toy car I had given him. Tony said, 'What a fascinating child! He looks Spanish to me,' and when Miss Rees was not there, 'I hope people will think I'm his father.' Before we left, Miss Rees and I walked round the garden together while she cut flowers for me to take home. We left Tony lazily bowling a ball down a shallow bank for Paul to retrieve and, almost before we were out of earshot, Miss Rees turned her gentle face towards me and said, 'That friend of yours has great charm; but isn't he a little dissipated? His face looks so worn. Of course, he's still very handsome, but there's something about his eyes. There's no hope in them. I shouldn't say things like this about a friend of yours, dear, only I don't want you to be unhappy.' I was touched at her concern and told her that I wasn't thinking of marrying Tony although he was steadier than he appeared. In any case it would be months before he was free. 'It's just that we are two people who have lost someone they love and I suppose we prop each other up,' I added lightly and, as I spoke, I realised that my feelings for Tony were far deeper than I had realised and I felt afraid.

Early in September we moved to this house Tony was renting from his friends. The owners had not been married long and the house was only partly furnished, but combined with our furniture it became almost fully furnished and seemed wonderfully luxurious to me. The house was amusingly decorated, mostly in white with just one wall or the ceiling coloured and the rooms were very light – lightness was the first thing you noticed. The double drawing room took up the whole of the hall floor, except for the passage-like hall, and the dining room and kitchen were in the base-ment, which was a semi and not dark. At the back of the house there was quite a large paved garden, with flower beds and a grape vine climbing up one wall and a beautiful willow tree, not a weeping one, but the kind you expect to see growing on river banks. Tony had not mentioned the garden and it came as a complete surprise.

A few days after we moved Marcella returned and I had to explain about Tony and how we were living together. I also told her about the drinking and she said resignedly, 'So we've got to go through that again, have we?' On the whole she took the fact that Tony and I were not married very calmly. She was in great awe of him and called him 'The Master' and he called her Biddy. I began to dread the thought of Paul returning. I imagined Tony shouting, 'Can't you keep that child quiet,' and both of them being jealous of each other with me torn between them. Actually it worked out far better than I expected. Paul slept in the room behind ours and sometimes woke very early in the mornings, particularly when the sun was shining. As soon as he became noisy I'd jump out of bed and rush him downstairs to Marcella so that Tony was not disturbed. This wasn't a great hardship because I was naturally an early riser. During the day Paul followed Marcella around or played in the garden and she said he was no trouble. Often, when I returned in the evening, Tony used to say, 'Don't put the child to bed immediately, I'm in need of some intelligent conversation,' and Paul would come in and, seating himself in the largest chair, would talk to us intently, using his hands to emphasise what he was saying. Unfortunately he usually spoke in a language of his own that we did not understand.

Now that we lived in South Kensington, there was no time to return in the middle of the day and walking to stations and standing in underground trains wasted a lot of my day. Tony kept asking me to give up my work and stay at home. 'The mornings aren't so bad, it's these long afternoons after I've eaten Marcella's eternal chops that get me down.' I said, 'I must have some money of my own. Find me a morning job and I'll leave.' Although Tony usually had an overdraft at the bank, he seemed to have plenty of money. I spent about two pounds a week of my earnings on our daily expenses. Our grocery and meat came from Harrods; it was put down on Tony's account, and he paid the rent of the house and Marcella's wages as well. He must have spent a considerable amount on his clothes; his suits were really beautiful and I sometimes stroked them when I had to go to his wardrobe. His pyjamas were real silk and his shirts and shoes were made-to-measure. He said his bootmaker had plaster casts of his feet and I was always meaning to see them, but never did. We must have got through a lot of money on drinking out, which was, of course, more expensive than drinking at home; but we did cut down on our dining-out now we had a proper home, and Marcella did most of the laundry, which was a help. Tony assured me that his expenses had hardly gone up at all; nevertheless I was always doing private sums on the edge of my drawing board.

Although Marcella was pleased to be back with me again, she was not really happy in South Kensington. She said there was no romance about it and the shops were dull. Harrods had no bargain basement and made her feel embarrassed and the other stores were just as bad. There was Buckingham Palace and she often trudged there in her high boots and gazed through the railings. She was once rewarded with seeing Queen Mary drive through the gates wearing sapphires and diamonds in her ears; but it was Oxford Street that she loved. Although she never complained, I think she found the stairs trying. The house was on four floors, and I had to plan her work for her, otherwise she was constantly climbing up the stairs, clutching cleaning implements or with Paul in her arms.

Tony often mentioned his sister Evelyn. He wasn't on very good terms with her, in fact, he hadn't spoken to her for over a year because of an incident at one of her dinner parties. He arrived drunk and uninvited after a quarrel with his wife and more or less wrecked the dinner party. Now they had become friendly again and I was taken to meet her at her house in Elm Park

Gardens. From the outside the house was perfectly hideous; but she had made herself a luxurious and beautiful maisonette in the upper storeys and the lower part was used as a day school for children under ten. I was afraid of Evelyn when I first met her because she was an intellectual lesbian type of woman, who drooped her eyelids and talked with vague allusions to people I had never heard of. Sometimes she gave a quizzical smile, but her face mostly looked as if it had been frozen. Surprisingly enough, she had an eight-year-old daughter, the result of a marriage that had lasted less than a year. The little girl attended her mother's school and spent her holidays with her father in the country somewhere. She was a beautiful child, tall and very fair like Tony, but shy and withdrawn, glancing quickly at her mother before she dared to speak. Evelyn was friendly to me in a patronising way, complimenting me on Tony's improved appearance and asking herself to dinner, insisting that she wanted to see my drawings and paintings (only she called them 'art work' in an amused, disparaging way).

She dined with us a week later. Unfortunately my journey home took longer than usual and she was already installed in the drawing room when I returned. While I fried chicken with rice and pimentos, Tony showed her over the house, proudly pointing out the cupboard I had decorated and a mural I had done on the kitchen wall. She said I was terribly, terribly clever in a damping way; but after dinner insisted on seeing more of my work. I reluctantly showed her some of my drawings and designs for backgrounds for the mermaid film we were working on and the kangaroo book I had illustrated; then to my surprise she offered me a job in her school as art mistress. She wanted me to teach simple crafts as well, raffia work and modelling in plasticine. Tony was eager for me to accept although the salary wasn't marvellous, twenty-four pounds a term, less than I was earning animating, but the hours were considerably shorter and there would be the long holidays. I reluctantly accepted her offer because I could see it would be better for us all if I was at home more.

SEVENTEEN

I STARTED MY ART classes early in the New Year and Tony's divorce came through about the same time. It was a subject we hardly ever mentioned, and, when he showed me the announcement of his ex-wife's marriage in *The Times*, I felt a horrible dark shadow come into the room and my breakfast stuck in my throat. I was sure the news would start Tony off on a severe attack of drinking, the kind that made him disappear for days. 'She hasn't taken long about it,' he remarked bitterly. 'It's hardly a week since the divorce went through. Special licence, I suppose.' He frowned into his coffee and pushed the cup away so roughly that coffee spilt on the tablecloth. 'Why didn't I think of doing the same? There's a marrying place in Marloes

Road. I'll go there this morning; so you'd better give me the particulars – you know, date of birth, full names, oh yes, and your parents' names, they'll need those too, I expect.' He hunted in his pockets for his pen and diary, looking at me expectantly. I said, 'I'm not going to marry you just to spite your wife; anyway I don't want to marry again.' That started our first real row and we fought like dogs over the breakfast table, with its marmalade pots, toast gone flabby, cold coffee and skinny milk. I threw a sticky knife at Tony when he shouted that I was 'morbidly obsessed with a dead lunatic' and he retaliated with a cup which broke against the wall. The kitchen was next to the dining room and Marcella, hearing dreadful sounds, poked her one-nostrilled nose round the door and hissed, 'I hope you're not insulting my girl,' and Tony shouted, 'Shut the blasted door. I'm only asking her to marry me.' The door started to close and Marcella's voice came through the chink: 'Now, stop all that shouting and swearing, sir. Miss Vicky knows what's right and will do it, whatever it is.' We looked at each other with our mouths turned down and suddenly we were shaking with laughter.

We were married ten days later and Evelyn gave a party for us, where I met some of Tony's more respectable friends. The only respectable friends I could produce were the Scobys and Dr Rees. It turned out that Violet and Evelyn already knew each other. I hoped they wouldn't discuss me together. We had no honeymoon because Tony was revising the book he had at last finished. It was long overdue at the publishers; in any case, January isn't an ideal time for honeymoons. The only difference being married made to us was that I didn't feel embarrassed spending Tony's money and we used the word 'we' more often; but I suppose the main difference was that, now we were a married couple, we were asked to dinners and cocktail parties and entertained in return.

Tony was now drinking far less than he used to, but we still had our nights out in pubs and nightclubs, where we met his hangers-on. I found it difficult to keep them out of the house. He hated these people when he was sober; but, when he had been drinking, he'd bring a taxi-load home and expect me to give them what he called a 'dormitory feast', and after the feast they would spend the rest of the night on the drawing-room floor until Marcella swept them out in the early morning. They left with books under their arms and silver ashtrays in their pockets and the lavatories were often filthy. I thought they were like the mistletoe that Gene had feared so much and hoped it wasn't starting to grow on me.

On the whole Tony and I were happy together and his drinking did not worry me so very much. I had been accustomed to it from childhood and looked on it as a sad thing that descended on people, just as schizophrenia had descended on poor Gene. I knew that Tony had a certain weakness of character; but there was much to admire in him – intelligence, generosity and his air of easy charm. The fact that he was nine years older than I was made me feel not exactly safe – because one could never feel safe with Tony – but looked after. I never reproached him with a long face after a drinking bout – how could I when I knew what he was from the moment I met him? – and I knew he hated himself afterwards. Sometimes in the night he'd be afraid and press his head against me, saying miserably, 'I must be all ruined inside, cirrhosis of the liver and the lining of my stomach all eaten away. Even if I stopped drinking, it'd be too late now.'

The quarter-day drinking had ceased and the only time I dreaded now was in between books. For a week or two after a novel had been sent to a publisher he felt wonderful and kept saying, 'Thank God we've got that out of the house. I can relax now.' Later he would become all deflated and feel he couldn't face starting another book; he had no ideas and had written himself out. That was when the drinking started and gloom came into the house until some vague idea would hold his attention and life would return to normal for another eighteen months.

Another thing that made me very happy was teaching in Evelyn's school: the children were so responsive. I started them on a mural of flowers on the white wall of a large basement room used for recreation. We used real flowers as models and, when they were scarce, vegetables, and the children would have painted all day if they had been allowed to. Unfortunately Evelyn made me touch up their paintings after the children went home. It was a pity and I felt dishonest doing it, but I could see her point. It was something to show the parents. Besides arts and crafts I had the terrifying job of taking the younger children to play in a nearby garden square. We had to cross a busy road to reach it and marshalling ten children under six across it was a shattering experience, although passers-by sometimes helped. I used to make them walk in single file with their hands on each other's shoulders. Once we were in the garden it was easy, because they were behind bars. When I had been teaching in Evelyn's school for a year Paul became a pupil and it worked out very well and gave Marcella a rest.

Paul had always loved being read to, even before he could follow what was being read to him. By the time he was three he knew many of his books by heart and if, out of boredom, we varied the words slightly he used to be furious. Sometimes I read him the book Gene had written for him in the asylum. Once, when it was Tony's evening for reading, he asked for it and Tony shouted down the stairs, 'Where's this new book about a roller-skating lion?' and I had to produce it. For some complicated reason I had kept it a secret, perhaps out of mistaken loyalty to Gene. After his spell of reading Tony brought the book downstairs, examined the illustrations and read it through again. He was so impressed with it, he thought it should be published. I mentioned the publisher of children's books that I had occasionally worked for; but he condemned them as 'small fry' and suggested taking it to his own publisher to see what they would make of it. This resulted in the book being published and, although it first appeared in troubled times, it sold well and earned nearly one hundred and fifty pounds, which I put into the post office in Paul's name so that he would have a surprise present from his father when he was old enough to understand. I hoped it would make Gene seem more real to him. I used to talk to him about his father; but he got him mixed up with God, whom he called 'God the painter'. Marcella used to tell him holy stories remembered from her distant childhood.

Blanche and John and their beautiful little boy, Stephen, returned from India. Before they went to Wales they spent a month in the nearby Bailey's Hotel and I saw them almost every day and their nanny used to bring Stephen to play with Paul in our garden.

Blanche and I used to watch them from the drawing-room window, their little heads bobbing among the flowers, and think how fortunate we were, Mornington Crescent seemed hundreds of miles and hundreds of years away. She liked Tony very much, saying she adored his baggy eyes and that marrying him was the first sensible thing I'd ever done. I told her a little about the drinking and she laughed and said there was always something: 'John has corns.'

Everyone was saying that a war was coming; they'd been saying it for years, first with Italy, then Germany, so I didn't worry much. Then Munich came and went and the pupils in Evelyn's school began to dwindle away because their parents were moving into the country or sending their children to boarding schools in areas they considered safe. The friends of Tony's from whom we leased the house wrote from America saying they were staying there while Europe was so unsettled and renewed our lease for another two years. After his leave John was sent to Aldershot and, although he never said war was imminent, I could tell he thought so because of their domestic arrangements. They had been longing to furnish their first real home ever since their marriage, but now they just took a furnished flat near Hyde Park and most of their personal belongings were sent to Wales. We went to hideous schoolrooms and were fitted with gas masks; but there were not any Paul's size. Tony said that, if ever he had to wear his, he was going to soak the nozzle in whisky first to drown the rubbery smell.

As war came nearer we saw long crocodiles of children with gas masks humped on their backs; the streets seemed to be filled with them. Then suddenly there was hardly a child left in London and, although the sun shone and shone, the parks were almost empty except for people digging long, straight holes, some said for trenches and others for mass graves. When John came to tell us he was driving his family to Wales the following day, I knew that war was really coming; it was only a matter of hours. He offered to take Paul and me with them; he said he had telephoned his mother and she was looking forward to having us, partly because she wanted to have the house as full as possible to keep evacuees away. We were to start early the next morning. I thought about the horrible gases that were coming, people said they would eat through the roof and eat into wherever we hid and there were death rays coming too; then I thought of Tony alone with these things, perhaps sitting with his whisky-soaked gas mask over his face, and knew I couldn't go on. So it was arranged for Paul to go in Nanny's care and we would pay her an increase of salary because of the extra work. It was the least we could do. Paul left on Saturday morning and on Sunday the war started with a false air-raid warning and ARP whistles madly blowing in the streets.

The blackout depressed Tony terribly. It depressed me, too, only it was worse for him because he loved to go out at night and now the streets were like a perpetual funeral. Evelyn was depressed as well because she had had to close her school. She would walk round in the evenings to sit in our dimly lit drawing room drinking gin with Tony while I sewed black curtains. Her daughter had been sent to relatives in Canada and she was alone in her huge house. Tony would say, 'No one will read my bloody books in wartime. I may as well enlist,' and Evelyn would gaze into her pink gin, worrying about the future: 'How can I afford to keep that great house on? We may as well face it, I'm ruined.' Then we would turn on the news although there never seemed any worth listening to. Underneath us, in the basement, Marcella sat knitting something strange and muttered about 'old nasty'. She wasn't very well and said her insides were all stirred up.

Gradually life became wartime normal. The blackout curtains were finished and the ARP warden stopped ringing our door bell and we used 100-watt electric bulbs again. Tony found himself working in a Ministry and forgot about enlisting and Evelyn worked in a branch of the FO and drank her pink gin in smart bars with high-up men. Everyone seemed to have work except me and it was dull at home with Marcella and her stirred-up insides. Most of our friends had melted away; even Tony's hangers-on were hiding so that they wouldn't be forced to work in factories or, even worse, find themselves pushed into the army. A few did become temporary policemen and slept in deserted houses when they were on night duty, and one had quite a success with a second-hand pram shop which he called The Chelsea Pram Mart.

We went to Wales for Christmas in John's car, John and Tony taking turns to drive; and suddenly, as I sleepily watched the scenery flash past, everything seemed familiar and we passed through the village that I'd left nine years before. There was grandfather's old house, with other people's curtains at the windows and the ivy all cut down, and the village shops hung with Christmas decorations. I thought I caught a glimpse of our Buffalo gardener, lame and walking with a stick, but I couldn't be sure, we were driving so fast. After we left Warwickshire, a fine snow began to fall and I hoped I would see Wales as Blanche had first seen it, under heavy snow.

My wish was granted and we arrived in the evening snow. We found Blanche, with Paul and Stephen assisting, decorating a tall Christmas tree in the great hall. It was difficult not to cry when I held Paul in my arms again and looked down onto his dear little bullet head. When we had parted nearly four months earlier, I quite expected never to see him again and now he was excitedly pulling me to the Christmas tree, then to the front door to show me there was more Christmas outside.

The house was fantastically large and had a neglected ballroom with a minstrels' gallery, where no one had danced for twenty years. Now it was used as a first-aid post with notices pinned on the walls. The Home Guard had taken over the old bakery and laundry and there were evacuees in the rooms over the stables; but I never saw any of these people, only the family, a butler with a wooden leg which made a noise when he waited at table, and two or three elderly maids in the kitchen. John's mother ran the house and, although it was of an unmanageable size and understaffed, it was unexpectedly comfortable. There was a fire burning in our bedroom and stone hot-water bottles in our beds; the bath water was reasonably warm and the maids were always charging about the passages with more hot water in cans with folded towels on top. The first thing you noticed when you entered the house was a delicious smell of wood smoke and beeswax and a great feeling of peace. John's uncle seldom sat in his book-lined study, but in a rambling sort of place called the estate room, which appeared to have been made by knocking several rooms into one. Part of it was devoted to fishing rods. He was a keen fisherman and was always inventing new spools and flies, which he made from anything he considered suitable, including human hair. He made one from Paul's while we were there.

On Christmas morning we pulled the children round the garden on a small sledge, then John remembered there was a huge homemade one in the stables and we tried it out on a sharply sloping field. This frightened Blanche and me because we always seemed to be missing trees and rocks by inches; but our husbands adored it and, although they were both nearing forty, they dragged this awful sledge about, searching for more and more dangerous slopes. The snow melted before we left and we were able to see the surrounding country either on foot or by car, sometimes taking a picnic lunch standing leaning against some huge rock on the sheltered side of the mountain. Clothes were no problem because there was a cloakroom full of communal tweed coats, raincoats and queer hats and boots and shoes of all sizes. There was a wonderful sheepskin jacket that Tony took over. He loved wearing it but said it must have been made from a ram's skin because the sheep gave him funny glances and the rams stamped and snorted at him every time he wore it.

Blanche returned to London with us. We both felt miserable because of parting from our sons and all through the long journey we kept wondering if we had done the right thing, being reassured by our husbands that we had. Sometimes I thought the war was just a dreary myth – to save electricity, perhaps. Thousands of women must have been feeling the same because most of the evacuees returned and the Fulham Road was as full of women pushing prams as usual. On a house agent's wall near South Kensington Station a disappointed flat-hunter had chalked, 'Plenty of cheap flats when the bombs fall'.

While we were in Wales, Tony had had an idea for a thriller, a spy story peppered with a number of murders. It was not at all the sort of thing he usually wrote; but the idea had taken hold of him and he longed to get it down on paper. He hadn't written a creative word since the war had started and the novel he had been working on was locked away in his desk perpetually frozen on page 98. Now, as soon as we finished dinner, he'd rush upstairs to his writing room and I'd follow with a Thermos of coffee, then spend the rest of the evening alone. It was well worth the dull evenings because Tony was so much happier when he was writing, feeling guilty and bored when he wasn't doing creative work. He would leave what he had written for me to type the next day, often scrapping half of it when he returned in the evening. I was glad to have something to do; but it didn't take up much of my time. I went to the film place where I used to work and found it deserted, just a few drawing-pins left on the walls and a pile of rubbish and an old broom in a corner. It seemed as if a piece of my life had vanished. I walked a little further to Charlotte Street and saw the house where I used to live, with its ever-open door, and found myself walking up the smelly stairs, passing the communal bathroom and glancing in to see if the bicycle was still in the bath. It was. I knocked on the Italians' door although it stood slightly open. It was so long since I had seen them I didn't like to walk in as I used to. I received a wonderful welcome and it was all just the same, with the laundry hanging across the windows, the rich smell of cooking combined with the scorchy smell of ironing, the vases of paper carnations, and the large baby with a dummy in its mouth. The family had expanded and they had taken over the room that used to be Paul's nursery and I was shown it with pride. The decorations had not been changed and there were the same stars on the ceiling; but the white walls were soiled now and the room was dominated by a hideous American cloth-covered sofa, which turned into a bed at night, with a battered cabinet gramophone standing beside it. We drank wine together while the family told me their experiences as evacuees in Hertfordshire and the trials they had been through. 'Give me the bombs any day,' the mother said as she poured rich, red sauce over spaghetti. 'The brute of a woman I was sent to was a vegetarian and tried to stop me bringing meat into the kitchen, wouldn't even have jelly in the house unless it was made from seaweed or some such rubbish. The children weren't allowed near her sickly little girl in case they had things in their hair. Some old bitch came round to comb them and, by an extraordinary piece of luck, nothing was found. We only stayed a week, though.' I wondered who lived in our flat, but didn't ask. Sometimes I thought that Gene and I were still there and I had turned into someone different.

EIGHTEEN

WE MOVED DOWN TO the basement when the bombs started falling. Except for the horrors of the fires, when it seemed as if all London was burning, we were not as frightened as we expected to be; in fact we were almost exhilarated, even when bombs fell near and shattered our windows. It was the following day, when we saw what had happened during the night, that we felt so awful – the torn houses exposing people's pathetic belongings; the thought of what had happened to the owners; the ARP men digging out dead bodies or carrying the living wrapped in grey blankets; the extraordinary things that had happened to the streets where we had walked the previous day. The bombing of World's End was a terrible shock. Poor old Marcella insisted on seeing the damage, then had hysterics. She slept in the basement hall under a Victorian square piano which looked remarkably like a coffin, not a nice thing to have fall on you, but she had great faith in it as a keeper off of falling ceilings. She was terrified and I had to sit up with her night after night; the guns frightened her more than the falling bombs. After the devastation at World's End, I took her to stay with Edward, where the nights were less disturbed. I only stayed for a single night because I felt that the house would be bombed unless I was in it willing them to keep away. I never saw Marcella again because she died a few months later from some internal trouble. I was surprised how much I missed her. We had been through so much together. She left me her life's savings, which amounted to nearly three hundred pounds, and I arranged for her to be buried in the village graveyard, beside my mother and grandfather, and years later Blanche and I went to see her overgrown little grave with convolvulus climbing up the headstone. It was exactly the kind of grave one would expect Marcella to have.

Blanche and John moved into a house near Guildford and it was the first time during their married life that they had had a real home of their own. They combed the sales for antique furniture and, when I went with them, which I often did, I couldn't resist buying something myself. I bought a set of Regency chairs with paintings of flowers and musical instruments on their backs and a small Queen Anne writing table which I still use as a dressing table. I was so happy to own these beautiful things; but all my buys did not turn out so well. Sometimes, when I examined the furniture I had bought, I was disappointed and it looked all wrong in our house. I easily disposed of it by advertising it in the local paper and usually made a profit. Everyone suddenly had money to spend, but there was little to spend it on, with almost everything rationed and meals in restaurants almost uneatable. One evening, I think it was our wedding anniversary, we went to a famous restaurant where they had pheasant on the menu, but, when the waiter brought it to our table, it was only Spam pressed into the shape of a bird's wing. Another time, we ordered champagne cocktails because most of the wines served in restaurants in those days appeared to have had salt added and it made one terribly thirsty. The champagne turned out to be Tizer with some sticky fruit added, the glass all stained brown. Meals in pubs were usually the best value, but took us a long time because it was difficult to get Tony out of a pub once he got inside.

When the air raids thinned out, we thought it safe to have Paul home and we only went down to the basement when things became very noisy. I found a school for him just off Gloucester Road and he went there in the mornings; but the difficulty was that we had no one to baby-sit at night. The woman who helped me in the house refused to come out of the Underground at night. She had a permanent home there on a platform on the Piccadilly Line and occasionally, when I was travelling late, I saw her sleeping there with her husband snoring by her side. To solve this problem we let Marcella's room to a girl from Tony's office who played the cello in her spare time. We deducted ten shillings from her rent every time she stayed with Paul and, as we only charged her thirty shillings a week, she seldom had any to pay. She looked forward to us going out because it was the only time she was allowed to play her cello. Tony hated it, saying it sounded like an entombed bumble-bee and made it impossible for him to write. He was still working spasmodically on his thriller, sometimes being wildly enthusiastic and other times saying that it was rubbish and a waste of time. It was the only creative writing he did during all the war years.

The war went on and on until it became a way of life, almost cosy in some ways, with families and friends gathering together to listen to the nine o'clock news. The announcers became almost as popular as the pop singers of the present day. There was something dreary called 'Make do and mend', but many women adored it. An enormous amount of jam-making and fruit-bottling went on; even the Zoo was full of bottled fruit and so was my kitchen, the jars dancing about the shelves when the raids were heavy. During wars English people tend to sing the most terrible songs, depressing sorts of dirges which are intended to be jolly. Then there were people who took a pride in using hardly any bath water, and that almost cold, and talking about Plimsoll lines and saying that all one's books should be turned into pulp. An old woman was fined for feeding ducks on a public pond and a light-hearted girl in the provinces was sent to prison for flashing a torch in boys' faces. Once I told a man at a party that my grocer occasionally let me have extra butter and he said that I was sinking ships. He was so angry that his eyes became crossed and I hurriedly left. Later I discovered that this man who thought I was sinking ships used to buy black-market petrol from dustmen who siphoned it out from their petrol tanks. Then there were people who loved to queue; they joined any old queue that was going.

Because I had a young child to look after I was exempt from war work, but I did fire-watch once a week. I never had the chance to put out a fire, though. I also collected magazines for the men on the nearest gun site and, when I could spare the sugar, I'd make them a cake; once, when John gave me several rabbits, I made a giant rabbit pie. Violet Scoby's hat shop was still functioning; but she now sold hand-made under-clothes as well as hats because so many women were wearing things called pixie hoods or tying up their heads in handkerchiefs, looking like puddings about to be boiled. She was fined for selling knickers with non-utility birds embroidered on them, which shamed her into working part-time for the WVS and wearing a new kind of hat.

People began to talk about D-Day and it was looked forward to as the most exciting day for years and gave one the feeling that the war was really about to end. Everyone was saying it was to be next week, next Wednesday, they knew for a fact that it was to happen on the first of May – and on a beautiful day in June, D-Day came. Tony and our girl lodger heard the news on their way to Gloucester Road Station and they hurried back to tell me. Tony said he was due to take a day off and told the lodger girl that she looked as if she had a headache and was to stay at home and play her cello while we went out together. I changed into a green dress I had been saving for something special and we went off and had the most perfect day. Everyone seemed happy and everything went right. Our lunch in a new Chinese restaurant was delicious; we wandered round the Summer Exhibition at the Academy because it was a nice old-fashioned thing to do, and we gazed into the shop windows. When I admired an early Victorian pearl bracelet with a fili-gree clasp, Tony insisted on buying it for me. It was that sort of day. We went to Hamleys and bought various toys for Paul; then took a taxi home to make sure we were there before he went to bed. We found him enter-taining Blanche and John and an officer friend; so we called the lodger girl away from her cello and made a party of it, drinking well into our month's ration of gin. Tony, who had been lying on the floor with Paul building a village of rubber interlocking bricks, ended the evening by suddenly leaping up and saying he felt in the mood to finish his book, even if it meant writing all night. Later, when I took sandwiches and coffee up to his room, he was so engrossed in his work, he hardly noticed me. At about three in the morning he came into our bedroom and told me the book was finished. We lay in bed talking and making love until it was light and it was a lovely ending to a happy day.

NINETEEN

THE FLYING BOMBS WERE a horrible surprise. For the first time during the war I was really afraid, not so much during the day when I could see them, but at night as we lay in the basement listening and waiting for the fearful moment when the engine stopped overhead and we'd dash to the cupboard under the stairs to get away from splintering glass. In a light-hearted moment I had had our windows re-glazed. As soon as the flying bombs started, while they were still called 'pilotless planes', Blanche took Stephen and Paul to Wales and John insisted on her staying there with the children, which annoyed her because she was so enjoying furnishing her house. Tony said, 'Of course you should be in Wales too,' but didn't urge me to go. I couldn't leave him alone in the house. Even our lodger girl had left us to stay with friends in the country, which was just as well, because the room where she used to sleep was completely destroyed.

One morning, after a terrible night spent in the broom cupboard, we got up early. It was a perfect morning with the clearest sky, free from clouds or flying bombs, so I laid our breakfast under the willow tree. As soon as I put the coffee percolator on the table, I heard the familiar drone overhead; then it stopped and I started counting as people did in those days, and thankfully saw it sailing overhead. Then something went wrong: it doubled back and landed in the square in front of the house. There must have been a violent explosion, only I can't remember hearing it, just the sound of tiles crashing down and the tinkling of falling glass. I was lying on the ground clutching the trunk of the willow tree and, although I was surrounded by broken glass, I was hardly cut at all. A few minutes later Tony staggered out of the house, clutching his head and white with plaster. The ceiling had fallen on his head as he was coming downstairs from the bathroom. We gazed at each other dazedly as the sound of the 'All clear' pierced our ears. Tony exclaimed bitterly, 'The bloody fools! It isn't all clear here – the house is a mass of rubble.' There were still odd thuds as more lumps of ceiling fell, so we stayed in the garden drinking unsweetened coffee from a handle-less cup, the only piece of unbroken china remaining on the breakfast table.

When the thuds stopped we went inside to see how bad things were. It was a horrible sight, with glass sticking from the walls like daggers and laths hanging down from where the ceilings used to be. The worst damage was to the front of the house; the top floor was wrecked because the chimneys had fallen in. We could see the sky in big blue patches. We found poor old Nero still warm, but dead, in a corner of the kitchen. He didn't appear to be injured and had most likely died of fright.

We camped out in the wrecked house for an uncomfortable week while we sorted things out. The furniture wasn't as badly damaged as we had thought at first, except for the things at the top of the house. We put all the landlord's furniture in one room and had it boarded up and our own things were sent to a warehouse in Wimbledon. I filled in war-damage claims and made tea for the workmen who came to clear away the rubble and nail pale blue cotton over the windows. It looked like the stuff architects use to draw their plans on and made a strange, unreal light in the broken rooms. The men who cleared the rubble told me harrowing bomb stories as they shovelled. Tony had been given leave from his office because his head hurt and both his eyes were black although they had not been hit by falling plaster. He had become all gloomy and, instead of trying to find us somewhere else to live, spent most of the days at Evelyn's. He did eventually find us a double bedroom at a pub called The Welsh Volunteer, a superior sort of place with a good dining room. Our room was large and clean, but depressing, with its 1910-bedroom suite, brown paint and ugly pictures on the walls.

Tony was in a bad way, as he always was after finishing a book, only this time it was worse because he was so tired of the war. The man he used to share an office with had been killed by a flying bomb and his black umbrella hung from a hook on the wall like a sleeping bat and after a few days of looking at it, Tony threw it from the window. It caught in a tree, still looking like a great bat. He was bored and frustrated in his work and hated keeping office hours. It was the first time he had worked in one and he kept saying that he wished he'd enlisted and been sent overseas. He had been able to put up with all these things until the house fell on him, after that he lost hope. Living in a pub in his depressed state meant he got drunk nearly every evening. He spent pounds in the bar standing people he'd never met before drinks and, when at last I managed to get him into the dining room, he was sometimes so unsteady that he sat on the floor instead of the chair and everyone would look. He hardly ate anything, just pushed his food around his plate, and, if I spoke, he gazed at me out of his huge bloodshot eyes and said, 'Quite.' Occasionally people asked us to dinner and we'd have a normal sort of evening, with Tony as he used to be, and I'd think that everything would be all right if only we could find somewhere to live.

After we had been living in the pub for nearly a month Tony suddenly started returning at odd hours and I'd often have to dine by myself. One evening I found him drinking in the bar with a neatly dressed woman with a white hat perched on her head. I imagined she was someone he had picked up in the bar, but she turned out to be a secretary from his Ministry called Madge Craig and he had brought her back to dine with us. They were both slightly drunk. I managed to get them into the dining room before they became any worse and they revived over the meal. Madge Craig, who had been hostile towards me at first, became gushingly friendly in a patronising way. Whenever I spoke she turned to Tony and said, 'Isn't she a poppet?' as if I were a quaint child instead of a woman of thirty. Apparently she had been a fan of Tony's for years and had even written to tell him so, but he hadn't replied to her letter. She smiled at him archly over her plate of chicken as she said, 'I'll make you suffer for that, you beast,' then kicked him under the table. I kicked her back. Tony, who had been sobering with every mouthful, looked acutely uncomfortable. Directly after coffee he suggested seeing Madge (he called her Midge) to Earl's Court Station. When she went to the lavatory to prink herself up, he shot into the bar to have a quick drink. I hustled him out again and we were both waiting for her when she emerged. She put her white-gloved hand on Tony's arm as she thanked me for a delightful evening. I told her not to thank me; it was Tony she should thank. I insisted on seeing her to the station, in fact I took her firmly by the arm and steered her out of the door with Tony following glumly behind. We walked to the station in an uncomfortable silence and after a few minutes Tony rushed ahead to buy her ticket, then stood waiting at the barrier with it in his hand. As she took it from him she whispered, 'Poor old Tony,' as if he were a hen-pecked husband, and lifted her face to be kissed. Tony lightly touched her cheek with the back of his hand and turned away. I called 'Goodnight, Miss Craig,' but she didn't answer. I longed to push her silly little hat over her face and kick her neat behind. As we left the station Tony said aggressively, 'All right, I know. I shouldn't have brought the blasted woman home.' I said thoughtfully, 'It doesn't matter. I like to know what I'm up against. This time it's something lethal dressed in mouse's clothing.' Tony snorted, 'Madge lethal! She's the kindest thing. You behaved like a bitch and made her nervous and silly. Usually she's such good company, and an affectionate little thing. She's had a hard time, you know. The man she was engaged to walked out on her a few days before the wedding and there was some other tragedy, I can't remember what.'

Fortunately the sirens started to wail and prevented me saying exactly what I thought of Madge Craig. We hurried towards The Welsh Volunteer although it was the last place I wanted to be killed in. The bar was closed and we went up to our room. Tony held a pillow over his head as a flying bomb passed over us. As we peeled the ugly folkweave covers from our beds, Tony told me that he had heard of a basement flat in the Boltons that we might be able to rent. It belonged to some people called Ware we sometimes met at parties. We always said to each other, 'You must come and dine with us one evening'; but the dining never took place. He had heard of this flat from Madge Craig, which contaminated it for me. She had acted as secretary to the husband at one time and they still sometimes met for lunch. It was at one of these lunches that Ware had told her he had bought a house and was about to convert it into flats.

The next morning, as soon as Tony left for the office, I telephoned the number he had given me and arranged to meet Mrs Ware at the house, which was still in the process of being converted. I found her in a distraught state due to frustrating builders, war-damage claims and permits. She was planning to live in the centre of the house, letting the top two floors and basement as self-contained flats. The basement was practically finished and consisted of two large, light rooms, a smaller one and a fair-sized kitchen. The bathroom was being made from an arched cellar and, although it was painted an attractive pink, it wasn't completely disguised. The living room looked out on to a large cement area, which got a certain amount of sun, and above it was a neglected garden where rose trees had run wild and willowherb and goldenrod grew in a lovely confusion. It looked beautiful from below. Mrs Ware was asking two hundred and fifty pounds for the flat and there were rates as well. It seemed a lot of money to me, more than we had paid for a complete house; but it was worth anything to get out of The Welsh Volunteer. At least the new decorations were included and I was in time to choose my own colour schemes for the main rooms. I agreed to take it and pay a year's rent in advance because I knew we both had money in the bank. The only good thing that could be said about the war was that there was plenty of money about and no unemployment. The woman who used to clean for us after Marcella left said that in spite of rationing the war was the first time in her life she had had enough to eat.

Tony sent Mrs Ware a cheque, then lost all interest in the flat. I did get him to walk round one Sunday; unfortunately it was a damp, dark day and he saw it at its worst. We only stayed a few minutes and never even got as far as opening and shutting the cupboard doors. He said, 'If it suits you, that's all that matters. I don't care where I live,' and clumped up the steps into the square. I pointed out the black angels round the bombed church spire. He wasn't interested. Sundays were usually dreadful now we had no home, nowhere to sit and all our books in store. If it was fine and Tony was in a good mood we'd go to the Zoo or Hampton Court. Once we took a boat and took turns to row and were happy for a few hours. I was convinced that when we were established in the Boltons this awful gloom would pass and Tony would start writing again. He wasn't drinking so much, but still returned at odd hours and I was sure he was seeing a lot of Miss Craig. It made it difficult for us to talk to each other properly; although we never mentioned her, she was always there.

Our furniture came out of store and was repaired by a man who specialised in that kind of work and made an excellent job of it. I went round the sales buying divans, carpets and china. I was able to buy new material for curtains because we had been given extra coupons after being bombed. As I had no sewing machine, I telephoned the Scobys to ask if I could use theirs. I tried several times but their phone appeared to be out of order, so I went to St John's Wood with my parcel of glazed chintz feeling slightly apologetic because I had not been near them for months. When I came to where their house should have been, there was only a bombed building and the houses on either side were in a bad way. I walked down the road a little way in case I'd made a mistake, until I saw by the numbers on the gate posts that I'd gone too far and returned to the bombed site. I wandered round the ruins and recognised pieces of the Scobys' dining-room wallpaper hanging from broken plaster, and I thought of Violet's wonderful hats all lying under the rubble where already sprigs of green were showing. I crossed the road to the nearest occupied house to enquire about the Scobys. I felt so sorry for the old people losing all their treasures and wondered where they were living – Violet perhaps at the ladies' club she belonged to. A brisk sort of woman wearing a man's blazer answered the door and, when I made my enquiries, asked me in, apologising for the drawing room which had half the ceiling missing. She told me in her brisk way that Violet and her parents had been killed by a flying bomb which fell directly on their house. It fell in the early morning, a day or two after the bombs started, and the sad thing was that they had planned to leave for the country that day. There was a car standing in the road already packed with their suitcases. Poor Violet had been found dead in the hall and her parents must have been still in bed when they were killed. Their bodies were almost unrecognisable. The woman went on talking; but I could hardly hear her because there was a ringing in my ears and my face had gone all clammy. I must have fainted because I found myself lying on a sofa and someone was splashing water on my face. I soon recovered and, feeling ashamed of myself, took a taxi to The Welsh Volunteer. It was years since I had fainted.

At last the flat was finished and, when I had arranged our things, it looked beautiful and homely too. I had made the small room into a bed-sitting room for Paul, and his surviving model aeroplanes, toys and books were waiting for him there. I whitewashed the area outside the living-room windows and filled it with tubs of early-flowering chrysanthemums, which helped to disguise the basement atmosphere. The day before we had arranged to move I filled the fridge with food. The landlady of The Welsh Volunteer had helped over this and Blanche had sent a chicken and a large basket of Blenheim apples. I filled the room with cut flowers and made up the bed and put out towels in the bathroom and felt so happy and grateful to have a home again. The only thing I left undone was unpacking the case containing Tony's books because I knew he would prefer to do it himself.

We left The Welsh Volunteer on a Saturday morning. The sun was shining through a mist and there was a smell of autumn in the air. As soon as we reached the Boltons, I left Tony to deal with the taxi and trunks and ran down to open the shutters and windows so that he could see it at its best. He was more interested this time and examined the rooms carefully, even climbing out of the window into the white-washed area, which I now called a courtyard. He sat down at his inlaid desk and started going through the drawers as if we had been living in the flat for weeks, and the strain of the last miserable months seemed to be melting away. I put my arm round his shoulder for a few moments and then, because there were tears in my eyes and I didn't want to appear emotional, went into the kitchen to prepare our meal.

Tony sat at his desk sorting his papers with great thoroughness. He asked for a wastepaper basket; but of course that was the one thing I had forgotten, so he used a cardboard box. He came to the novel that had stayed frozen on page 98 for five years and I cried, 'Don't tear that up,' and he replied, 'No, I'll read it first,' and put it aside thoughtfully. This seemed a perfect sign that our life was returning to normal. Usually the workmen above made the most appalling din; but today they were doing something quiet, playing cards perhaps, and at lunchtime they all trooped away and we had the house to ourselves.

We drank brandy with our coffee; the landlady had let me have a small bottle, also a bottle of gin which I was saving until the evening in case Tony became restless. I sat on the floor with my back resting against his chair and felt completely relaxed. Madge Craig had vanished into the mist. I said, 'Let's do something lovely tomorrow. Do you think we could borrow a car?'

Tony didn't answer immediately and I rested my face against his knees. Then he said in a strained voice, 'I shan't be here tomorrow.' I turned and looked up into his twisted face and he cried, 'Blast you! Don't look at me like that with your silky brown eyes. I know I'm murdering you.'

'Is it Madge Craig?' I whispered with my face against his knees.

'Not really. She's a temporary thing I need at the moment. It's something that happened when the house fell on me. God knows what, but I've felt completely different ever since. Moody, impatient and a brute to you. Guilty too. I want to be by myself for a time and go abroad if it's possible. It's the dreariness I hate, the utter dreariness, Billy Brown and the "squander bug", "Roll out the Barrel", the whole bloody lot.'

I said, 'If you live by yourself it'll still be there.'

'I suppose so,' he said slowly. 'But I'll be free to get drunk, walk the streets all night or go to bed with a tarty woman if I feel like it. I know you're marvellously patient with me, but the look of misery in your eyes and your skin all strained across the cheekbones makes me feel a monster.'

'If you feel like that, perhaps you'd better go. How long have you wanted to get away from me?' I asked bitterly.

'I've told you, since that bomb fell. I was completely happy with you before that, happier than I've ever been. It's not you, it's the war combined with my unfortunate character. I've always been my own enemy.'

We sat silent for what seemed hours, Tony occasionally running his fingers through my hair, physically close, but utterly separate. I thought, 'Whatever happens we must part on good terms so that he will feel free to return.' I asked where he planned to live, desperately hoping he wasn't moving into Madge's flat. He said he'd taken a service room in Argyle Street and, looking thoughtfully at the crate containing his books, said, 'It's absolutely impersonal. I don't think there is even a bookcase there. I'll only need my clothes. Of course, you're to keep all the furniture.' Then he went on to money. He wanted to give me an allowance. I couldn't help saying that if he didn't want me, I didn't want his money. I'd manage perfectly on my own. He smiled at that and said we'd discuss it another time; but for Paul's sake I must accept money from him and legally he was bound to keep me. We sat silent until the room was dark, then he went away. It was quite simple because all his things were still in suitcases in the hall. It was just a matter of finding a taxi.

TWENTY

ALTHOUGH I DID NOT care for gin, I got drunk for three successive nights until there was no more gin. I drank it neat and hoped it would burn holes in my insides. Then I tried beer; but it did not work so well and I gave up my life of drink. When I was recovering from my last hangover, John came and found me still in my dressing gown, sick and with my black hair in damp wisps – and I expect my breath smelling horrible. I told him that Tony had left me, but instead of the sympathy I expected, he said, 'Poor chap, he always was unstable. It's amazing really how long your marriage lasted. Now go along and clean yourself up and I'll take you out to lunch.' He took some papers from his briefcase and settled down at the table in a businesslike way and I tottered off to the bathroom. I realised that it wasn't only drink that was making me so shaky, but lack of food. All I had eaten during the last three days was a tin of tomato soup and a few apples. It took me an hour to get ready. John went on calmly working at his papers, even continuing to write for a few minutes after I appeared in the room, all clean and well brushed. He took me to his club and, after I'd steadied myself with a brandy, I enjoyed my lunch and felt able to talk about the future without crying. I didn't want to disgrace John in his club. He suggested that I went to Wales for a few weeks so that I could be with Blanche and Paul. He said he was leaving for Wales in two days' time and we could travel together.

The visit to Wales was a wonderful idea and I felt better immediately I arrived. I hadn't seen Paul for over three months and he had altered a lot in the time. The freedom of the country suited him. He rode a bicycle to the village school every morning and had learnt to swim in the lake and was mad on fishing. Old Mr Clifford Jones had given him a fishing rod and they often went fishing together and sometimes I went too. Blanche was expecting another baby in the early spring; but her pregnancy hardly showed and we went for long walks together followed by the two boys and various dogs. We usually ended up in the orchard, where we munched apples and talked and talked as we always did together; but we hardly mentioned Tony and I tried not to think or worry about him during the day. I couldn't help myself thinking at night, particularly when I woke to find he wasn't there.

I stayed in Wales for a fortnight, then returned to London in a hurry. I had a new worry now which I kept to myself: I was almost certain I was pregnant. I went to a doctor I did not know with a foreign nameplate on the door, and found he was an Indian with long brown fingers which frightened me even when they were enclosed in rubber gloves. He said that I appeared to be about seven weeks pregnant, but it was difficult to be certain at such an early stage, and suggested tests. I didn't need tests, I knew. I went home and drank coffee with castor oil floating on top. It didn't work the way I'd hoped. I tried boiling baths and Epsom salts and felt very ill indeed although nothing happened. I had been with Tony for over eight years and there had never been any sign of a baby and now we had conceived one without love in the hideous bedroom of The Welsh Volunteer. It was impossible to look for work with a baby hanging over me and I was determined to lose it. I tried not to think of it as a beautiful fair child looking like Tony, and feeling so sick made it easier for me to hate it. I suppose Tony would have returned if he had known I was pregnant; but I didn't want a reluctant husband living with me from a sense of duty.

I didn't know who to turn to for advice until I remembered the last time I had seen my Italian friend she had mentioned that there was a Polish abortionist living in the same Charlotte Street house. She had remarked that it was very handy although she preferred having her babies; some of her friends patronised him and he had a nice little business. I found him living on the first floor in a single, large room. He was a man with a coarse red face and only one arm and his remaining hand had bitten nails. There was a horsehair sofa in a prominent position near the window, also a long deal table, and I wondered which he used for his abortions. Neither was bloodstained. I had to beat about the bush a little before I could bring myself to say what I wanted and I called him 'doctor', which pleased him. He eventually agreed that he did occasionally 'help ladies' and, if they liked to give him a little token, he didn't refuse. Ten or fifteen pounds, in notes of course, was very acceptable. He wanted to examine me with his one hand. I said it was not necessary until I had discussed the matter with my husband; I'd return in a few days . . .

I went home feeling dirty and depressed, really tainted with mistletoe which would stay on me for ever. I hadn't exactly caught it, but brought it on myself. I found the Wares in the process of moving in and was glad to do what I could to help them, to forget my miseries. I started pushing their furniture around with amazing energy, hoping it would bring on a miscarriage. I had the embarrassment of telling them that Tony had left me. They must have known about it already because Isobel Ware said, 'Oh, has he gone off with that Craig woman? She's a menace, an absolute nymphomaniac. He'll be back soon. No man can stand her for long.' Her husband looked embarrassed and suggested it was time we went out for a drink and I remembered Tony saying Madge Craig was a friend of his.

It was Isobel Ware who gave me the name of another abortionist, a qualified doctor, which was reassuring. She said that although she had not been to him herself, several of her friends had and his treatment always worked. She told me the name of one of her friends so that I could use it as an introduction. I made an appointment over the telephone and then waited for three dreadful days until it fell due. The doctor lived in a decaying part of south London and his house stood in a neglected garden with red buses flashing past. In spite of its dingy outward appearance the house was surprisingly clean inside, with a reassuring smell of floor polish, and there were family photographs dotted about the waiting room. I was shown into the surgery by a jolly little maid who called me 'dear', and I wished she could have stayed with me;

I longed for some female support. The doctor didn't look at all sinister; he was a chubby man with a high colour and small black eyes. It's a strange thing, the three abortionists I have met all had coarse red faces. One would expect them to look pale and furtive, perhaps with a black monocle in one eye or a twitching cheek.

The small surgery was dominated by a horrible chair with queer leather horns sticking out at the sides; they were intended for women to hook their legs over while they were being examined. Before I got into this fearful chair, I gave the abortionist a bundle of pound notes which he carefully counted. Perhaps he had been cheated at some time. After examining me he told me I was nine weeks pregnant. By this time I was in such a state of nerves I was shaking and biting my fingers; so he showed me all his electric gadgets in the hope of calming me down. I believe there was even one to dry out noses with streaming colds. I had to climb back into the chair for the operation. It was not too painful, just a gruesome kind of vibrating, like an alarm clock going off inside me. I think he did it with one of his electrical gadgets.

When I reached home, there was a parcel waiting for me. The publishers had sent a copy of Tony's thriller, *The Whirlpool*, which was about to be published. There was a photograph of him on the back and, when I opened the book, I saw it was dedicated to me. I turned the thin, wartime pages and read the words I knew so well. I remembered typing Chapter Seven under the willow tree on a perfect spring day; most of Chapter Nine had had to be retyped because of Tony's alterations and the part where the heroine had been nailed down under the floorboards used to have coffee spilt on it. I gazed at Tony's beautiful, unhappy face and held the book against my cheek and thought, 'If only we could be together again I wouldn't mind having cancer.'

The doctor had told me his treatment would take anything up to twenty-four hours before it acted and there would be a certain amount of pain when it did. I was terrified, not so much of the pain as of what on earth would happen. There would be blood and some poor little thing that had been living. There was also the thought of dying alone. The pains started during the night and lasted for a searing two hours and then I was free of this unwanted child. I felt disgusted and degraded afterwards and for days imagined I smelt of dead birds however many baths I had.

TWENTY-ONE

I FOUND WORK IN a place where they turned useful and useless things into junk. There was a pile of white china jerries and, when the handles had been knocked off, I and a few other girls painted flowers on them. We painted flowers on tin lids which were sold as ashtrays; but the first cigarette that came in contact with them must have burnt the paint off again. We painted lobsters and shrimps on tiles with felt stuck on the back and sprays of flowers on cheap wood trays, and I could imagine how messy they would look after a few days' use, particularly when hot tea and coffee pots had stuck to them. There was such a shortage of worthwhile things in the shops, people bought anything, particularly if it looked bright.

The flying bombs died down and things became so quiet I decided it was time Paul came home; we had been separated too long. The Wares' children were now living with them, a girl of eight and twin boys, and we had agreed to help each other with child watching. I seldom went out in the evenings because people seemed to shy away now Tony and I had parted. Evelyn asked me to an occasional party from a sense of duty. I didn't enjoy her parties much because boring men always attached themselves to me, the hopeless kind that goggle at you through thick spectacles and talk about sex or their mothers. It was difficult to shake them off without a husband. A dreary young man with a beard and very little hair started calling on Sundays. It seemed as if the hair from his head had accidentally dropped to his chin and he was followed by a dog who looked like a mad rocking horse. On Sundays he would wander round and round the Boltons with this mad dog and every now and then they would come to rest against the iron railings above my flat. He would ring my bell at hourly intervals; but I only let them in if it was raining heavily. The dog scratched and scratched and would soon be as bald as its master. When it wasn't scratching, it was sneezing. I hoped Paul would scare them away when he returned.

John brought Paul home from Wales, and the sad thing was, he didn't seem happy in London. He missed the freedom of the country and his bicycle and fishing, and, of course, it was a shock to find Tony had gone. He said there was nothing to do in London. He half-heartedly made a few model aeroplanes and at the weekends we trailed round the museums or sailed boats on the round pond. He didn't care for his new school either and preferred the village school where there was no Latin. It was the first time he had come across it. He went to the same school as the Ware boys and, although the fees were higher than I could afford, it was well worth it because Isobel Ware took them backwards and forwards and let him play with her children until I returned from work. Isobel had a vague, casual air, but was kind underneath and a very good friend to me.

Soon after *The Whirlpool* was published I received a cheque for a hundred pounds and the publishers told me that Tony had arranged that I was to receive all the royalties from the book. I was touched by Tony's thoughtfulness and felt it would be ungrateful to refuse the money, which I knew he could spare. I still had most of Marcella's legacy and the rent was paid well in advance. On the other hand, I was spending far more than I earned painting rubbish. The four pounds a month from Gene's father had ceased to arrive over a year before. I supposed he must have died, perhaps killed by a bomb, or he might have become short of money in his old age.

Gradually we settled down. Paul began to enjoy his school and became devoted to the Wares' daughter, Ann. I used to take them to a skating rink on Saturday afternoons and we developed a passion for it. I took up painting again and sent my work to exhibitions; it was sometimes hung, never very well, usually behind a door or in a narrow passage. Once I even sold a painting, although it had been hung practically in the lavatory. I began to make new friends and go out more and often went all day without thinking of Tony once. It was during the night and when I first woke in the morning that I missed him most. When we parted we had agreed not to see each other, if possible, for six months; but before the time ended Tony sent a telegram asking me to meet him for lunch at a Chinese restaurant we used to go to. Although I took a lot of trouble over my appearance, I dreaded the meeting. I felt I wasn't ready for it and suddenly realised I didn't really want him back. I'd been too hurt and, although I loved him and wished him well, I couldn't face living with him. When I saw him standing in the entrance hall of the restaurant, my heart did turn over; but over lunch I noticed things I'd never minded before – the slight trembling of his drinker's hands, the unhealthy colour of his skin and a deadness about the big blue eyes. There was a sort of film over them. At a first glance he appeared wonderfully handsome, but a second glance showed he was a wreck of a man. We didn't kiss, we just held hands. We couldn't even speak for a few minutes and, when we did, it was in strained jerks. We slowly relaxed and became normal together and exchanged our news. I didn't tell him about the abortion because it would only hurt him unnecessarily and make him feel guilty. We talked about our work, Paul and the people we knew. He surprised me by saying that a few days after he had left me, he realised he had made a terrible mistake and had rushed round to the Boltons at eight in the morning, only to be told by the workmen that I had gone off with a man, and it was weeks before he realised that the man must have been John and I'd gone with him to Wales. He told me that he was controlling his drinking again. He'd been terribly ill for a few days and it had scared him. He also said he'd given up Madge – I wasn't sure that I believed this. He was very keen to see Paul and it was arranged that they would go out together sometimes. It was a difficult situation to explain to Paul and so far I'd only told him that Tony was working away from home.

After the first lunch together we saw each other frequently and sometimes he came to the flat and helped himself to a book or two from the crate which was still standing in the hall. We called it the Bolton Library. We became very good friends, better friends than most married people; but that was all. If we had lived together again it would have been a travesty of how it had been and I would not have had the patience and love to help me deal with the difficulties.

In the spring it was obvious the war was about to end and the V-2s had been like the last growls in a dog fight. Most people were full of ideas about what they would do when the war was really over. To some it meant a husband returning, to others a hope of a home of their own again and, to most of my friends, the prospect of travel and a change of scene. Tony was expecting to be sent to America on some mission. Although the people at the Ministry must have had some idea that he was an alcoholic, he always had the sense to keep out of their way when he was drinking; in any case it usually took place after office hours and his work seldom suffered, only his health. He so wanted this American job, he took a week's leave and spent it in an Alcoholics' Home and when he came out took to drinking milk.

At the end of February Blanche had a baby daughter and a few weeks later returned to their house near Guildford. It had been let furnished for months and there was the usual trouble about cigarette burns and scratched table-tops, and also a large round hole that had been cut in the front door for a cat. The baby was christened Amanda Victoria, Victoria after me. I was a godmother. I felt very proud when I held her in my arms at the christening, but so regretted my abortion. It was a thing I usually managed to keep at the back of my mind. Blanche did not seem so cheerful as usual and sometimes her eyes looked as if she had been crying, but remembering how easily she was moved to tears, I didn't worry. In any case I was rather distressed in my own mind at the time. Tony and I had decided against having a divorce because it meant that the King's Proctor would prevent us seeing each other for months or even years. Some divorces took as long as two years and there were queues of people waiting for them and we didn't want to add to the queue. Ever since we had parted Evelyn had been badgering us about having a divorce although neither of us wanted to marry again; she said it was only fair to me. I think the real reason was that she felt our relationship was untidy. Now that Tony was going abroad and we would not be able to meet in any case, she had at last talked him into it and it weighed on my mind like some frightful examination. Tony only had to provide the evidence and money, but I had to appear in court and have the shadow of the King's Proctor hanging over me. Tony said we must keep it a secret if possible or he'd have Madge Craig on his back. She was having an affair with a Polish officer, but this didn't prevent her giving him reproachful looks when they met in passages at the Ministry and she often telephoned him, saying she was lonely and needed his advice. He said, 'Once she's got her hookers into you, it's hard to shake her off. Poor girl, she should have been called Ivy.'

Tony stayed in England long enough to provide faked evidence for the divorce; then he left for the United States. In spite of the King's Proctor, who had been a reappearing shadow during my life with Tony, we spent our last day together packing and wandering about London. We went to Chiswick Mall, where Tony had lived as a boy. We sat on the huge ruin of a black boat and sniffed the lovely mud-smelling air, a very special smell if you have been brought up by a river. We looked at Tony's old home where 'at certain tides we could feed the swans from our windows' and the church where he had been christened and which he had attended as a child. 'In my memory there were always bumble-bees buzzing against the windows, only there can't have been in winter' and 'Evelyn and I thought Mother so devout with her eyes glued to her prayer book. It was years before we discovered she was reading a leather-bound copy of *Alice in Wonderland*.' He said that his mother had died quite young. 'My father was a human icicle and froze Mother to death. As soon as he entered the house it was as if a north-east wind was blowing. Evelyn has the same thing in a diluted form.' It was seldom Tony mentioned his childhood. In the evening we dined at Evelyn's and shocked her by going home to the Boltons together.

I felt bleak after Tony left. There was the case of books still standing in the hall and a soiled silk shirt in the linen basket, but that was all. The drawers of his desk were completely empty and his things from Argyle Street were stored at Evelyn's. The lawyers were grinding away at our divorce and I had already had two perplexing interviews in a dark office near the law courts. I had a great longing to be with Blanche, so telephoned to ask if we could stay with her in Guildford for a few days. She agreed to have us, but didn't sound enthusiastic, and the more I thought about our telephone conversation the more unwelcoming she seemed. Then I remembered she had no nanny and looked after the baby herself in rather a fierce way, not allowing anyone else to touch her, so I put her abruptness on the telephone down to tiredness.

Blanche seemed pleased enough to see us when we arrived. I had scarcely seen the house because they had been there so little and now she showed me over it with pride. It was a perfect little Queen Anne house, hardly more than a cottage really and very easy to run. The garden was delightful too, with an enormous weeping ash tree in the centre; Blanche said it was like a tent in summer and they often had their meals there. There was also a walnut tree and a tiny apple orchard. Paul and Stephen were happy to be together again and spent hours playing croquet and riding bicycles and timing themselves with a stopwatch. Everyone should have been happy in that lovely home; but there was something wrong and I could feel that Blanche was keeping something back, something she couldn't bear me to know. Then, when I was alone with John one evening, he told me the truth. Poor little Amanda Victoria was practically blind. Her eyes had been damaged in the early days of Blanche's pregnancy, when she had had an attack of German measles, and, as far as they could tell, she had hardly any sight at all. 'Poor little thing. She smiles and holds her hands out to a torch or burning match and turns her face towards the window when the sun is shining,' John said as we walked round the garden in the dusk. Blanche was putting Amanda to bed and the boys were building a house in the walnut tree, hoping to finish it before dark. 'There won't be any tree-climbing for Amanda,' John remarked sadly as we stood watching them clambering about, carrying large chunks of wood and the coal hammer. 'Of course when she is older and can wear special glasses it will make a tremendous difference and she may even lead a normal life. We can only wait, but Blanche is taking it badly. She can't stand anyone knowing about it, because she feels that, once they do, it will become an established fact. She just can't face up to it – I'm hoping that now you know, you'll be able to help her.' I was so shocked there was little I could say. In any case, I hate people who belittle sorrow, saying it is God's will and will all come right in the end. I don't know how I managed it, but I was able to comfort Blanche and she was even making tearful jokes about the baby wearing minia-ture contact lenses before I left.

A few days after Paul and I returned to London, the war ended. It was good to know that the air raids were finished and that people were not being killed any more, but peace seemed to me a dreary anticlimax. I had expected too much after looking forward to it for so many years. The lighting in the streets was the only change and people even wrote to the papers complain-ing about it, saying that it was a waste of electricity and the lights should be turned on late and cut off early. Rationing went on just the same and food became even more scarce. Tony sent food parcels from America and it was marvellous opening them and seeing all the glittering tins and bright packets. Then an American officer arrived with a small parcel containing nylon stockings, the first I'd seen, and a self-winding watch for Paul. Tony wrote fairly frequently and seemed to be happier than he had been for years, his only worry being the difficulty of controlling his drinks, 'The strongest I have come across for years and they almost pour it down your throat.'

I gave up painting rubbish and through friends managed to find work in a studio that made advertising films, and, besides doing the work I liked, earned more. I did find it a little hard working all through the summer, particularly when the sun was shining. I'd got out of the way of regular work and kept remembering past summers which seemed so happy in retrospect.

A few days after VJ Day I had to appear in the divorce court to obtain my decree nisi. It wasn't such a shattering experience as I expected, in fact it was quite interesting listening to other people's broken marriages, but horrible when I had to stand in the box myself. My solicitor had told me that on no account was I to smile, for some reason it put the judge's back up. I never felt less like smiling, but every now and then a ghastly twitch came on my lips and once a definite grin. The divorce went through all the same, and eight months later became absolute. It was as if Tony and I had never been married, there was so little to show for it. Even the letters and food parcels had ceased.

TWENTY-TWO

LIVING ON MY OWN gave men the idea I was sex-starved and ready to go to bed with anyone; even John Ware, my landlord, used to make advances if we were alone together. The unmarried men sometimes suggested marriage, only they were usually the unattractive ones that no one else wanted. I did become engaged to a middle-aged art dealer called Leon who owned a small gallery just off Bond Street; but the engagement only lasted six weeks. Although he was eighteen years older than me, I found him quite attractive and liked the idea of queening it in an art gallery. Some of the artists who exhibited their work there were famous although they didn't look it. You would have hardly noticed them in a restaurant and they only became interesting when they talked. The sad thing was, Leon wouldn't let me speak to them if he could help it. He would introduce me as, 'This is Vicky, she doesn't know a thing about painting,' and once, 'She only cares about dogs,' and sent me into a horrid little cubbyhole to make tea. I was not sure if he was jealous of my sharing his famous friends or jealous of them taking me away from him. He was extremely generous in some ways, even giving me twenty-five pounds for one of my paintings, which I'm sure he didn't want, and he was thinking of setting me up in an antique shop after we were married. It was over small things that he was mean. Drink was one of them and we always had water with our meals when we ate out; when he gave a party to celebrate our engagement, the guests were offered watered wine with decaying fruit floating in it. Although he was not allowed to sleep in the gallery, he had converted a basement room without windows into a makeshift bedroom and slept there in a late Victorian four-poster bed hung with camphor-smelling oriental hangings he had bought in a sale. He planned to move into my flat when we married. He got on quite well with Paul, who was at an awkward age, with perpetual holes in the heels of his socks and a row of leaking fountain pens across his chest. He was still devoted to Ann Ware and they used to explore London together on Saturday afternoons. Leon was impressed with Paul's drawings and bought him some canvas board and oil paints. It was the first time he had used oils and there he was in his holey socks, aged twelve, painting at his father's easel, looking extraordinarily like him.

When Leon came to dinner, I always served wine although I knew he objected to it. He used to say drink was the cause of much suffering and I'd say, 'I know. No one has suffered from the effects of drink as much as I have,' and drink another glass to annoy him. He liked a white cloth on the table and used to talk about coming home to a well-cooked meal served on a white cloth when we were married. I wasted seven coupons on the tablecloth and had to wash and iron it every time he came. Many years before he had had a little German wife and was hoping I'd turn out like her. Sometimes he could be very amusing and I'd think that our marriage was going to be a success; then he'd behave in a fussy, mean way and I'd hate him. When he suggested turning my living room into a workshop to make picture frames in, we had a bitter quarrel and for days I slammed the receiver down every time he telephoned. When he arrived at the Boltons with a chicken and flowers, I forgave him, and we stayed engaged for another week until I saw him lying in his camphor-smelling bed on the first summer day of the year. It was a perfect Saturday morning and the leaves on the trees were just showing green; the parks were filled with flowers and I was hoping that perhaps Leon would take me to the country. I went to the gallery and there he was lying in this smelly basement bed saying he felt ill and blowing out air from between his lips in great sighs. Completely unmoved, I said I was sorry he was ill and went away immediately, his querulous voice following me up the stairs. I never saw him again although he sometimes sent me messages through friends; one of them was that he was sorry for me because I had broken our engagement.

For the first few years after my divorce I had no serious money worries. I lived simply and my main expenses were Paul's education and the rent. The rent was usually covered by the royalties from *The Whirlpool*, which had sold well for over a year, then appeared in a cheap edition. It was a blow when the publisher's cheques dwindled and finally ceased. Even then I was able to carry on for a time with the remains of the money Marcella had left me and it wasn't until Paul was fourteen that we became really poor and had to count every penny we spent. He was now a day boy at a suburban school. The only subjects he shone in were art and languages. The headmaster thought it unlikely that he would pass his school certificate and suggested an art career would be the best thing for him. As this was what Paul wanted to do in any case, that was one problem solved; but there were many others, all due to lack of money. Clothes were a nightmare. Paul grew out of his so quickly and in a way I did, too, because skirts suddenly came down almost to the ground and mine were knee-length. To earn a little more I worked in a restaurant three evenings a week and Paul helped our grocer on Saturdays.

Old Mr Clifford Jones died and John inherited the estate. He retired from the army and the family moved to Wales, which meant I didn't see them very often except for Christmas and a week or two in the summer. Paul spent his long summer holidays with them and fished and rode his cousin's pony to his heart's content, a welcome change from living in a basement and delivering grocery. Sometimes I felt a little bitter when I thought about the contrast in the cousins' lives. Stephen was about to leave his expensive prep school and was due for Winchester, his father's old school, and Amanda had a French governess. She now wore tremendously strong spectacles and managed to live almost a normal life although she was practically blind without them. To see anything clearly she had to hold it an inch or two away from her eyes; but it was extraordinary how much she managed to see, particularly in the open air – in the house she was inclined to bump into things. The boys adored her and took her about with them on the pillions of their bicycles. She was completely fearless and had learnt to swim when she was four years old; in fact she was quite a problem because she wanted to do everything the boys did.

When Blanche saw how shabby Paul's clothes were, she took him to the nearest town and bought him a complete new outfit, then insisted that in future I was to buy everything he needed from a shop where she had an account and charge it to her. This was a weight off my mind because I knew Paul minded looking different from the other boys at school. One winter term he used to hide his coat in the coal hole after he left the house because he had been teased for wearing one that was much too small for him. When I discovered this bundle among the coal, I pawned the pearl bracelet that Tony had given me and bought him a new coat with the money it fetched. I was never able to reclaim it. Once I was in a dairy and a woman picked up a pound note and asked if I had dropped it. I thanked her and put it in my bag although I knew it wasn't mine. I felt degraded afterwards and never dared enter the dairy again in case the pound's real owner had turned up. Another time, when I was in charge of the till in the restaurant where I worked, the drawer wouldn't close properly and, as I was scraping out the back of the till, two dirty pound notes appeared which must have been there for weeks. I kept that money too.

I worked in the restaurant three evenings a week, from seven until eleven. The pay was small, but the tips made up for it and I was allowed to eat anything I liked. Except that I got rather tired, I enjoyed the work and meeting new people who told me their life stories on slack evenings. It was a middle-class place that served pub-like meals: steak-and-kidney pudding, joints, sausages and fried fish followed by jam tart or cabinet pudding. The kitchen wasn't properly ventilated and there was usually a strong smell of cooking and hot dripping that hit you in the face as soon as you opened the door. There were old-fashioned tea and coffee urns on the counter and I used to burn coffee beans in the gas jets to drown the smell, without success.

One evening after work, when I was running down Gloucester Road with a newspaper held over my head to keep off the rain, a man in a car stopped and offered me a lift. From the light of the street lamps I could see he was fat and middle-aged with a harmless frog-like face, so I accepted his offer and we reached the Boltons in a few minutes; but when I thanked him and was about to leave the car, he started talking and saying he was lonely in London. He came down from the north on business once or twice a month. The only people he met were businessmen and dance hostesses. 'Nice girls, you know, but out for your money and you can't talk to them. They don't give a damn.' We sat there smoking while he talked in his northern voice and, half listening, I wondered if my hair smelt of dripping. He asked me to have dinner with him the next evening and I accepted. It was a long time since I'd been to a good restaurant.

This man from the north became part of my life. His name was Thomas Wrigley and he was connected with steel. Unhappily married to a domineering wife, he found consolation in other women – only one at a time, though. He was naturally monogamous, in fact almost prudish, and complained that it brought on his stammer when he had to tell a dirty story. He became my lover, if you can call a man you don't love a lover. I went to bed with him for purely mercenary reasons although in time I felt a great compassion and friendliness towards him and was pleased when I saw his chunky figure, topped by the frog-like face, waiting for me in restaurant foyers. Sometimes he lunched in my flat and occasionally spent the night there when Paul was away; but more often we dined together in his suite of rooms in a well-known hotel. I listened to long stories about his business associates. He didn't seem to trust them much and they were always referred to by their initials. We went to sentimental films and musicals together, ate wonderful meals and, of course, there was 'love'. I found it hard at first, dreading it all the evening, poor clumsy man; but gradually I felt this kindness towards him, and it became easier. He gave me an allowance, which was never mentioned between us, the money appearing in my handbag at regular intervals. I hoped it came out of his expense account. There were hampers too, which used to arrive unexpectedly, containing things like tinned chicken, shortbread, caviar, peaches bottled in brandy and crème de menthe. I would have preferred real food, but we loved opening them. Paul used to ask who sent these extraordinary hampers and I said it was an old lady called Madam Crammer and almost believed in her myself in time.

Having Thomas Wrigley for a lover made a big difference to my life. I was able to give up the restaurant and only work during the day on the animated films, work I really liked. It also meant that we could live reasonably comfortably. I could give Paul a proper breakfast before he went off to school, not fill him up with stodge as I frequently had to do in the past. He was able to have pocket money like other boys and no longer spent his Saturdays delivering grocery; also he could bring his friends home – before it was impossible because they ate so much. Another luxury was that we were able to use as much gas and electricity as we wanted, an important item if you happen to live in a basement.

I was Thomas Wrigley's mistress for nearly three years. Then he went to Hamburg and, after we had exchanged a few letters, I heard no more from him and imagined he'd become attached to some German woman. By this time Paul was seventeen, very tall and like his father except that he had my high colour in his cheeks, looking a little like an overgrown Pinocchio. He was studying at the Camberwell School of Art and received a small grant, which was a help now Thomas Wrigley had gone. I had to take up night work again and waited in a small coffee bar all hung with bamboo. It was called The Chinghai and the tables were so low the customers were almost sitting on the ground unless they climbed the precarious stools arranged round the bar. This kept the older people away and the customers were mostly students, young lovers or people wanting a snack meal in a hurry. Sometimes Teddy boys from the rougher parts of Chelsea took over and there were fights, but they always behaved decently towards me, even offering to pay for broken cups and saucers when tables were overturned. Saturday evenings were worst and Paul and Ann often came to give me extra courage. Paul was always asking why we were suddenly so short of money and I said that it was the increased cost of living and heavy reductions from my salary due to increased income tax and National Insurance.

In spite of the long hours of work and money worries I was fairly happy. I had a wonderful feeling of achievement every time I looked at Paul. In spite of all the difficulties, I'd managed to rear and educate him and now he was almost independent and I'd nearly won through. Even if I died, he'd be able to manage.

Although I spent so little time in it, I loved our flat and all it contained and again there was the feeling of achievement that I had managed to keep it going. When I left the coffee bar in the middle of the night, I'd feel so tired I could hardly walk home; but, as soon as I switched on the light in the living room, the tiredness went and I would kick off my shoes and read for half an hour, looking up from my book every now and then to rest my eyes on all my dear possessions.

On Paul's eighteenth birthday, I was able to give him a post office saving book containing a hundred and fifty-seven pounds – the money Gene's lion book had earned. I had often been tempted to spend some of it, but knew that if I had once nibbled into it, it would have all melted away. To Paul the money seemed a fortune and wild ideas such as buying a second-hand car and travelling round the world filled his head for days, but eventually he bought an old motor bicycle, which gave him a lot of pleasure, and put the rest of the money into the bank to be spent on travel when he finished at Camberwell. Before he banked the money he gave me a surprise present of a most expensive sweater, the chunky kind of thing his girl friends wore with their tight black trews. I was shy of wearing it in The Chinghai in case the customers thought I was trying to appear younger than I was, so wore it during the day in the studio where I worked.

TWENTY-THREE

ONE MORNING, AS I WAS arranging my hair, I saw three thick white hairs running through the black like frozen rivers. Then I examined my face carefully for other signs of age and noticed a very slight blurredness and odd lines that looked as if they had been drawn there, and I saw that my eyes seemed to have shrunk a little and the whites did not look so fresh. I drew up my sleeves and examined my elbows because I'd heard strange things happened to them as one grew older. They looked normal to me. For years I had thought of myself as aged twenty-seven and not quite young any more and now I realised I was almost middle-aged. Forty-one, perhaps that was middle-aged. I comforted myself by thinking of film stars and actresses who were still beautiful in their fifties, and there was the Duchess of Windsor who had upset the English throne when she was over forty; but all these women had fabulous sums to spend on their appearance and I had nothing. I thought about old age and trying to struggle along on my pension and perhaps dying in a lonely little room in a bed with dirty sheets and wished I hadn't loved and married such fragile men.

I wondered if it was too late to marry again, to marry for security and friendship, not for love. There was no security with the kind of men I loved. All the men I met through my work were much younger than me, both in the studio and at The Chinghai, and, since Thomas Wrigley had gone away, there had been no more lovers. A tiny man who looked like a fox terrier used to follow me home in the evenings, but that was all. Now that it was firmly fixed in my mind that I was forty-one and not twenty-seven, I began to find working twelve or so hours a day far more tiring than it used to be and I longed for beautiful clothes to make the best of my looks while they lasted. I tried out new hairstyles and manicured my hands, wearing gloves of rubber or cotton when I was working at home, and I put my breasts in a black uplift bra which made them ache at first.

I was still at the aching stage when E. M. Dadds came to The Chinghai. It was deserted except for a pair of lovers in a corner. He gave the rubber plants and bamboo a startled glance and started to retreat until he saw me scowling at him, then asked if I served coffee. While I worked the machine he tried one of the low seats and finding it too uncomfortable, smiled ruefully and tried a high stool facing the counter. He said he had been directed to the bar by a mechanic in a nearby garage where a long nail was being extracted from one of his tyres. It was the first time he had been in a coffee bar and didn't blend well. When the regulars came in they eyed him thoughtfully and, as I gave a queer his coffee, he asked, 'Is he your father, dear?' He left after that and I never expected to see him again; but he turned up the next evening and showed me this great nail that had become embedded in his tyre and told me his name – E. M. Dadds, the E. M. standing for Ernest Montgomery. To my surprise he became a regular customer, calling most evenings soon after I arrived, staying for about a quarter of an hour, then driving off to his Putney home. The other customers heard me calling him Dadds and he became known as my father and soon everyone was calling him Dad. They'd say, 'Can you give me a lift as far as the Fulham Road, Dad?' or 'Is this record too noisy for you, Dad?' Although parents were not encouraged in The Chinghai, they treated him with a certain respect. One evening, when I wasn't busy, I showed him over the huge cellars under the bar. Years before the place had been a bakery and the cellars went under the road, cave after cave of them, with iron ovens like poor old prisoners rusting away in the damp darkness. E. M. Dadds became strangely excited after his visit to the cellars; he was trembling when he came out and kept pulling at his coat collar. He blurted out an invitation for Sunday. Would I come for a drive with him? I refused at first because Sunday was the only day I spent at home with Paul; then I remembered he was taking Ann to lunch with friends in the country, so agreed, although the thought of wasting my only free day on E. M. Dadds gave me a stifled feeling.

When Sunday came, there he was waiting with his car outside Putney Bridge station. He wasn't a bad-looking man, well built and athletic looking in spite of a rather pale face. His head was on the small side and his black felt hat had hardly any brim, which made his head appear even smaller in contrast to his broad shoulders. He shook hands with me and it was the first time I had touched him. We drove round Richmond Park in his Austin car, which smelt new although it was pre-war. There was a feather duster lying in the back to flick it with. We had luncheon at a Hampton Court restaurant and he gave me a sherry first, which I was grateful for after my experience with Leon. He talked easily in a pleasant voice. His main topics were sport and cars, things that meant little to me; but I smiled and ate my food while I wondered what the Wares would say when I told them I'd be a little late with the rent this month. Paying a year in advance had been dropped some time ago. We sat over our coffee while he told me about the sports clubs he belonged to, golf, tennis and squash; one was called The Bonhomie. Then he suggested showing me his flat, which he said had a magnificent view from its windows. I looked at him with caution and he appeared quite wholesome and not a sexy old man, so we drove to an Edwardian house that had been converted into flats and walked between the laurel bushes and up the red and black tiled steps, entering the house through a massive front door. It must have been a particularly well-built house before it was shaken up by bombs during the war – the builders had replaced most of the ceilings with plaster board that echoed and magnified sound. His flat was on the second floor and it was true about the magnificent views and the rooms were large and well proportioned, but they were furnished with an ugly incoherence of furniture, the only unity being an equal ugliness. He told me that he had been living in this flat for twenty years. At first he had shared it with a sister; but a year or two earlier she had married a clergyman who had recently been widowed and since then he had been on his own. 'It's rather depressing really,' he said. 'I come home to an empty flat and arrange a simple meal for myself. The woman who cleans does the shopping, just buys what she thinks I need, you know. Sometimes I think I'll move into a club, only it's a pity to give up a rent-controlled flat and Putney suits me. I belong to these sports clubs and there's the Heath and Wimbledon Common almost on my doorstep. I'm fond of walking, always was an outdoor man.' He was interrupted by the sound of high heels tripping over linoleum, then a trickle of water followed by the unmistakable sound of a lavatory plug being pulled. We both glanced upwards, but said nothing. He wanted me to stay and watch television with him, but I said I must go home to Paul. It had started to rain and I suddenly felt sad and homesick. He drove me back to the Boltons and accepted my invitation to meet Paul. I really meant that he was to come another day; but he misunderstood me and we went down the steps together. Paul was home and we found him sitting on the floor with a mug of tea in his hand surrounded by the Sunday papers. To my surprise they got on very well together and soon disappeared into Paul's room. The idea was that E. M. Dadds wanted to see Paul's paintings and drawings; but when I went in half an hour later, they were looking through old numbers of *Motor Sport* and in their enthusiasm might have been the same age. In spite of a certain ponderousness there was something slightly boyish about E. M. Dadds and, when he was enthusiastic about anything, he would rub the back of his close-cropped head with his hand, laughing from time to time.

After that Sunday visit he often called at the flat and, as he came to the coffee bar most evenings, I saw quite a lot of him; but only in small doses because his visits were always short. It wasn't long before he realised my difficult financial position and was deeply shocked. I don't think he had known anyone as poor as me before. Then he saw me pocketing tips in the bar and that shocked him too. He started leaving ten-shilling notes folded up small, which I found acutely embarrassing, although I pounced on them as soon as he left. They just about paid for our grocery.

On fine Sundays he took me for bracing walks, 'To get some clean air into your lungs,' and we'd walk among the deer at Richmond or round the windmill on Wimbledon Common. We didn't talk much, just breathed the clean air; but sometimes he took my arm. I'd think, 'What am I doing with this man, wasting my Sundays?' It was as if I had lost my identity. One afternoon as the light was dying we stood by a lake or it may have been a large pond. It was completely quiet as if we were the only people in the world. The quietness was broken by E. M. Dadds asking me to marry him. At first I thought he was asking me to become his mistress because he had such an embarrassed, guilty manner and was rubbing the back of his head as if he were going to knock it off. He went on about us both being lonely people and how much he admired me and he thought it would be a good thing if we married as quickly as possible, just a quiet wedding and there was no need to tell his sister until after the ceremony. I asked him to give me a month to think it over and he said, 'All right, little lady, I know it's a big step to take,' and my heart sank even more because I knew I would be a fool to refuse him.

I immediately wrote to Blanche to ask her advice, begging her to come to London so that she could see E. M. Dadds for herself. Then I told the Wares about my offer and sat in their drawing room drinking innumerable sherries and talking with tears in my eyes about love. The Wares were realists and said that love after forty was difficult to find. Anyway, where had love led me? To poverty and overwork, with only the old age pension to look forward to. They had seen E. M. Dadds thundering down the basement steps and thought he looked 'a decent chap, quite good-looking in a ponderous way. You must dig him out of the Putney flat and buy a house. It's a pity he's so attached to fresh air or you could buy one round here, but Putney with a car wouldn't be too ghastly. You'll be crazy to turn him down.' Paul considered the marriage a good idea too. 'We'll have to do a bit of adjusting, but he'll be out all day and it's good of him to say I can come along as well. I like him, he's so straightforward and I know he'd look after you properly. I suppose he's a bit healthy and hearty, not quite your type of man; but he's good. You can't help respecting him.'

John and Blanche came from Snowdonia to inspect him and liked what they saw. Blanche said his name was the only drawback, but perhaps I could get him to change it. She didn't want to address envelopes to Mrs E. M. Dadds. They stayed in London long enough to see me safely married and the Wares gave us a small reception. They must have been delighted to regain possession of the basement after my long occupation. It was worth a great deal more than I had been paying for it and sometimes I wondered if that was why they were so keen on my marriage.

After a subdued honeymoon in the Lake District we returned to the Putney flat, which was in a chaotic state due to my favourite pieces of furniture being stacked in the drawing room, and, although we were expecting them to be there, I could see E. M. Dadds was put out. He had given me permission to sell a few of his hideous things, but only a very few, and a horrible roll-top desk was to remain although I offered him Tony's beautiful marquetry one. He had agreed to my having the room decorated; but, when I discovered the only colour he wanted was something called Old Bath – or perhaps it was Bath Stone – I left it the colour it was and concentrated on curtains and chair covers. I decorated the bathroom and kitchen myself. The kitchen was huge and sunny and looked onto the garden and I painted it lime and white and hung red and white striped curtains at the windows. I used it as my living room when I was on my own – and I was on my own a lot because Paul did not come to Putney with us after all. He decided to move in with three other boys who had a flat in Earl's Court Road and his new stepfather made him a small allowance. This was a disappointment for me and it seemed as if I'd exchanged Paul for E. M. Dadds. I was supposed to call him Monty, but to myself he was always Dadds. I met his sister, a formidable woman a few years younger than her brother, with the same iron-grey hair and upright figure. Our marriage must have been a shock to her and although she was polite to me she kept shaking her head and saying, 'It's you I blame, Monty.' As she only visited us about twice a year she wasn't much of a problem.

I really wanted to make Dadds happy and tried not to upset his habits. He was very set in them. I cooked the kind of food he liked and watched television with him when I'd rather be reading and went for long Sunday walks. The only thing I refused to do was to take up any form of sport. Once he brought a strange woman home. She was wearing a 1912 straw hat and overgrown schoolgirl's clothes although she was over fifty and she turned out to be a bowling queen and he hoped she would persuade me to take up the game. I had often longed to have enough time to paint and now I had it; but I found something had gone from my painting; it had become neat and dead and I was always reaching for small brushes. I became interested in gardening and took over some of the flower beds I could see from the kitchen window and got a certain contentment from them in spite of the fact that gardening often meant that I became involved in long conversations with the other tenants, all middle- or old-age widows. I tried hiding behind clumps of pampas grass when I saw them coming, but they always found me.

I regretted my marriage at first acutely, then dimly. I wasn't happy or unhappy, just feeling as time went on, 'Good, I've got another day, week or month or year over.' When I passed The Pines, I'd often wonder if Swinburne had felt as I did, deadened, but grateful. I had little affection for Dadds, only respect and a certain gratitude.

The love part was not very difficult because he expected me to be completely passive, and to take my mind off what was happening I'd say:

Maître corbeau sur un arbre perché
Tenait en son bec un fromage.
Maître renard, par l'odeur alléché,
Hé! bonjour, Monsieur du corbeau,
Que vous êtes joli! Que vous semblez beau! . . .

to myself. If I was fortunate I'd only have to repeat it all through twice.

TWENTY-FOUR

FIVE YEARS AFTER WE were married Dadds retired. Before that he only played 'Tea for Two' on the piano on Sundays; but now he played it every day. I was only alone when he was out playing tennis or squash – for some reason he had given up golf. We ate our main meal in the middle of the day. He was fond of sausages with mashed potatoes. 'There's no waste with sausages,' he'd say as he smeared them with mustard, and at first I thought he was referring to their shape. On Sundays there would be the inevitable joint and two vegetables followed by a pie, and, after he retired, he'd come with me when I did the shopping, often choosing the joint himself. He had become increasingly interested in the domestic side of our life and was obsessed with waste. It wasn't that he was mean, just careful. I was allowed to spend as much as I liked on clothes as long as they were good and would last. It made me long for bad clothes that wouldn't. He bought me a refrigerator, second-hand, but in excellent condition, and hoped it would curb this tendency of mine to waste food – slices of tomato left over from the salad, the remaining potato or sardine, or the last rasher of bacon gone cold and stiff, even cold porridge; all these things were perfectly edible and he liked to open the refrigerator and see it filled with plastic plates and saucers each containing some little mess. Sometimes he went through the contents of the dustbin and pointed out food that had been needlessly thrown away among the tea leaves and ashes – slices of lemon that had decorated the fish or chicken's gizzards which could have been used in soup. When the winter ended, he drained off the antifreeze to use again next year and he stuck paper over all the holes but two on the scouring-powder tins so that I didn't sprinkle out too much at once. Often when a kettle was boiling in the kitchen, he'd sense it and come in to see that I hadn't filled it with more water than I needed. Sometimes, when he wasn't there, I'd boil up kettles and leave them to get cold.

When we were first married, Paul used to come to Putney most Sundays, often bringing Ann Ware or some other friend; but gradually I saw less of him, particularly after he left the art school and was working with a firm who did window displays. Then he suddenly married Ann without telling anyone, and, when a baby arrived hardly seven months later, we all realised why, except Dadds who had no idea how long babies took to be born. Paul had bought a tiny house in a narrow street leading from Earl's Court Road. It must have originally been a workman's cottage; but he had to pay four thousand for it and had an enormous mortgage to pay off. Fortunately he was earning a good salary. In spite of early parenthood and the mortgage Paul and Ann were happy and the baby was an endearing little black-haired boy, very much as Paul had been. I loved to visit them and seemed to be always welcome, perhaps because I restrained myself from going too frequently.

Dadds and I seldom quarrelled in spite of his interfering in domestic matters. He was an even-tempered man and just in his way, generous if we went out in the evening, always booking good seats in theatres and taking me to good restaurants afterwards. We had an evening out about four times a year – on our birthdays, wedding anniversary and special days of that sort. I expect people who saw us thought we were a happy couple and I think he was happy; it was only I who had become deadened.

About four years after he had retired Dadds began to wilt. He tired easily and complained about his throat, and suddenly his clothes didn't fit him any more. When I urged him to see a doctor, he gave his boyish grin and, rubbing the back of his head, said that all that was wrong with him was old age. We went to Wales for Christmas because I thought the mountains would do him good; but the long drive tired him and he spent Christmas in bed. Blanche and John were shocked when they saw the change in him and a doctor was called without his permission. The doctor insisted on his going to a local hospital for treatment and he stayed there for a fortnight; then John drove us home. Poor Dadds never drove his car again. He went into the private wing of a hospital in the Fulham Road, very near The Chinghai where we had first met, which had been turned into a launderette now. I would have been glad to sit there after my visits to the hospital. Sometimes Paul came with me and I'd return to his little house and spend the night there and play with my grandson, now a sturdy boy of four. It was miserable at Putney, with the old ladies tapping on the door and asking after Dadds.

He kept asking to come home and, as there was little they could do for him in the hospital, they agreed. I fetched him home in a hired car and the driver helped him up the stairs for the last time. He never left the flat again, just sat about in his dressing-gown gazing through the windows and sometimes on good days playing 'Tea for Two'. When the time came for him to be in bed permanently, his sister came for weekends and they shut the door and talked about money. It seemed such a long, cold winter.

Although Dadds knew he was dying, he still worried about waste and would give a whispered cry, almost a hiss, when I sprinkled too much Vim into the washbasin as I cleaned it, and from his painful bed he sometimes got whiffs of the expensive bath cubes I was using. He said a handful of soda would do just as well. Once he woke in the night in spite of being heavily drugged and, seeing a streak of brilliant light under the door, knew that I had left the landing light burning away needless electricity. He kept his finger pressed on his bedside bell until I came running from my room, thinking something terrible had happened. His voice had almost gone and he made such agitated gestures I thought him delirious until I woke up properly and realised what was causing his distress.

One morning, when I was arranging spring flowers in his bedroom, he took my hand and looked at me so kindly, as he whispered in his broken voice about his will. It seemed to worry him. Every morning after the visiting nurse left, he liked me to read *The Daily Telegraph* out loud, the financial pages in particular, also the weather reports – he was devoted to them and the previous day's temperature both Fahrenheit and Centigrade gave him a lot of pleasure. When I'd finished reading and we had discussed what I had read, he'd start talking about his will again and pleadingly he tried to explain that he had left the bulk of his money to his sister because he knew she would look after it for him: 'You see, my dear, I'm sure you'd waste it, be through my life's savings in a couple of years or, even worse, marry some scoundrel who would waste it for you. Of course, there will be something for you and the best thing you can do is to buy an annuity with it. Remember, an annuity. My sister will advise you.' I hated this talk and almost hoped he would leave me nothing and I'd be free. I'd jump up and say the soup was boiling over and he'd have visions of the kitchen stove with the gas unnecessarily high and soup, the only food he could eat, pouring all over it. Then there would be complaints because I had cut two slices of bread when I knew he could only manage one. Poor man, he had to take a drug before anything went down his throat, to deaden the pain.

He could still watch television for short periods, usually the sport and news programmes; he found plays too tiring. In his last days he became obsessed with the idea of seeing the Boat Race for the last time. When I brought him his morning tea, he'd croak,

'I haven't missed it, have I?' He now had a nurse who lived in the flat because he needed so much attention at night. Except for her meals she wasn't much trouble and I was glad to have someone to share the responsibility. I was so afraid of his dying when I was alone with him. On the day of the Boat Race we propped him up and put a glass of weak brandy in his hand and sat beside him watching his enjoyment. When it was over, he rubbed the back of his head and grinned triumphantly as he wrote on his pad, 'I made it.' I had to leave the room to hide my tears. I only cried once more for E. M. Dadds and that was when I found among his papers an envelope containing a great nail and the date on the envelope was the day we had met for the first time.

Dadds died the day after the Boat Race. He became unconscious during the night and lingered on and on – every breath appeared to be agony. I didn't know death could be so horrible.

TWENTY-FIVE

THE OLD LADIES WENT to the funeral and it was as if they were mourning their husbands again, they wore such heavy black and cried into their little white handkerchiefs so much. For days afterwards they brought cups of lukewarm tea and flabby biscuits to my door and begged me not to go away. 'You are one of us now and we must all stand together.' They were afraid of change and someone new coming to the house. Dadds's sister stayed with me for a week and I was grateful to have her, with poor Dadds lying so cold – though strangely handsome, rather like the Duke of Wellington. She arranged the funeral and paid for it out of the money she had been left – twelve thousand pounds, which was not as much as she had expected.

I was to have the insurance money, which seemed a fortune to me – three thousand, four hundred pounds, including bonuses. He had left me the contents of the flat and, rather touchingly, his treasured car to Paul.

The landlord, whom I had only seen twice before, called to pay his condolences. He looked like an undertaker and I had heard that he had lost one of his lungs and wrote for church papers. He said in his flat, sad voice, 'I presume you will not stay in this big flat all alone,' and I was about to tell him I couldn't wait to leave it when I noticed an expression in the large, light eyes. It was as if I'd received a small electric shock. I replied, 'Oh, I expect I'll stay, it's so expensive to move.' Then he suggested paying something towards the move. 'Would fifty pounds cover your expenses?' he asked softly. 'I'd like to help you as Mr Dadds was such an old and valued tenant.' I agreed that fifty pounds would certainly pay for the move but I'd have to pay at least five hundred premium for even a tiny flat. He said that of course he couldn't let me have such a large sum and I agreed that of course he couldn't, so I had better stay on as the other widows had. A look of despair came over his already depressed face and we sat in silence for at least ten minutes before he offered me two hundred and fifty to get out. I accepted it.

I sold Dadds's furniture, only keeping the things I had brought with me from the Boltons, and that brought in another hundred and twenty pounds, which meant that I had three hundred and seventy pounds to burn, in fact to waste. Before Dadds's sister left, she had spoken to the bank about investing my insurance money and I was to have a miserable little income, the kind old ladies starve on genteelly; so I didn't tell her about this lovely wasting money I had.

I gave all the old ladies presents before I left. The poorest one had the television set and the others things they had admired in the flat. It had been arranged that I was to stay with Paul for a week or two; then I was to go to Wales. Blanche and John were expecting me to stay for the entire summer, but I was making secret plans to do something quite different. It was so long since I had done anything I wanted to do, I was afraid that even people I loved would crush me.

Blanche had recently learnt to drive and said she would take me to Wales if I could trust her driving, which was still rather erratic. She was in London buying linen for Amanda's wedding. She was engaged to a friend of her brother's – a young doctor from Harlech with independent means. Amanda, in spite of being practically blind, led an almost normal life, particularly in surroundings she was accustomed to, only losing confidence in cities, where the sounds and smells confused her. She was a beautiful girl, very much as her mother had been only not so tall, and she had her mother's dress sense, choosing her clothes with the greatest care. One was always forgetting how poor her sight was and being surprised when she nervously clutched one's arm in a busy street.

I planned to stay in Wales until the wedding, perhaps staying on a day or two afterwards, then take a MacAndrew's boat to Barcelona, stay there for about a week, then take a boat to Athens and end up at Mykonos, staying there as long as my money lasted. This journey had been planned with the help of a sympathetic travel agent I had taken into my confidence and meant that besides staying in Spain and Greece, I'd have a glimpse of France and Italy. The longing to travel I had had as a young girl had suddenly come back to me.

On my last day in the little house in Earl's Court I rather defiantly told Paul and Ann the arrangements I had made. Instead of the shocked disapproval I had expected they thought my holiday an excellent idea, only asking me to return in September. Then it turned out that they had also been making plans and I was included in them. As a sideline Paul was going to sell and decorate furniture, the furniture to be painted by both of us and to be sold in a nearby shop he had taken from the September quarter. 'I haven't mentioned it to you before because I only signed the lease this morning. I can't believe we have really got it. It's exactly what I wanted,' Paul said excitedly. 'There's a large workroom behind the shop and a small flat upstairs that would just do for you, and you and Ann could take turns in serving in the shop.' Enthusiastically he showed me the designs he had made, some modern and almost geometrical and others, which appealed to me far more, of flowers and Cupids and clouds, and some lovely designs for bed-heads and chests. We walked round to look at the shop from the outside. Unfortunately it was closed and the keys with the agent, so we pressed our faces against the dirty window, which now displayed coarse china, flower pots and dead moths lying on their backs, but we saw it filled with newly painted furniture. The flat above looked larger than I had expected and there was a stretch of flat roof where I could grow plants in tubs and urns. The shop faced south-west and there were no tall buildings to block out the sun. I was so pleased with it, I almost regretted I was going abroad.

Blanche and I drove off together at six o'clock the next morning, before the roads were groaning with traffic. Even then, driving with Blanche was a shattering experience, particularly when she told me that she hadn't passed her driving test and I was to be her co-driver although I couldn't drive. We stopped at a lorry drivers' open-all-night café for breakfast, a most efficient place with road maps under glass on the table tops. As we ate tinned tomatoes fried with streaky bacon, I told her about my holiday and the shop. Then it turned out that she had plans for me as well. She thought it would be a good idea if I stayed in Wales permanently, living with them and working as a part-time secretary for John, typing his letters and helping him with the estate papers. She insisted that it would take such a weight off his shoulders and the house was going to feel so large and lonely after Amanda married. Stephen was in Aden soldiering for five years before coming home to take over the estate; in the meantime, John, who was over sixty and arthritic, was finding it rather a burden. 'We really do need you and it would be much better than working in the poky shop in Earl's Court, with your hands all ruined with paint. You'd hate if after a few months and be worn out. Don't you remember how tired you were before you married Dadds?'

I lit a cigarette to give myself time. I'd given up smoking while I was married because Dadds used to say, 'Have a gasper' every time he offered me one and now I had taken it up again although it was so expensive. I was touched by Blanche's offer, but couldn't accept it. I far preferred the 'poky shop' in the slightly slummy street to a mansion built among the dripping trees of Wales. I refused as tactfully as I could; but Blanche's eyes filled with tears as she exclaimed crossly,

'Oh, you're always drawn to slums and poverty. Living in Charlotte Street and basements and now over a shop, it's a sort of disease you picked up in Camden Town. Perhaps John will be able to talk you out of it.'

We drove away from the café in silence although a man shouted at us when we narrowly missed his stationary lorry. The misty sky was clearing and it promised to be a beautiful day, far too good to quarrel in, and by the time Blanche was having trouble with a flock of sheep on the brow of a hill we were on speaking terms again. The journey was taking longer than it should because we had to go miles out of our way to avoid busy towns. At midday we noticed that the verges on the sides of the roads seemed to be broader and more luxuriant, with tall buttercups and giant parsley gently swaying in the summer wind, and there was something familiar about the neat orchards and flat fields. Studying our map we realised we were about to pass through the village where we had lived when we were young. We had both driven through it before; but we had never stopped because we felt it wasn't the right time. Now we passed the farm where they used to give us bantam's eggs and once cakes tinted blue for tea and down the hill into the village, where we accidentally knocked a man off a bicycle. He wasn't hurt and, when he saw our stricken faces, he was quite nice about it although his back wheel wasn't round any more. We had been looking for Grandfather's house and hadn't noticed him. We felt a little shaken and turned up a quiet road that led to the church and stopped outside its gates. 'Shall we go in?' Blanche asked as we stared at the familiar tombstones. 'It's quite thirty years since we walked up that path,' I said nervously, 'and I expect the door is locked.' Blanche got out of the car, saying she was going to look at the family graves, and I watched her pass through the gates; after a few minutes I followed her. The churchyard was neglected, the ground deep with long-stemmed daisies and grass trailing across the graves. Some of the headstones were so old and thin that large holes had come in the stones like strange windows. 'There's Mr Hobbs's grave,' I whispered, 'and that little cross is Mrs Busby's. Do you remember she wore hats like giant buns?' 'Look at old Mrs Willower's grave; the stone's got all crooked and it's covered in thistles,' Blanche exclaimed as we walked through the long, damp grass. We had ceased to whisper. 'Grandfather and the Greats should be somewhere near here. You know, I can hardly remember him although he was so good to us. Did he have a moustache?' 'Yes,' I replied thoughtfully. 'I seem to remember a white one like feathers.'

We came to the graves that stood out in their neatness – a polished grey headstone for Grandfather and a bleak white cross for Mother. Blanche cried, 'Look!

How well kept they are. It must be Edward's work. Now I have seen Grandfather's tombstone I can remember him quite clearly, it's so like him.' 'I suppose so,' I agreed, 'grey and upright.' We turned to Mother's white cross. 'How new it still looks! Poor thing, she was younger than either of us when she died – a year younger than you are now, Blanche – forty-seven. We weren't very sympathetic, were we?'

'No. I didn't even like her.'

'Did John tell you I was drunk for three days after Tony left me?' I asked in a low voice. 'I might have been the same as Mother if he hadn't saved me.'

'Did you mind about Tony so much?'

'Yes, terribly at the time, although it was Gene I really loved. I was happy with Tony and still miss him in a way, but I'd hate to meet him again, all old and perhaps drink sodden. It's years since he published a book, so he may have died. I don't think he ever returned to England.'

Blanche said, 'Do you realise we have had five husbands between us, not bad for simple country girls.' And then, almost regretfully, 'And you've had lovers.' I thought of my unloved lovers, the solid Thomas and Leon of the camphor-smelling bed, and was glad Blanche had never seen them. 'I almost had a lover in India,' she said wistfully, 'and then I couldn't go through with it because of John. I loved them both, you see.' I envied Blanche her goodness and she envied me my lovers. I wished I'd led a better life and hadn't been so touched with mistletoe. I wasn't covered with it, but I'd definitely got some.

Just behind Mother's cross, a dear little grave caught my eye. It was smaller than the others and there was convolvulus climbing up the sloping headstone. Then I saw it belonged to Marcella Murphy and drew Blanche's attention to it. I knelt down to pull up a few nettles and at the same time said a hazy prayer for her. Blanche with a faint smile said, 'I wonder what happened to her little black boots; perhaps she was buried in them.' We couldn't imagine her without them. From behind the church we could hear someone digging and clods of earth being thrown up. 'Come away,' Blanche said, 'I don't know what it is, but this place reminds me of Garibaldi biscuits.' Suddenly we were laughing and crying at the same time. We turned away and walked down the flagstone path towards the car.